TOMORROW IS HERE

TOMORROW IS HERE

SPEECHES

NAVID KERMANI

TRANSLATED BY TONY CRAWFORD

polity

Originally published in German as *Morgen ist da* by Navid Kermani
© Verlag C.H.Beck oHG, München 2019, 2021

This English edition © Polity Press, 2022

The translation of this work was supported by a grant from the Goethe-Institut.

Polity Press
65 Bridge Street
Cambridge CB2 1UR, UK

Polity Press
111 River Street
Hoboken, NJ 07030, USA

All rights reserved. Except for the quotation of short passages for the purpose of criticism and review, no part of this publication may be reproduced, stored in a retrieval system or transmitted, in any form or by any means, electronic, mechanical, photocopying, recording or otherwise, without the prior permission of the publisher.

ISBN-13: 978-1-5095-5056-2 (hardback)
ISBN-13: 978-1-5095-5057-9 (paperback)

A catalogue record for this book is available from the British Library.

Library of Congress Control Number: 2022932467

Typeset in 10.75 on 14pt Janson Text
by Cheshire Typesetting Ltd, Cuddington, Cheshire
Printed and bound in the UK by CPI Group (UK) Ltd, Croydon

The publisher has used its best endeavours to ensure that the URLs for external websites referred to in this book are correct and active at the time of going to press. However, the publisher has no responsibility for the websites and can make no guarantee that a site will remain live or that the content is or will remain appropriate.

Every effort has been made to trace all copyright holders, but if any have been overlooked the publisher will be pleased to include any necessary credits in any subsequent reprint or edition.

For further information on Polity, visit our website:
politybooks.com

Contents

Editorial Note vii
Preface viii

On the Presentation of the Special Award of the
  Erich Maria Remarque Peace Prize to the Iranian
  Writers' Association 1
On the Death of the Unborn Sofía 10
On the 65th Anniversary of the Promulgation of the
  German Constitution 17
On Receiving the Joseph Breitbach Prize 27
At the Public Commemoration of the Victims of the
  Paris Attacks 48
On Receiving the Peace Prize of the German
  Publishers' Association 56
Eulogy for Rupert Neudeck 77
Eulogy for Jaki Liebezeit 83
On the 20th Anniversary of the Founding of the
  Department of Jewish History and Culture 88
On Receiving the State Prize of North Rhine-
  Westphalia 108
Eulogy for Djavad Kermani 120
Eulogy for Karl Schlamminger 131
On the 70th Birthday of FC Cologne 139
In Memory of Egon Ammann 145

Dinner Speech at the Investment Conference of Flossbach von Storch AG	160
Keynote Address to the Congress of the International Association for Analytical Psychology	181
Statement before the Opening Reading of the Harbour Front Literature Festival	211
On Receiving the Hölderlin Prize of the City of Bad Homburg vor der Höhe	216
On a Concert by the WDR Symphony Orchestra in the Broadcast Series 'Music in Dialogue'	233
On the 75th Anniversary of the Founding of the State of Lower Saxony	239
Epilogue: On My Bookseller, Ömer Özerturgut	251
Notes	257

Editorial Note

Except for five speeches and the preface, all of the twenty texts collected in this book were first published in German in other places: in newspapers and magazines, in yearbooks and jubilee volumes, as brochures or e-books. One of the speeches was also printed in one of my earlier books, *Between Quran and Kafka: West-Eastern Affinities* (Cambridge: Polity, 2016). However, most of the early printings diverged from the original spoken versions, which are retained in the present book. This English edition is based on the German edition published by C. H. Beck in 2021. Twelve speeches which appeared in the German edition have not been included here.

All of the speeches were read before presentation by friends, relatives, hosts or colleagues, and all the final versions incorporate their corrections, objections and comments. Although it would be fitting to list them all, after twenty years I can no longer remember who checked and improved which particular speech. For that reason, I would like here to mention only those readers to whom I sent almost all my manuscripts over those twenty years, asking them what they thought of them: my editor Ulrich Nolte; my late publisher Egon Ammann; my friends Carl Hegemann and Stefan Otteni; and Katajun Amirpur.

Preface

Of all the forms of public communication, the most peculiar seems to me to be the delivery of a prepared speech. When a person speaks without a script, whether at a lectern or as a member of a panel, they finish their ideas as they are speaking, all advance preparation and practice notwithstanding. They can react to the incomprehension, the sympathy, the surprise, the boredom, the displeasure they read in the faces of the audience or hear in the form of interjections, applause and coughing. They can hurl interjections of their own at those leaving the room before the end, and in many cases that makes the speech all the more lively, especially if the protest becomes a dialogue, heated though it may be.

At an author's reading, on the other hand, one of the conventions is that the text being read aloud does not directly address the listeners present. Hence the reading is a more pleasant format for most writers, more closely aligned with their working situation. The reading adheres to the stylistics of written text; the speaker's modulation is not aimed at any particular addressee. For that reason, the speaker rarely looks up to make eye contact, to establish a connection with the listeners. I myself, at least, instinctively tend to concentrate during my readings on the book lying on the table in front of me, shutting out everything that impinges on me from outside. Even the clicking of a camera – which wouldn't bother me during the introductory remarks or the conversation with the host afterwards – can be so disturbing that I interrupt my reading to ask people not to take photographs. It looks affected when that happens, I know, but it is still better for the audience than if I were to go on being distracted and annoyed by every click.

A written speech is a contradiction in terms, and the thing designated by those terms is still more paradoxical: the speaker speaks to a specific audience, directly addressing the listeners present in the salutation and in the delivery, but what the speaker seems to be saying spontaneously has actually been thought out in advance, word for word. In a way, the speaker is imitating an extempore speech. Naturally, the speaker can deviate from the script if a new idea occurs to him; he can respond to listeners who interject comments or applaud. But afterwards he generally goes on with his speech as planned, reading the text as he prepared it well ahead of time, even if he now realizes that different words would be more fitting. If the discrepancy between the written thoughts and those of the moment becomes too great, the speaker can also put aside the script completely. In writing the speech, however, he is not likely to have planned an improvisation, since that brings with it new imponderables. No, the intention in writing a speech is to imagine a situation so well, although it is still in the future, that you will say at every moment exactly what you want to say – only more precisely, more elegantly and more profoundly than you ever could spontaneously. Because speaking from a script is by no means simply deficient, as speakers are occasionally told: putting a text in writing, and thus making it literary, can also be an advantage and, on many occasions, or for some rhetorical talents, may be imperative. The impromptu speech is not necessarily more free. In order to be artful, persuasive and memorable, it must – if only to fit in the speaker's own memory – follow rhetorical, homiletic rules and topoi – that is, literally, 'commonplaces'. In the best case, because the prepared speech permits more complex sentence structures and thematic sequences, it gives the mind more space. It is admirable that people speak without a script in Parliament, let's say, and the listeners gladly tolerate a certain amount of imprecision, awkward syntax or polemics born of the fervour of the moment. But it is no less imperative that, in a speech about Auschwitz, let's say, no word is spoken rashly. To be exact, we are talking about two different genres, and so the present volume contains not speeches but texts which have been delivered publicly.

A person writing a novel or an essay also takes the readers' reactions into account. Hoping he knows the reader's expectations, the author plans to fulfil, disappoint or disregard them. Writing a speech is no different in this respect: the speaker at his desk allows the imagined applause, annoyance, disappointed expectations, and even the protest he anticipates at certain points, to take their places in his train of thought. The difference from a book or an essay, of course, is this: a person writing a speech has the advantage, or the disadvantage, that he will experience those reactions in person. The author looks at the people he is addressing and immediately notices, as a rule, if they bristle, lose the thread, approve enthusiastically, or roll their eyes. In the worst case, the speaker will wish he could vanish into thin air – something not given to any speaker so far, unfortunately. The suspense and the strain that I feel at the beginning of every speech come from the uncertainty whether the audience will actually follow the ideas that I have already set down – and the knowledge that, even if they turn away, figuratively or literally, I will have to persevere.

When, for example, I stepped up to the lectern in St Paul's Church in Frankfurt in 2015 to deliver my thanks for the Peace Prize of the German Publishers' Association, only a few friends with whom I had discussed my manuscript knew how the speech would end: that I would ask my listeners to stand up to pray, or to meditate on their wishes, for Father Jacques Mourad, Father Paolo Dall'Oglio and the other hostages in Iraq and Syria. Thus I imagined, as I began to speak, the embarrassment that would be mine when the audience remained sitting in spite of my request. I was also nervous because my script was about twice as long as the time allotted for the ceremony, which was being televised live, and the speaker who had introduced me had already gone over time. By the end of my speech, I imagined, there would be hardly anyone left to stand up, and the television crew would long since have gone off the air. Only as I gradually gained confidence, because I read the attentiveness in the faces of the audience and heard the silence between my sentences, my fears dissipated and I was able while I spoke to think of Father Jacques Mourad, Father Paolo and the other hostages, with whom I was carrying on my inner dialogue. The strength, the love and the courage of desperation that the speech may have conveyed did not come from me, I felt; they came – and this was what kept me going and enabled me to ignore the organizers' expectations, the listeners' possible fatigue and the television programme – the strength, love and courage came from the prisoners in Syria and Iraq.

Thus there is another paradox in delivering a speech that has long since been written down: although the reactions that the speaker witnesses are quite immediate, the speaker is the more persuasive the more apathetic he is to the audience and the less he cares about the audience's expectations. I have often experienced, both as a listener and as a speaker, that you are more likely to reach other people the more you are in touch with yourself; that is, the more your statement expresses an inner concern – 'Here I stand; I cannot do otherwise ...'. The opposite can be observed on any anniversary or formal occasion when the speaker is speaking not as an individual but as the representative of a nation, a religion, a business, a city or a congregation of mourners. Literature never comes about vicariously; it is individualistic in the extreme; otherwise it is not literature. It can express common afflictions, longings and demands only by finding the most personal and distinctive words: those moulded by the individual's life experience, personality and situations. But the less literary a speech is, and the more it is influenced by external pressures to be balanced out – the concerns of advisors and advocates, political constraints, commercial expectations, concessions to diplomacy or respect – the greater is the danger of sound bites, stereotypes, run-of-the-mill truths which no one would contradict and which are immediately forgotten. The highest art of public oratory would be to speak for many while saying what only one single person can say: to be literary and at the same time representative. This paradoxical challenge was not obvious to me, as my older speeches especially attest; hence few of them are included in this collection. The self-confidence to retain my own style in speech as in writing, with its rhythmic idiosyncrasies and its convoluted sentences, is something I had to acquire, and so is the chutzpah to say unfitting things at a ceremonial gathering – indecent things, all too heartrending things, discursive, personal, even banal things – if they happen to be important to me at the moment.

It is only natural that, in retrospect, there are some things I would state differently, in spite of the strength of my conviction at the time, and that I have occasionally erred, plain and simple. A speech, more than a book or even a newspaper article, is written for a very specific moment, a specific place and a sharply circumscribed audience. Later, elsewhere and for an indeterminate readership, the world necessarily looks different. Furthermore, an essay, a novel or an academic study may be revised after its publication, but at the lectern there is only the spoken word. I have taken the liberty here of making minor corrections of wording only in those speeches that were not recorded on their public delivery; in other cases, I have to live with my own mistakes and inadequacies, which, of course, are displeasing to me more than anyone. The hopes for the reform process that inspired the Iranian Writers' Association in 1999 have long since been dashed. In my 2014 speech to the Bundestag, I should have pointed out the distinction between refugees in the sense of the Geneva Conventions and the comparatively few victims of political persecution who are the subject of Article 16 of the German constitution. I would also have spared myself some objections if I had given an example to clarify exactly what I meant with my criticism that, since the reform of Article 16, 'asylum has practically ceased to be a fundamental right in Germany' (note that I did not say it had 'ceased to exist', as some have misquoted me), because in substance, alas, I was right: under the third-country rule, human rights activists who are in danger of arrest, torture or execution at home technically have no legal way to apply for asylum in Germany – unless they arrive here by parachute. The following year, when hundreds of thousands of refugees sought shelter in Germany, the vast majority of them were not victims of political persecution in the sense of Article 16, and, even if they had been, they would not have been claiming a fundamental right. They were admitted at the discretion of the German government, and it is still a subject of controversy today whether it was legitimate to take such a momentous decision without parliamentary approval.

And so on: in the Peace Prize acceptance speech, as in many earlier and later publications, I should have denounced Shiite extremism and the Iranian policy in Syria more explicitly so that my condemnation of Wahhabism could not be discounted as a Shiite position. In the eulogy for my father, hastily written while I was still overwhelmed with grief, I probably mentioned myself a few times too often. In the eulogy for Karl Schlamminger, who died the night after my father's funeral, I ought to have said so much more to do justice to his work, his character, his family and his love. The list of mistakes and possible improvements goes on, and the question I faced in preparing this publication was not which errors I must correct, but whether each speech as a whole, with all its inaccuracies, shortcomings and references unfamiliar to an English-speaking readership (who are not as well versed in the history of FC Cologne, for example, as the guests present at the club's internal jubilee celebration were) – whether each speech seemed important enough to be printed in this form (although, as the fan I am, I must say FC Cologne is of global importance in itself). In truth, that is not the case with all the speeches I have given – or have had to break off to improvise. Many of those commentaries which received the greatest attention at the time proved dispensable because they dealt with current political developments. Some of my literary speeches – on Lessing, Goethe, Kleist and the idea of Europe – are not included in this English collection because they are already published in expanded versions in *Between Quran and Kafka: West-Eastern Affinities* (Polity, 2016). Strangely enough, the more intimate speeches in particular, the more personal ones, seemed to the publisher, the translator Tony Crawford and myself to be of general significance, and for this reason they make up a greater proportion of the English edition of *Tomorrow is Here* than of the German first edition. In any case, I hope that this book will speak to readers some of whom could hardly be more remote, geographically and temporally as well as linguistically, from the original audience, for therein lie the purpose and the power of literature. And public oratory is one of its genres.

On the Presentation of the Special Award of the Erich Maria Remarque Peace Prize to the Iranian Writers' Association

Osnabrück City Hall, 3 July 1999

Mr President of the Bundestag, Mr Mayor, dear Ms Sari, dear Mr Golshiri, ladies and gentlemen,

Over thirty years ago, Iran's most important writers met in Tehran to found the Iranian Writers' Association. They resolved to apply for official recognition and presented their application to the competent official in the Ministry of Culture. The official agreed to consider the application. But he never sent an answer. Many other officials succeeded him. After a while, they no longer wore ties, but had beards instead. Yet they never said what decision they had reached.

Since the Iranian writers' first attempt to found an independent association, Iran has undergone a revolution, an eight-year war, tens of thousands of executions, the return of hundreds of thousands of Iranians from exile, the emigration of millions of Iranians and a simultaneous influx of at least 3 million refugees from other countries, an unprecedented economic crisis, internal power struggles, political assassinations, terrorism by the state and by the armed opposition, the unending persecution of those who think differently from the rulers and, over and over again, hopes that have turned out to be in vain. The time could not have been more turbulent; a time in which no stone has been left standing, and still, more than thirty years later, the Writers' Association is in the process of being founded. That is a continuity one might be tempted to snicker at, if it weren't for all the epochal disappointment that comes with it.

Of course there were phases, especially just before and just after the revolution of 1979, when the writers were able to meet and issue joint statements in relative safety, but those phases were short in comparison with the long period underground when they met only in private homes, the years when the friends could never be sure from one meeting to the next whether they would all still be free, alive and in the country. Thus the history of the Iranian Writers' Association could be told as one of oppression: a history of dangers, a history of the people murdered, arrested, tortured, driven into exile. But there is also a history of resistance to be told: a history of patience, of defiance, self-assertion and the power of literature. If, after thirty years, a Committee to Found the Iranian Writers' Association still exists – or exists again – that is not only an indication of the adversities to which writers in Iran are exposed; it is also an indication of their persistence.

That dictatorships deny writers the right to associate in an independent federation almost goes without saying. But that the writers have pursued their intention over such a long time, that they have insisted, under the most difficult conditions imaginable, on the single, central demand of all writers in the world – the freedom of the written word – is not something to be taken for granted. We must bear witness to it, because it shows what literature is capable of. I do not say: human beings; I do not say: what resistance fighters, freedom lovers, intellectuals are capable of. I say: what literature is capable of, because this history begins with literature and must end with literature. 'We are writers,' reads the first sentence of the protest declaration of autumn of 1994, in which 134 Iranian authors demanded the abolition of censorship and the authorization of the Writers' Association. 'We are writers.' It sounds like a trivial statement, but in fact it was a manifesto and a contentious demand. In a country ideologized by the revolution, where every television quiz show tests political beliefs and every book is censored for its political convictions, it is a tedious and a highly political struggle to reconquer spaces for the personal, the artistic, the apolitical, and to insist: We are writers, nothing else.

And yet there is another reason why I spoke of the power of literature. No matter how wise and courageous the statements writers might make on the political situation in their country – if they did not write great novels, poems, stories, plays, who would listen to them? It is poetry that makes their struggle for freedom of thought an existential struggle, because it is a struggle for their existence as poets. And it is their literary work that lends their protest the authority that not even the most powerful can ignore. This is the only explanation for the efforts which two state security systems have made – that of the monarchy and that of the Islamic Republic – to silence this quite small core of one or two hundred authors. This is the only explanation for the special departments of the various intelligence agencies, the coordinated arrests, the rabid sentences, the military-style campaigns in the state media to which the Writers' Association has been subjected from its inception.

As I said, that inception dates back more than thirty years: to the year 1967. Even without an official authorization, the writers in those days rented an office where they could meet regularly for literary circles, readings and discussions. But the first arrests began soon afterwards. Gholam-Hossein Saedi, Abbas Milani, this year's prize laureate Hushang Golshiri, and Ali Ashraf Darvishian, who is also present today, are among those who, in the late sixties and early seventies, were arrested and in some cases tortured for demanding freedom of speech. Some of you may not know the names I mention, but those who are familiar with the Persian literature of our time know that practically every major contemporary author I could name has been active in this Association, fought for this Association, whether Ahmad Shamlu or Simin Daneshvar, Mahmoud Dowlatabadi or Simin Behbahani, and also the winner of this year's Erich Maria Remarque Peace Prize, Hushang Golshiri.

In 1977, the regime loosened the reins to avert the impending rebellion. The writers resumed their public activities. The same year saw the most noteworthy days in the history of the Writers' Association, and perhaps in the history of the German Goethe Institute as well. For ten autumn nights, some sixty of Iran's most important writers assembled in the garden of the Goethe Institute in Tehran to read their texts, give speeches, and discuss literature and politics. Night after night, thousands of Iranians flocked to the poetry readings. There is something magical about those ten nights. It was cold; it was often pouring with rain. But the people held out for hours under umbrellas and tarpaulins to hear new poetry and avant-garde prose. When you talk to Iranians who attended those ten nights, whether as speakers or as guests, you immediately perceive a light in their eyes, and you hear adjectives that you would ordinarily expect to find in love stories. It must have been a great moment indeed, a moment of consummated love, when the writers were able to meet their readers unhindered. There have not been many such moments in the history of modern Iranian literature.

The revolution of 1979 at first brought the poets the freedom they had hoped for. Some of them – including Simin Daneshvar, Ahmad Shamlu and Hushang Golshiri – decided to go and visit the Leader of the Revolution, Ayatollah Khomeini, to present the ideas and demands of the Writers' Association. It must have been a very disappointing meeting. Khomeini was disgruntled and didn't understand what the poets wanted from him – perhaps he didn't want to understand. By the time the writers were outside his door again a few minutes later, they knew that this Leader had a different revolution in mind than they did. In 1980, just a year after the deposition of the shah, the familiar attacks on literature started up again, now no longer in the name of the Nation and the Crown, but in the name of the Faith and the Leader of the Revolution, who cried, 'Break their pens!' The poet Said Soltanpour was arrested and executed. Many others had to surrender their teaching posts or were prohibited from publishing.

It would be more than ten years before the Writers' Association resumed its regular meetings. Half a generation of poets had emigrated or died, and another generation had entered the literary stage, among them Abbas Maroufi and Amir Hassan Cheheltan, who are here today, and Fereshteh Sari, who will accept the prize today in the name of the Writers' Association. Not until the spring of 1994 did the writers publish another declaration, this one in protest against the arrest of their colleague Ali-Akbar Saidi Sirjani, who would die in his cell eight months later, allegedly of heart failure. In October of the same year, the writers went a step further, drafting the 'Declaration of the 134', which demanded the abolition of censorship, the recognition of human rights and the authorization of the Writers' Association. The declaration drew worldwide attention. I was in Iran at the time, and I remember being rung up by the cultural editor of a German daily. What surprised him most, the editor said, was that there were 134 opposition writers in Iran at all.

That was the perception of Iran in Germany at that time: it was seen as a theocracy with a compliant population of fanatical masses. This perception has since changed radically. The Western public has learned of the existence of an inventive art scene, important filmmakers, courageous intellectuals. They have taken note that the majority of the Iranian population desires democracy, freedom and a more open foreign policy. They may differ in their estimation of the chances of success, but they are amazed at the social movement which is shaking the ruling system. The writers have been instrumental in changing those perceptions, not only with their 'Declaration of the 134' but also with the interviews, statements and articles they have published in the international press since then.

When people talk about the Iranian reform movement today, it often seems as though it began two years ago with the surprising election of President Mohammad Khatami. Yet this movement formed much earlier in the society, in the schools and universities, in the colleges of theology, among women and among intellectuals. Khatami's landslide victory, against the declared will of the Leader of the Revolution and in spite of the state's propaganda machinery, was the result of this broad social movement, not its beginning. The discontent among the population had been tangible before; the first uprisings had taken place, and independent journals such as *Kiyan*, *Gardun* and *Adineh* had outlined the demands that are openly debated in Iran today.

The writers were and are only a part of this broad movement, and they are by no means the only people who have made sacrifices: critical theologians, student representatives, members of religious minorities have been persecuted no less brutally in recent years, although awareness of their fates is often only marginal in the West. Thus today it is left largely to the clergy and religious intellectuals to confront the ideology of the Islamic Republic and to initiate the discussion most feared by the guardians of the Islamist order: the discussion of secularism, human rights and democracy. The writers cannot be responsible for developing or discarding theories. But it is the writers who lend a voice to the desire for freedom – a voice that is heard in the world, because they speak the language that is understood in all cultures: the language of images, rhythms and stories, of surprise, of shades and ambiguities, the language of poetry. Their responsibility is to describe the people's fear so accurately that it can be known and to express the people's hope so promisingly that all people may take part in it.

Because the ruling elite felt the ground trembling beneath their feet, they prepared to strike once more. A new wave of repression began soon after the 'Declaration of the 134'. The translator Ahmad Miralai was murdered; so was the journalist Ghaffar Hosseini. Both of them had signed the Declaration. Others either were coerced by the secret police to withdraw their signatures or fled the country. The publisher Ebrahim Zalzadeh and the professor Ahmad Tafazzoli were also killed. The attempted murder of twenty writers on a trip to Armenia, the suppression of critical journals, the flogging and imprisonment of Abbas Maroufi, the kidnapping of Faraj Sarkohi – the terror in which the rulers took refuge was born of their fear, not their strength. Faced with the example of the Soviet Union, the examples of Ceauşescu and the Truth Commission in South Africa, they tried to suppress the struggle for freedom before it became too powerful, and to intimidate the writers in particular through sheer terror.

Last autumn, there was another series of murders. In addition to the political opposition leaders Dariush and Parvaneh

Forouhar, the victims once again included two members of the Writers' Association, Mohammad Mokhtari and Mohammad Puyandeh. The fates of two other intellectuals are still unknown: Piruz Davani has been missing since the summer of 1998; Majid Sharif was found dead the same year. But then came the reaction that the murderers and those who command them least expected: instead of withdrawing in fear and resignation, the people fought back. Tens of thousands came to the funerals of the murdered intellectuals. The students demonstrated; newspapers demanded in bold headlines the investigation of the murders; the writers addressed the national and international public; politicians declared their solidarity with the people under threat. The public pressure forced the secret police to present an explanation that was unprecedented in Iranian history: the secret police admitted that they had committed the murders. The confession set off a political earthquake which led to the first local elections in the history of Iran, and for the first time an Iranian government explicitly supported the founding of the Writers' Association.

We should judge this government by whether it keeps its word, because the Association which is being honoured today with a Special Award of the Erich Maria Remarque Peace Prize has not been founded yet. It is still in the process of being founded, as it has been for over thirty years. To judge by the recent news, it may be a long time yet before independent political parties, associations and institutions, and among them a Writers' Association, will exist in Iran and before violence as a means of political contention will finally have been done away with. But in the end – and if it takes another thirty years – in the end the swords that are still being drawn today, that may kill again tomorrow, in the end they will melt in the searing patience of the people, among them those people who believe in literature, in images, rhythms and stories, in surprise, in the shades and the ambiguity of life.

I thank you; I thank all the members of the Iranian Writers' Association, and especially the murdered members Ahmad Miralai, Ghaffar Hosseini, Mohammad Mokhtari and Mohammad Puyandeh.

On the Death of the Unborn Sofía

Church of St Thomas Aquinas, Berlin, 27 April 2003

Dear Maria, dear Gereon, dear Felix, dear friends,

Sofía Charlotte Hamm was a quiet child, quieter than her brother Felix. She evidently felt comfortable in the loving care of her parents, who surrounded her with their voices and their hands. The only thing that excited her was when her brother Felix spoke to her. Then she stretched out and kicked her legs with joy. There was a special bond between the children. Sofía looked quite like her brother, too. She had the same nose, the narrow mouth, the same dark, full curls that had surprised their parents at Felix's birth, and she had the same long, thin lips as Felix. If she had grown to be a woman, those lips would certainly have driven her admirers mad. But Sofía did not grow to be a woman; she remained an angel. She died on the 11th of March. That was three weeks before the date the doctors had predicted for her birth. There was no reason for it: Sofía was healthy, 49 centimetres long, one centimetre less than Felix at his birth. She was slender, a pound lighter than her brother, yet her face seems to me somewhat broader than his: proper chubby cheeks she had, converging at the bottom to a pointed chin. Like her mother, Sofía was a very pretty girl.

We don't know why Sofía died before she was born. Medicine can answer that question only with statistics, and its figures can only mask our helplessness. The only thing we have an inkling of is *why* we cannot explain it. Sofía was alive: she had eyes, ears, a little nose; she could feel with her fingers, taste with her tongue and express by her movements when something pleased or displeased her. Her heart beat. She could perceive our world; she reacted to the signals by which her parents and her brother spoke to her. But at the same time she still belonged to another world in which the logic of our understanding has no force – a transcendent world.

What distinguishes our world? The fact that everything in it is, in principle, explicable. We can understand why a child grows up and an old man dies; we know the biological laws by which a plant grows and a flower wilts. Everything has a reason for *becoming*. Yet our understanding cannot explain why something *is*. Because, to be something, it must first be nothing. But we don't know anything about being nothing – we don't even know whether to imagine it as a not-being, or as a different kind of being. And what would that be – that not-being? We know how a person *is born*, but we don't know how it is *not to be born*. We know *why a person dies*, but we don't know *what death is*. If our world is characterized by the fact that everything in it is, in principle, explicable, then the world beyond it is distinguished by its fundamental inexplicability. And Sofía still belonged to the world beyond ours. Although she had come into our world, she had not yet closed the door behind her. Because she lived between two worlds, she was an angel. And because she was an angel, she was not subject to any of the reasons that govern us people. We can feel her, and sometimes even see her. I know with certainty that she is here among us – but we cannot explain her presence any more than we can her disappearance.

Angels are known in every culture: they are those beings who can leave the other world without losing it and move in our world without belonging to it. Angels embody the possibility of an in-between. With one wing they touch Heaven; with the other wing they brush our souls. And angels are pure: every culture says so; they do no one ill; they are good in the strong sense of the word. That is why most religions say that children go directly to Paradise. Even those who, unlike me, don't believe in angels may accept them as a metaphor for a moral and aesthetic purity. After all, that is exactly what we do when we speak of angels, or of God: we express in parables what language cannot say; find an expression for what has no explanation in our world alone – the first and last things, which some of us feel, but none of us know.

During her first pregnancy, Maria painted a series of red pictures that seemed to show something like an exploding ball of energy. That, as it turned out, was a fairly succinct idea of Felix. During her second pregnancy, when she was pregnant with Sofía, Maria also painted a series of red pictures. But this time they showed something like a female figure standing gracefully on slender feet. The strange thing about this geometrical figure was the arches spreading out in the upper third of the picture, sometimes wider, sometimes smaller. Perhaps it wasn't a woman, but a bird. Now we know that the arches were actually wings fluttering. And at the same time it is a woman, a girl, a little child. Without knowing it, Maria had drawn the outlines of an angel. It was a picture of Sofía in Heaven.

As we can see on the invitation to this observance, the drawing of Sofía is not exactly a portrait. It is a geometrical figure; it is an outline; it is like a shadow produced by hatching. That is probably as it must be; it's probably impossible to draw anything but the shadow of angels. That is quite a bit. It is more than it would be possible to draw of God, the absolute Other. Angels are different from people, but they also are people: they have human features; they can feel and rejoice, they care and empathize as no god could. We can draw at least the shadows of the angels, unlike God, because they cast their shadows on our world: we have an idea what they look like; we can imagine it – but we cannot draw a picture of it. In Judaism it is said, 'You don't recognize an angel until after he has gone by.'

All images of angels in art history and in the culture industry teach us that anyone who gives angels an exact appearance must inevitably be lying. The shadow doesn't show what angels look like. But it shows that they exist. And so it is with Sofía. We got to know something about her, but it isn't anything precise. We don't know how she would have become if she had gone on living. But we feel how much we have lost by not getting to know her better. We got an inkling of her. That is quite a bit – it is much more than we will ever know of other angels. And, at the same time, it is little: precisely because we had an inkling of her nature, her beauty, it is dreadfully little.

I am not here to give consolation. That is more than I can do. The death of a child is sheer horror – although only for us, most likely; not for Sofía, who remained where she would have returned one day in any case, in Paradise, or in not-being, or in the Paradise that not-being may be. But, for the survivors, her death is horror: for her parents, her brother. And for many others, Sofía's death is a loss that they can never measure: for the friends she will not meet, for the admirers she will not desire, for the colleagues she will not work with; and for the neighbours she will not live next door to, for the people she will not love; and for the children whose mother she will not be. There are no pious words or philosophical thoughts that can make sense of Sofía's premature death – none that I know, at least. All I can do, all we can do, is to share Maria's, Gereon's and Felix's pain, knowing that it will not make their pain any less.

I cannot give consolation, but I know that there can be consolation. Consolation is the love that we give and receive. The loss of a person we love makes our sight keener for the gift we have been given up to then. That too cannot lessen the pain, but it helps us to bear it. And there is also consolation in two things which seem contradictory, but which can go together: in forgetting and in remembering. As we remember Sofía, she goes on living. As time helps us to forget our despair, we can go on living. That is why we are here today: to remember, with Maria, Gereon and Felix, the girl we did not get to know, and to begin the life that will go on. Permit me to quote the German poet who knew most about angels, Rainer Maria Rilke:

> To the angel praise the world, not the unsayable; to *him*
> you cannot boast of feeling the sublime; in the universe
> he has more feeling to feel, and you are a newcomer. So
>   show
> him a simple thing that, wrought from generation to
>   generations,
> lives as something of ours, beside our hand and in our
>   sight.
> Say the things to him. He will stand more astonished; as
>   you stood
> before the rope-maker in Rome, or the potter on the Nile.
> Show him how happy a thing can be, how guiltless and
>   ours,
> how even keening grief resolves to be pure shape,
> serves as a thing, or dies to be a thing; and hereafter
> blissfully escapes the harp. – And these things, living

by passing, understand that you praise them; ephemeral,
they entrust a salvation to us, most ephemeral of all.
Desire we might transmute them wholly, in our invisible
    hearts,
into – endlessly – us! Whoever we are in the end.

On behalf of Maria, Gereon and Felix, I would like to thank you all for coming and for sharing the pain, the love and the memory with them. So many people have stood by these three in the past few weeks, bestowing great kindness on them, that I must ask you to forgive me for not addressing each one of you personally. On behalf of all of us, I want to thank at this point only Felix, who probably saved Maria's life when she was in danger of bleeding to death. Felix, alone, left his home and rang the neighbour's doorbell, even though it was so high that he had to jump as high as he could to reach it. We owe our thanks also to Maria's and Gereon's neighbour Rob Groth, who saw to it that Maria got medical care, within minutes, and just in time. Maria, Gereon and Felix have also asked me to thank the children Naomi and David, who steadfastly took care of Felix when his mother could not take care of him because she was unconscious. And we thank Selina, who awaited Sofía almost as joyfully as Felix did, and always kissed Maria's belly during her pregnancy, and her mother Melanie Müller von Hindenburg. When Felix lived with her in the days that followed the death of his sister, Selina was herself a sister to him.

And I would like to thank Maria, Gereon and Felix for the love and strength with which they cared for and looked after Sofía during her short visit on Earth. Their love and strength will be an example to us in our own difficult hours.

I said, all we can see of angels is their shadow. I ought to have said: we ordinary people can see only their shadows. Maria, Gereon, Felix spent a day and a night with Sofía.

When Felix saw his sister, he asked, Where are her wings? The other angels will bring them when they come to fetch Sofía, Gereon explained to him. Felix wanted to know everything: Would the wings be glued on or screwed on? They just grow out when you go with the angels, said Gereon. Now she has gone with them, and she has surely grown the wings that Maria had unwittingly drawn. What remains in the urn that Isabel Hamm has made are ashes – not Sofía's ashes, Felix told me, but the ashes of the candles that the angels had with them when they took Sofía with them to Heaven.

I said, all that we ordinary people can see of angels is their shadow. But there is a photograph of Sofía, and in it we can see her lying swaddled in a blanket, her hands resting on her chest. Since Maria sent it to me, I have taken out this picture to look at it again and again. The peace that is in her face is not of an earthly kind. To me this is a photograph from Heaven, and, if it doesn't lie, she is comfortable there.

This observance began with a song invoking the angels. It ends now with a song that Sofía always heard as she lay in Maria's womb. It is by the band The Durutti Column and is called '4 Sophia'.[1] Now it is no longer a song 'for' Sofía, but Sofía's song: the song in which we meet the girl we never got to know.

On the 65th Anniversary of the Promulgation of the German Constitution

In the Bundestag, Berlin, 23 May 2014

Messrs Presidents, Madam Chancellor, honourable members of the Bundestag, your Excellencies, dear guests,

Paradox is not one of the customary stylistic figures of legal texts, which naturally strive for the greatest possible lucidity. A paradox is necessarily enigmatic in nature; it is appropriate where an unambiguous expression would be tantamount to a lie. For that reason it is one of the most frequently used devices of poetry. And yet no less a legal text than the constitution of the Federal Republic of Germany begins with a paradox. For if human dignity were inviolable, as the first sentence states, then the state would not have to uphold it, much less defend it, as the second sentence requires. Dignity would exist independently, untouched by all power. By a simple paradox, hardly noticeable at first glance – dignity is inviolable and yet needs to be defended – the German constitution reverses the premises of previous German constitutions and declares the state to be, not the telos, but the servant of the people, of all human beings, of humanity in the strong sense. Verbally, it is – I hesitate to call it brilliant, because that would be aestheticizing an eminently normative text – it is only perfect.

And we cannot explain the impact, the incredible success of this constitution without acknowledging its literary quality. In its substantial features and statements, in any case, it is a remarkably beautiful text, and was meant to be so. It is well known that Theodor Heuss, the first president of the Federal Republic, rejected the original version of the first article on the grounds that it was bad German. But *Die Würde des Menschen ist unantastbar* is a superb German sentence, so simple, so complex, immediately obvious – 'human dignity is inviolable' – and yet all the more unfathomable the more we think about the sentence that follows it: *Sie zu schützen ist Aufgabe aller staatlichen Gewalt*; 'it is the duty of all state power to defend it'. The sentences cannot both be true, but in combination they can come true – only in combination; and, indeed, they have come true in Germany to a degree that few or none would have thought possible on 23 May 1949. Comparable in the German language perhaps only with the Luther Bible in this respect, the German constitution has created a reality by the power of the word.

'All persons shall have the right to free development of their personality' – how odd it must have seemed to most Germans, worried about sheer survival in the rubble of their cities; how odd they must have found the prospect of developing something as intangible as their own personality – but what a compelling idea it was at the same time. 'All persons shall be equal before the law' – the Jews, the Sinti and the Roma, the homosexuals, the disabled, all those on the margins of society, the dissenters, the strangers: until then they had been unequal before the law, so they had to be made equal. 'Men and women have equal rights' – the weeks and months of resistance to this article in particular is the clearest proof that, in 1949, men and women were not thought to have equal rights; the sentence acquired its truth only in practice. 'Capital punishment is abolished' – this was not the will of the majority of Germans, who in a survey favoured retaining capital punishment by a majority of three to one, yet it is widely approved today. 'All Germans shall have the right to move freely throughout the federal territory' – this sentence was almost embarrassing to the members of the Parliamentary Council in view of the refugee crisis and the housing shortage, and sixty-five years later freedom of movement is guaranteed throughout not only reunified Germany but half of Europe. The Federal Republic may 'consent to such limitations upon its sovereign powers as will bring about and secure a lasting peace in Europe' – this article anticipated, in 1949, a united Europe, and more: the United States of Europe. And so on: prohibition of discrimination, freedom of religion, the freedom of art and science, freedom of speech and assembly – when the constitution was promulgated sixty-five years ago, these were statements of principle rather than descriptions of reality in Germany. And at first it did not look at all as if the Germans would hear the appeal that lay in these both simple and forceful articles of faith.

Public interest in the constitution was, in retrospect, disgracefully small, and approval among the population was marginal. When asked when Germany had fared best, 45 per cent of the German respondents in a representative survey chose, as late as 1951, the German Empire, 7 per cent the Weimar Republic, 42 per cent the period of Nazi rule, and only 2 per cent the Federal Republic. Two per cent! How glad we must be that the politicians who attended the beginning of the Federal Republic were guided in their actions not by surveys but by their convictions. And today?

I have no doubt that the members of the Parliamentary Council, should they be watching our commemoration from some celestial seats of honour, would be content and very much surprised at the roots that freedom has put down in the past sixty-five years in Germany. And they would probably notice and nod approvingly at this significant detail: that the promulgation of the constitution is being commemorated today by a child of immigrants, and one who belongs to a different religion from that of the majority. There are not many states in the world where that would be possible. Even in Germany a short time ago, let us say on the fiftieth anniversary of the constitution, it would have been difficult to imagine the commemorative speech in the Bundestag being delivered by a German who is not *only* German. In the other state whose passport I hold, it is still unthinkable, in spite of many protests and many victims in the name of freedom. But I would also like to say from this podium, Messrs Presidents, Madam Chancellor, Honourable Members, dear guests, and not least to his Excellency the Ambassador of the Islamic Republic, who is also watching today, although not from a celestial seat: it will not be sixty-five years, or even fifteen years, before a Christian, a Jew, a Zoroastrian or a Baha'i as a matter of course delivers a commemorative speech before a freely elected parliament in Iran.

This is a good Germany, the best one we have ever known, the president of the Federal Republic said recently. I cannot dispute it. No matter what period of German history I consider, there is none in which people lived in greater freedom, peace and tolerance than in our time. And yet the president's statement would not flow so smoothly from my lips. Why is that? One might dismiss such unease at expressing pride in our country as typical German self-loathing and, in doing so, overlook the very reason why the Federal Republic has become liveable and even lovable. For when and how did Germany – the Germany that was viewed with suspicion because of its militarism as early as the nineteenth century and that appeared to be thoroughly dishonoured after the murder of 6 million Jews – when and how did it regain its dignity? If I had to name one day, an isolated event, a single gesture in German post-war history which seems to merit the word dignity, it was – and I am sure a majority of the Bundestag, a majority of Germans, and also a majority of those in the celestial seats, will agree – it was Willy Brandt's genuflection in Warsaw.

That is even odder than the paradox that begins the constitution, and probably unique in the history of nations: this state attained dignity by an act of humility. Is not heroism usually associated with fortitude, with virility and hence with physical strength, and most of all with pride? But here a man showed greatness by stifling his pride and shouldering guilt – and, what is more, guilt for which he personally, as an opponent of Hitler and an exile, was least responsible – here a man proved his honour by his public shame; here a man so conceived his patriotism that he knelt before Germany's victims.

I am not given to sentiment in front of the screen, and yet I felt as so many did when, on his hundredth birthday, the films were replayed of a German chancellor who steps back from the monument at the site of the Warsaw Ghetto, hesitates a moment, and then, to everyone's surprise, drops to his knees – I cannot watch that even today without tears coming to my eyes. And the strange thing is: along with everything else, along with the emotion, the remembrance of the crimes, the unending astonishment, they are also tears of pride, of the very muted and yet definite pride in such a Federal Republic of Germany. That is the Germany I love: not the boastful, strong-man, proud-to-be-German or Europe-finally-speaks-German Germany, but a nation exasperated with its history, dissatisfied and struggling with itself to the point of self-incrimination, yet which has grown wiser through its error, has outgrown pageantry, humbly calls its constitution a 'basic law', prefers to show strangers a bit too much friendliness, too much trust, than ever to lapse into hostility and insolence again.

It is often said, and I have heard speakers say it at this podium, that the Germans should finally return to a normal, relaxed attitude towards their nation; that it's now long enough since Nazism was overcome. And I always wonder what those speakers mean: there never was a normal, relaxed attitude, even before Nazism. There was an excessive, aggressive nationalism, and as a counter-current there was a German self-criticism, a plea for Europe, an appeal to world citizenship (and also to world literature for that matter) which was unique in its determination, at least in the nineteenth century. 'A good German cannot be a nationalist,' Willy Brandt said confidently in his Nobel Lecture: 'A good German knows that he cannot refuse a European calling. Through Europe, Germany returns to itself and to the constructive forces of its history.'

Since the late eighteenth century, since Lessing at least, who despised patriotism and was the first German to use the word 'cosmopolitan', German culture has often stood in diametrical opposition to the nation. Goethe and Schiller, Kant and Schopenhauer, Hölderlin and Büchner, Heine and Nietzsche, Hesse and the Mann brothers – all of them struggled with Germany, saw themselves as citizens of the world and believed in European unity long before politicians discovered the project.

It is this cosmopolitan line of German thinking that Willy Brandt continued – not only in his struggle against German nationalism and for a united Europe, but also in his early plea for *Weltinnenpolitik*, a 'global domestic policy', in his commitment to international development, and during his chairmanship of the Socialist International. And it puts the Germany of today in a perhaps not very advantageous light when, in television debates before the parliamentary elections, practically nothing is said about foreign policy, when a constitutional body trivializes the upcoming European elections, when the developmental aid of such a strong economy is below the average of the OECD states – or when Germany admits just 10,000 of the 9 million Syrians who have lost their homes in the civil war.

After all, the involvement in the world that Willy Brandt exemplifies has always implied, conversely, more openness to the world. We cannot commemorate the constitution without remembering the mutilations that have been inflicted upon it here and there. In comparison with the constitutions of other countries, its wording has been changed unusually often, and few of those modifications have done the text good. What the Parliamentary Council expressly put in general and overarching terms, the Bundestag has burdened from time to time with detailed regulations. The most severe deformation is that of Article 16, linguistically and otherwise. The very constitution in which Germany seemed to have codified its openness for all time now locks out those who are most urgently in need of our openness: the victims of political persecution. A wonderfully concise sentence – *Politisch verfolgte genießen Asyl*, 'Persons persecuted on political grounds shall have the right of asylum' – was amended in 1993 into a monstrous provision of 275 words, stacked wildly one on top of another and closely convoluted just to hide one thing: the fact that asylum has practically ceased to be a fundamental right in Germany. Is it really necessary to recall that Willy Brandt, whose name brought approving nods from many of you throughout this chamber, was a refugee, an asylum-seeker?

Today too there are people, many people, who depend for their safety on the openness of other, democratic countries – and Edward Snowden, whom we have much to thank for in regard to the defence of our fundamental rights, is one of them. Others are drowning every day in the Mediterranean, several thousand every year, and very probably during this celebration. Germany does not have to receive all them that labour and are heavy laden. But it does have sufficient resources to defend victims of political persecution instead of shrugging off the responsibility onto so-called third countries. And out of properly understood self-interest it should give other people a fair chance to apply for immigration legally, so that they don't need to resort to the right of asylum. For there is still no sign, twenty years later, of the unified European refugee law that was talked of in 1993 in justifying the amendment, and the textual abuse alone that was inflicted on the constitution is painful enough. The right of asylum was robbed of its substance; Article 16 was robbed of its dignity. May the constitution be cleansed of this hideous, heartless stain by its seventieth anniversary at the latest.

This is a good Germany, the best one we have known. Instead of closing itself off, it can be proud that it has become so attractive. My parents did not flee Iran for political reasons. But after the coup against the democratic Mosaddegh government in 1953, they were glad, like many Iranians of their generation, to be able to study in a freer, more just country. After their studies they found work, they watched their children, grandchildren and even great-grandchildren grow up; they have grown old in Germany. And this whole big family, now grown to twenty-six people, counting only direct descendants and their spouses, have found happiness in this country. And not only we: many millions of people have immigrated to the Federal Republic of Germany since the Second World War; counting the expellees and the ethnic German immigrants, more people than half the current population. Even compared with other countries, that is a tremendous demographic change which Germany has had to master within a single generation. And I think, on the whole, Germany has mastered it well. There are cultural, religious and, most of all, social conflicts, especially in the metropolitan areas; there are resentments among Germans and there are resentments among those who are not *only* German; unfortunately, there is also violence and even terror and murder. But, on the whole, life in Germany is decidedly peaceful, still relatively just, and much more tolerant than it was as recently as the 1990s. Without actually noticing it, the Federal Republic has accomplished a magnificent work of integration – and I have not yet mentioned reunification!

Perhaps there could have been a little more recognition here and there, a visible, public gesture especially towards my parents' generation, the generation of the 'guest workers', for all they have done for Germany. But, conversely, perhaps the immigrants too have not always made it sufficiently plain how much they appreciate the freedom in which they share in Germany, the social balance, the professional opportunities, the free schools and universities, an outstanding health-care system by the way, the rule of law, a sometimes painful and yet precious freedom of opinion, the freedom of worship. And so, in closing, I would like to speak in the name of – no, not in the name of all immigrants: not in the name of Djamaa Isu, who hanged himself with a belt almost exactly one year ago today in the Eisenhüttenstadt refugee camp, for fear of being deported to a so-called third country without consideration of his request for asylum; not in the name of Mehmet Kubaşık and the other victims of the National Socialist Underground, who for years were libelled as criminals by the investigating authorities and the biggest newspapers in the country; not in the name of even one of the Jewish immigrants or returnees, who can never consider the murder of almost their entire people redressed – but in the name of many, of millions of people, in the name of the 'guest workers' who have long since ceased to be guests; in the name of their children and grandchildren, who naturally grow up with two cultures and, at long last, with two passports as well; in the name of my literary colleagues, for whom the German language too is a gift; in the name of the football players who will give everything they've got for Germany this summer in Brazil, even if they don't sing the national anthem; in the name of the less successful, the needy and even the delinquent, who belong just as much to Germany as the Özils and the Podolskis; especially in the name of the Muslims, who enjoy rights in Germany that, to our shame, are denied Christians in many Islamic countries today; thus in the name of my devout parents and an immigrant family of twenty-six – I would like to say, with at least a symbolic bow: thank you, Germany.

On Receiving the Joseph Breitbach Prize

Stadttheater, Koblenz, 9 September 2014

Dear representatives of the state, the city, the Foundation, the Academy, and the family of Joseph Breitbach; dear Egon, dear Martin; ladies and gentlemen,

The novel that receives a distinction today, *Dein Name*, is at its core a book of the dead. It commemorates the people in my life who died. I doubt whether the dead need anyone to keep their names in memory. What I learned as I wrote my book is that we need them – that something in us dies if we don't invoke them: the life we shared with them. The novel is finished; I tried several times to continue it, only to realize that I was getting caught up in repetitions; the story I set out to tell seems to have been told, and its incompleteness is a part of it. But the people – they keep on dying, and the older I get, the faster they die: the book of the dead, since it must strive for completeness, only ends with my own death. And so I would like, instead of explaining the novel that is receiving a distinction today, to recite the chapters that have been added since its publication.

But I cannot commemorate the dead as I did in *Dein Name*, with their names and all their details, to repeat the phrase of Ingeborg Bachmann[2] which became a refrain in the novel; down to the most insignificant observations, and their physiognomy down to photographic precision: too many people have died in the past three years, the time is too short, and a public speech is not an appropriate form. No, I will limit myself to the five who have died who are directly connected with *Dein Name*, some of whom in fact appear in it, although without their names, because they were alive, as friends, as relatives, as colleagues: let my acceptance speech be about how each one of them made the novel possible in the first place, influenced it, made it take an unexpected turn, and how each of them is connected in my life with each of the others, although they did not know one another, didn't even live on the same continent, didn't speak any language in common, and each of them thus creates the enormous web of relationships that we call I. That is what's meant, I believe, where the Talmud and the Quran say, in almost identical words, that killing one person is like killing all humanity. Each human being is a humanity.

The first to die, three months after the novel's publication, was Heinz Ludwig Arnold. Most of you will know him as one of the most important commentators and editors of German post-war literature; some of you also know him as your friend Lutz. I was still a student, writing on the side for the *Frankfurter Allgemeine Zeitung*, when Lutz wrote me a letter to ask me to introduce him to contemporary Persian literature. In reward for a small favour, he remained a loyal friend his whole life long, supported me where he could, reviewed my dissertation on the Quran, although its subject matter was foreign to him, and read my *Book of the Listeners Slain by Neil Young*, whose subject matter he must have found stranger still. He corrected the manuscript and sent it persistently, with his letterhead and his renown, to publishers, until I finally received an acceptance for my first literary publication.

What was curiously strange about Lutz, and at the same time admirable, was the submission with which he faced death. All the obituaries paid tribute to the man of action who, at twenty, became Ernst Jünger's secretary and, at twenty-three, founded the journal *Text und Kritik*; who soon published the *Lexikon zur deutschsprachigen Gegenwartsliteratur* [Encyclopaedia of contemporary literature in German] and later the *Lexikon zur fremdsprachigen Gegenwartsliteratur* [Encyclopaedia of contemporary foreign-language literature]; beyond number the broadcasts and essays and books that he wrote; and then the juries, lectures and seminars, a whole enterprise with its own staff sometimes numbering in the dozens, yet always standing on his own two feet, always independent, because a person like Lutz never let anyone tell him what to think, and, to the end, as if all that were not enough for one life, he also edited the new edition of *Kindlers Literatur-Lexikon* [Kindler's encyclopaedia of literature], with the help of his wife, his staff, dozens of experts and hundreds of authors – the last edition of *Kindler* that will ever be published, because no one in the world will ever again undertake such a task, such exertion, precision and coordination. Lutz was not religious, even at the end; he was almost surprised himself that he felt no such impulse; baulked just three days before his death at Heinrich Heine who, in his mattress tomb, claimed to have found a God after all. But what is characteristic of religion – the religious attitude – he, of all people, whose force of will seemed inexhaustible, had miraculously acquired that: now let another will be done; Thy will be done. He liked my observation that he had become, unintentionally so to speak, free of intention, as the religions prescribe. At the same time, he persevered in his disbelief in Eternity: a person simply disappears bit by bit, it seemed to him, until nothing remains. No complaint came from his mouth; at most, the observation that some situations are just rotten: getting up, going to the toilet, nausea and – most tormenting – the difficulty breathing, which led to anxiety attacks that he just couldn't help. Lutz himself was not anxious; only his body was on occasion.

His submission, which I admired, puzzled me at the same time. I had always assumed, and it fit with the observation in my novel, that people who are religious – regardless of any particular religion, or even God necessarily; what I mean is the awareness that all of this that exists is only a lesser existence – I had assumed that religious people have an advantage, at least in regard to the ultimate questions, because they have a certainty where a person, on dying, enters the absolutely uncertain, and they have prayers at hand where their own words fail. Lutz, who was himself surprised at the failure of any faith to materialize, rebutted my assumption as a prejudice, and with it one of the assertions of my novel. If he had died sooner, just four or five months earlier, *Dein Name* would have taken an atheistic turn at the end.

As I sat with him, his round body collapsed like a wrung-out skin, the only hope left in his eyes that of a quick disappearance, I also sensed, to my surprise, something of happiness, or, to be more exact, I felt that we the younger ones, who owe Lutz so much, would later remember these days as, in a way, happy. In a last exertion, he had put all his literary affairs in order and also provided for his wife and, most importantly, for his daughter. The feeling that everything had been taken care of, the pain bearable, thanks to the morphine, except for the occasional difficulty breathing; although the really unpleasant situations were more frequent with each passing day, they were still interspersed with peaceful hours right up to the end; fully conscious, with his family by him, and visits every day from friends who travelled to Göttingen from far away – to die in this way, to celebrate one's own death, is not given to many. If God, in Whom Lutz did not believe, is just, then such luck can only have been deserved. The great communicator of German post-war literature, its most industrious servant, received his reward, not in the form of his medals and prizes, although he took a childlike delight in such recognition. In the last weeks of his life, the loyalty he had shown was returned to him.

I always had the feeling that my literary texts impressed him as something learned or bold, like my academic texts, rather than as something personally moving, and that it was more out of friendship than enthusiasm that he supported me for so many years, encouraged me, gave me the benefit of his advice and his contacts, and was sincerely indignant at attacks and certain criticisms. During my last visit, just two days before his death, he listed the typographical errors he had discovered in *Dein Name*, most curious among them the confusion of Grass's *Dog Years* with Kempowski's *Dog Days*, which I swear no one else had noticed.

But at the funeral – vain as it is, I have to mention it – one of the speakers reported that, at the end, Lutz read by turns in three books: the *Decameron*, the *Divine Comedy* and *Dein Name*. He hadn't told me so explicitly, but on my visit I also had the feeling that perhaps my novel did not impress him as much as my earlier literary and academic texts; rather, my book of the dead moved him personally in a way that an author might wish, but a friend certainly would not. For when I gave Lutz the book on the 27th of August 2011, it was already plain that he would be the next one to be named, with his name and all his details, down to the most insignificant observations, and his physiognomy down to photographic precision. Although at the time we still expected him to have several months, perhaps even a year or two, of bearable life, his face already showed that humility that I had not known in him before. He knew that I would commemorate him, and I knew it. For that reason, we didn't speak of it. When I returned to Göttingen at the end of October, we didn't talk about the book; only about typographical errors and reviews, which he was annoyed with, as ever. All he wanted was for me to read him a little bit of it.

Of course, there is no consolation for parting. Lutz himself sent me away the next morning when he realized that the bad hours were beginning, the hours that got worse every day. I quickly gathered up my things. Farewell, said Lutz. You too, I thought, although Lutz did not believe in immortality. May his soul rejoice: Heinz Ludwig Arnold, born the 29th of March 1940 in Essen; died the 1st of November 2011 in Göttingen.

*

The next one to die, almost a year later – such a long time without death grows rare in the second half of a lifetime – was my old headmaster in Siegen, Volker Eckardt. I can say this much with certainty: if it hadn't been for old Eckardt, I never would have finished grammar school. And if I hadn't finished grammar school, I wouldn't have gone to university and read Middle Eastern Studies, and if I hadn't read Middle Eastern Studies, then my life would have taken such a completely different course that it wouldn't have been my life at all – the life of the man standing before you – but someone else's life, probably that of someone very strange to me. To give just one example – the nearest one to hand – of how I became the person who is accepting an important literary prize today: Heinz Ludwig Arnold would not have written to me if I hadn't read Middle Eastern Studies, hadn't finished grammar school, hadn't run across old Eckardt, out of all the headmasters in Siegen.

Because what had happened was that, at fifteen, I was expelled from school, the Prinz-Johann-Moritz-Gymnasium, and then applied to all the other grammar schools in Siegen one after another, but none of them had a place for me. This went on until I was beginning to panic, and my poor parents too, and we began to look into the schools in neighbouring towns, and how long I would travel, with what buses and trains, to get there every morning and back again in the afternoon. It is not important at this juncture why I was expelled from school; it's not the stuff of a heroic saga in any case. The important thing here is only that I finally rang the Gymnasium am Rosterberg, was given an appointment for an interview, and found myself for the first time face to face with old Eckardt, a tall man with a still taller forehead, reddish hair grown a bit too long, fluttering out behind his ears almost to his shoulders, his limbs clad in a dark-blue, old-fashioned suit, which made him more Hölderlin than hippie, or a character from an Erich Kästner novel. And I had hardly sat down when Eckardt said, I'll take you. And I – I must have been so surprised that I could only stammer, Why? And then old Eckardt told me that old Schütz, the head of the school I had been expelled from, had rung him up and warned him, Eckardt, not to admit me, and Schütz had rung not only him, Eckardt, but the heads of all the grammar schools in Siegen. And then he, Eckardt, had thought, What a weasel! – meaning Schütz; in that case he jolly well would admit the nipper, meaning me. But he expected of me, he said, that from now on I would always go to class – on time! – and not fool about so much: 'You must give me your hand on that, now.' I stood up and promised old Eckardt, who was a head or two taller than me, and gave him my hand and my word, and I did not always keep it – there would be trouble with old Eckardt often enough – but I kept it well enough that, four years later – it is fool's pride to mention such a thing, but here, in my commemoration of Eckardt, it is part of the story – I passed my exams with full marks.

By that time old Eckardt was no longer head, but a bigwig on the district school board. That was a story in itself.

When old Eckardt got promoted, the school threw an unbelievable fete for him: every single class thought up something, rehearsed and performed something really imaginative, much of it very amusing; recitals, songs, sketches – old Eckardt was wonderful to imitate, the way he burst into a classroom, unannounced if possible, with his outstretched arm and floating hair, to make sure everything was in order, and old Eckardt himself, great big Eckardt in his old-fashioned blue suit, sat there with misty eyes, in the front row of the hall, and just couldn't believe it. Then old Eckardt was gone, far away on the district school board, in another town, and to be honest we soon got used to the idea that someone else would be head, and thought about who we would prefer among the staff. And grumblers were also heard among the students who thought the fete a bit much and said old Eckardt hadn't been as great as all that, and had had his favourites, after all. Of course I had to disagree – I who was known as one of Eckardt's favourites. No, old Eckardt was not always fair; he could hardly hide his poor opinion of some teachers; yes, he had his favourites among the students – but when you're one of them, you don't think equality is so all-important any more.

Everyone had got used to going on with our lessons even if Eckardt no longer stormed into the classrooms, hair flying, and we were expecting the appointment of his successor, when one morning I heard from a classmate: Old Eckardt is back! What? How? Yes, Eckardt was back, had broken out of the bigwigs' jail and returned to his office, without consulting the school board. 'I nearly suffocated under all those files,' he growled when I waylaid him in the corridor. 'Couldn't breathe without you scallywags about.' And then something happened, or rather didn't happen, which old

Eckardt had perhaps expected when he returned to us with flying tresses: no cheering broke out. The school had just honoured him a few weeks before with such a rousing send-off as is rarely seen, every year giving its best – but it had been a send-off for all that. If the feelings at the farewell fete had been so strong, the compliments so extravagant, it was in part because the students thought they were losing him: such exuberance towards a sitting head would have been altogether awkward. But now he was back, from one morning to the next. Without quite knowing why, we were all a bit perplexed. The grumblers even said they'd been given the run-around.

Whether Eckardt too felt that his reception was less cordial than his farewell had been I was not bold enough to ask. In any case, he did not stay long: naturally the school board did not approve his reappointment – definitely not in that way. Old Eckardt must have known they wouldn't even as he got in his car in the chief town of the district to drive back to his headmaster's post at Rosterberg – all told, his return had something sadly quixotic about it; it was doomed to be a futile act of revolt against the odds, and then it failed even to draw the expected support of the students. This time, old Eckardt left our school more quietly – not with a fete, not even a small adieu: from one morning to the next, old Eckardt was gone.

Ten or fifteen years later – I had finished at university and was on the staff of the *Frankfurter Allgemeine Zeitung* – I heard on our answering machine his deep, creaking voice with the familiar cadences of Westphalia, if not the Siegen area: *Ja*, I hope I've reached Navette – you have to imagine my name pronounced the Westphalian way: not Navid, much less the Persian Naveeed, but Navette, and old Eckardt in particular always stretched the first vowel: Nayvett. *Ja*, I hope I've reached Nayvett, ehm, I mean, Mr Kermani. This is Eckardt, your old head from Siegen. As the head of a grammar school of course he had always been a reader of the *Frankfurter Allgemeine Zeitung*, and so he had seen my name, found out that I lived in Cologne, and got my number from directory enquiries. You mustn't call me Mister, I said straight away to old Eckardt, and from then on I visited him and his wife regularly, at first in the chief town of the district, where he had just been pensioned as a school board bigwig, and later in Münster. Once old Eckardt and his wife came to an award ceremony: I saw him towering over most of the other guests at the reception with his grey but now still longer hair, now really more hippie than Hölderlin, and I heard him from across the room creaking loudly as he told a stranger about little Nayvett, the nipper he had admitted even though he'd been warned against him. You won't find a head like that, such a headmaster as I had, even in an Erich Kästner novel. May his soul rejoice: Volker Eckardt, born the 27th of February 1929 in Münster; died there the 27th of July 2012.

*

I have written at length about Aunt Ghodsi in *Dein Name*, although without mentioning her name. For her husband was Mr Ketabi, whose name heads the fifth chapter, and what I recount there of his life is also the life of my Aunt Ghodsi, my summer holidays at their house in Tehran, their visit to Germany, and finally the years in which Aunt Ghodsi cared for her sick husband and in which, for all her care, all her self-sacrifice, she was still able to seize some freedom: drawing out her shopping by a few minutes; her aquagymnastics in their apartment block's pool; her ladies' circle, which she insisted on attending right up to the end. And the melancholy smile that she occasionally cast my way when the conversation lagged because, although the silent Mr Ketabi could still hear us, he was no longer interested in anything – her melancholy smile too suggested freedom, the freedom of her thoughts, even if her husband's illness forced an almost twenty-four-hour duty upon her, which she accepted without complaint and carried out in exemplary fashion.

The love of Iran that took literary form in *Dein Name* is not an intellectual love: it does not come from reading, much less from political or social conditions. Büchner and Kafka were always much closer to my heart than Hafiz and Rumi, and I certainly identify more with West Germany as a community than with the Persian Empire or the Islamic Republic. The love that took form in *Dein Name* is the love of a little child. If there is anything I associate with Iran, it is a tremendous tenderness and warmth in personal interactions that I perceived among my relatives, the men included, and more often among the women, first among them my Aunt Lobat, whose death I described in *The Terror of God*, but also her youngest sister, Aunt Ghodsi, whom we always stayed with in Tehran. Her daughter, who is five days older or younger than I – I still can't keep that straight – was my best friend in Iran, and so I sometimes stayed on by myself for days at Aunt Ghodsi's house when my parents had business out of town.

I don't want to derive any culturalist theories from it, or do any injustice to other peoples – and, in retrospect, I must not overlook my status as a guest, which shielded me from all reproach – but the utter gentleness, the perfect softness of the language and the gestures that I heard, saw, felt on my skin, even on my head, which Aunt Ghodsi liked to stroke for minutes on end, during the summer holidays at her house – I had never known that in German adults. I know the silken sound of endearments only from Iran, the delicate sing-song in Aunt Ghodsi's sentences, always ending on a slight lift in her voice, so bright, so friendly. Although I stayed many days or even weeks in her house in Tehran, I never heard a sharp word from her, or even an impatient one; in fact I don't even know what her sharp or even merely impatient word would have sounded like, although with her own children she must surely have been strict at times. Or is child-rearing imaginable with no anger, no rebuke at all? I can't imagine it, and yet I never saw such a thing from Aunt Ghodsi, although she had four children.

At most, she reminded us occasionally that we ought to make less noise after lunch because Mr Ketabi was taking a nap, or to eat the fruit that she peeled for us without being asked. She never punished us. And the strange thing was, looking back on it today: unlike all the anti-authoritarian child-raising that I later observed in Germany, it worked; it worked thanks to the unreserved love she showed us. I had such trust in Aunt Ghodsi, who in those days was in her forties, not yet old, but to me an absolutely adult person – I had such trust in her that it never would have occurred to me intentionally to do anything she wouldn't like. My own parents, whom I knew as a child how to infuriate, were much more strict with me. My parents were probably strict because I was disobedient, but as a child I would have explained my disobedience in any case as a rebellion against their strictness. I obeyed Aunt Ghodsi, on the other hand – I would have reasoned as a child – because she did not exercise the least coercion.

As a child, of course, I did not know the concept of anti-authoritarian child-raising, which only works, for that matter, when the authority is so self-evident, as Volker Eckardt's was, that it doesn't need to be demonstrated. But I did notice as a child the contrast between scolding and non-scolding adults, and I distinctly associated the scolding ones with Germany – not only the German adults but also my own parents, although by the standards of the time in

Siegen and vicinity, where the 1968 movement had not yet arrived, they were giving us an altogether liberal upbringing. Conversely, I associated parents who did not scold with my summer holidays in Iran. My childish perception probably turns all the available statistics upside down. And I don't need any statistics to know that corporal punishment is still shockingly common in Muslim families; a peek behind the façades of my own multicultural neighbourhood in Cologne is enough. As a reporter, I witness the tyranny that reigns in many Middle Eastern countries. I am ashamed of the mercilessness of many people who espouse Islam. I am writing this month against the thraldom that a so-called Islamic State imposes on people, the mass executions, the torture, the stonings, the expulsions and the forced conversions. I know about the physical punishments that are provided for in the Quran itself. I am not ignoring that; I am searching for the causes of the violence which the world, with good cause, associates with Islam. But I myself – I grew up with resolutely Islamic relatives who were as resolutely gentle as my Aunt Ghodsi. I cannot wipe away this influence, as tempting as it seems some days to despise the land and the religion of my parents.

I suspect that those Iranians, Turks or Arabs who appear in the Western media today as accusers of their culture of origin had different relatives from mine: whipping, punishing relatives. I cannot hold it against them if they identify the violence that was done to them with their culture. But I cannot do otherwise than to associate the same culture with compassion. For compassion, to me, is more than just a word that occurs at the beginning of every surah, every prayer, and hence every journey, every long drive, every reading, and this acceptance speech. Compassion is what I experienced in the summer holidays among my relatives, the men included, and the women still more. May her soul rejoice: Ghodsi Ketabi, born the 21st of January 1932 in Isfahan; died the 28th of February 2013 in Tehran.

*

Friedrich Linpinsel was one of those strict parents I mentioned a moment ago. That doesn't mean I didn't enjoy visiting the Linpinsels, whose son was friends with my brother and whose daughter is now my sister-in-law. Strict did not necessarily mean unfriendly or unpleasant. Strict was just different from what I knew from my summer holidays in Iran. Strict meant rigidly kept mealtimes with fixed seating. Strict meant a raised voice once in a while. Strict meant: better not do anything wrong! Nonetheless, strict adults could also be nice or make jokes that all the children laughed at. Mr Linpinsel was that kind of a strict, but nice, and even rather jovial adult.

When I think about it today, my brother must have been an odd kind of friend: always bringing along his little brother, eleven years younger than him, when he visited the Linpinsels. I don't know exactly why I went along, but I did, and I enjoyed it. Mr Linpinsel can't have been as strict as I remember him being, otherwise his children would never have been allowed to bring so many friends home, and not only friends, but also their friends' siblings – or at least me. It is true that Mr Linpinsel's opinions were strict: his religion strictly Catholic, his politics staunchly Christian Democrat, his newspaper strictly *Frankfurter Allgemeine Zeitung*; he held communism to be the Devil incarnate and detested the peace movement – which would sweep me along in my adolescence – as a band of naive and, worse, unkempt nitwits. Yet it wasn't this or that opinion that was disconcerting to me, but the fact that Mr Linpinsel seemed to have a definite, unshakable opinion on everything: every word a final judgement. What he disclosed of his work and, more specifically, his conception of his work as the chief prosecutor of Siegen, was enough to instil in me a lifelong fear of the law: woe betide anyone who faced a prosecutor like Mr Linpinsel.

Over the many years, the decades, of our acquaintance, there not only grew trust, until he seemed to like me almost as a son, and I respected him as a father; our opinions too, which as a fifteen-year-old I would have considered irremediably incompatible, gradually came closer together. In tortuous discussions with his parish priest and our Islamic clerics, he was persuaded to agree to his daughter's marriage to a Mohammedan, and the newspaper I wrote for was none other than his beloved *FAZ*. In his old age he praised his alliance with our Muslim family as a gift of God, and to my fifteen-year-old daughter I am just as reactionary today as Mr Linpinsel was to me at fifteen. To the last, when we weren't criticizing the *FAZ*, we discussed German politics, Adenauer and Strauss, Schmidt and Kohl, Schröder and Merkel, and though we rarely agreed, least of all about Brandt, I have long since ceased to hold his strictly Catholic, staunchly Christian Democrat camp, which is not what it once was, to be the Devil incarnate.

I would like to illustrate by an example how my coordinates have shifted, in part because of Mr Linpinsel. My politics were shaped by two influences: the revolution in Iran and the Green-alternative movement in Germany. In both milieus, anti-Americanism was taken for granted. As the son of Iranians, I associated America with the shah, SAVAK, the coup against the democratic Mosaddegh government. As an adolescent in Germany, I associated America with imperialism, the Contras, and the coup against the democratic Allende government. The Allende argument was a long shot, I admit: in 1983 in Siegen, I knew little more than the name. The overthrow of Mosaddegh, on the other hand, is, to most Iranians of my generation, and still more to the older generation, an event which leaves America with tangible guilt for the shah and all the violence that followed. Thus, in one part of my biography at least, there were reasons to be against America: there was an experience that affects our lives even today. Without the coup against Mosaddegh, my parents would not have emigrated, and there would have been no Islamic revolution.

Mr Linpinsel had had the opposite experience. He had been in the war, first on the eastern front, later in the west, where he had been taken prisoner by the Americans. Just as his fear of the Russians was fed by experiences beyond my imagination, Mr Linpinsel experienced Germany's alliance with the West as his personal good fortune. He described in full detail the magnanimity of the Americans who had restored to him – their enemy! – his dignity and even his enjoyment of life. The Americans could have humiliated, annihilated, enslaved him – Mr Linpinsel would not have been able to object. Instead the Americans had treated their prisoner of war as a young man who could work for a better future for his country; they had offered him a clean bed, given him decent food, supplied him with books and reasonable clothes, taught him English, even given him – their prisoner! – access to higher education in America; and released him as a German citizen cured of the nationalist conceit. It was only through Mr Linpinsel that the liberation of Germany became part of my own family history. Perhaps that is why in *Dein Name* I rediscovered the American school that my grandfather attended in Tehran at the turn of the twentieth century. I notice in any case that, in all the major foreign policy debates in which I have publicly taken part in recent years, from the Iraq war to Ukraine and Syria to the 'Islamic State', I have dissented from my own left-alternative milieu: war may have been the wrong means, but liberation is never the wrong goal.

On his deathbed, Mr Linpinsel spoke of almost nothing else but war. I have never seen a person so soft, shockingly tender in his words and his touch, defenceless and grateful. The strict Mr Linpinsel of my childhood, the chief prosecutor with the staunch opinions – he was no more. I had grown old, an adult through and through, but he was growing steadily younger, as young as a recruit. His body in a thin gown such as one apparently wears on one's deathbed, lying on his side, his bent legs bare, he returned to the present only briefly, grasped my arm, caressed it, thanked me again and again for my visit, as if I wouldn't naturally visit him, and conversed a bit more before sinking back into his memories. He wept when he was at the front and smiled blissfully when he was captured again by the Americans. Germany had been rescued. May his soul rejoice: Friedrich Linpinsel, born the 20th of November 1923 in Königsberg, died the 27th of March 2013 in Wilnsdorf.

*

I have mentioned the *Frankfurter Allgemeine Zeitung*, the major daily newspaper from Frankfurt, so many times already. Frank Schirrmacher's death this summer taught me that God doesn't care about closure. Schirrmacher supported me as a student, and after my doctorate he offered me a contract; he sent me abroad on assignments that no daily newspaper would pay for today, and he asked me long before the 11th of September 2001 whether I would go to the Middle East as a cultural correspondent. That was the prospect that was far more enticing than an academic career: spending the next few years in Cairo. Schirrmacher seemed to be quite stuck on me. It didn't occur to me that he could come unstuck again.

Schirrmacher had a gift that I hadn't seen in anyone else before then: the gift of creating the impression that you had his full attention. No matter what was going on around him, in the outer office, the bustle of the newsroom; no matter what he might have been thinking about two minutes ago – when we sat knee by knee on the sofas of his office, he seemed to have switched off the outside world like a television set. The fact that Schirrmacher was one of the first to realize what an overload the brain is subjected to by the new communication media must have had something to do with his own ability to concentrate so totally on a single object, a single person – although I was just a student, and had bought a jacket expressly for the appointment, and he was one of the shareholding editorial board of the respected, and also somehow dreaded, *Frankfurter Allgemeine Zeitung*, the major newspaper associated with the enemy camp. Entranced, his small mouth half open, his eyes on me as if unblinking, his torso bent forward, he nodded as if I had just explained to him how the Earth was created and asked questions with such enthusiasm that I was persuaded of – more than just his understanding: his agreement. He gave me a tour of the editorial offices, knocked on the doors of the colleagues he most urgently wanted me to meet, and was not above taking me up or down a floor to the sports section because I had mentioned an interest in football.

Only much later did I learn that Schirrmacher was able to switch into an input mode almost at the push of a button, or that he was like a child absorbed in his play: it probably had nothing to do with the people present; it was more the topic that fascinated him – in my case, the world of the Middle East. His later lack of interest, accordingly, had no more to do with me than his earlier interest had. He was just mesmerized by the next new topic – neuroscience and the natural sciences in general this time – and by the new people who went with it. I didn't notice that; all I saw was that my articles began to slide towards the back pages and were being grotesquely shortened. In a polite, almost reverent letter, I pointed out to him the carelessness with which my texts were being treated lately. I still assumed that this was just a series of misfortunes, petty matters, actually, that an editor-in-chief could not be bothered with, and that I would soon be moving to Cairo. Days and weeks went by without an answer from Schirrmacher. Finally, an editor intimated to me that no answer would be forthcoming. On the spur of the moment, I sent my resignation to the *Frankfurter Allgemeine Zeitung*.

I have reported from several war zones since then, and have certainly been exposed to dangers. But if I had to name a moment when I personally displayed courage, it was that resignation. I turned down a future that looked as if it was tailor-made for me. I had just finished my degree, just become a father; I had no security of any kind, no salary and no other professional plans. And yet it was a lovely feeling when I dropped my resignation in the letterbox near our house, and didn't even have anything to do for the hours that followed: as young as I was, I would certainly have time to set a new course in life.

I don't need to dwell on the contempt that Schirrmacher subsequently showered upon me. That was apparently his way of dealing with people who turned away from him; perhaps an expression of disappointed affection, perhaps just wounded vanity; in my case, to be sure, there was also the accusation of ingratitude. It wasn't dignified; it was, in an almost poignant way, petty and weak. Perhaps the same childlike quality that made his curiosity as a journalist so great also made him so childish in anger. It hurt nonetheless, and it harmed my books for a long time afterwards. An editor who shared the same fate a short time later said to me, If you turn your back on Schirrmacher, he'll throw an axe at it. That's exactly what it was like: an axe that I still feel today between my shoulders. But even that is a kind of contact.

Some of you may remember the controversy about the Hessian State Cultural Prize in 2009. At that time, it was the *FAZ* that defended me, with all its conservative prestige, against the minister-president and the two church leaders. And that, I know for a certain fact, saved my neck as a public figure. For, otherwise, the accusation would have clung to me that I had insulted Christianity, I of all people. That was – it could only have been Schirrmacher personally who took my side when I needed it. Yet we never spoke, or even e-mailed, about it, neither at the time nor later.

I always thought, from the day of my resignation on, that our falling-out was much too silly to last forever. The attention he had given me – that was not a trick. The gratitude that I owe him – if only for the fact that, if it weren't for Schirrmacher, I never would have done the reporting that so much of *Dein Name* is concerned with – in fact, I never expressed that gratitude. I always read his editorials and fancied that he must miss my articles. I always thought: one day we will sit knee by knee again, he and I. And now, barely begun, our story has already come to its end. May his soul rejoice: Frank Schirrmacher, born the 5th of September 1959 in Wiesbaden; died the 12th of June 2014 in Frankfurt am Main.

*

If I imagine just these five people in my life who have died in one room, at the same table – the literary critic, my old headmaster from Siegen, my aunt from Tehran, the chief prosecutor, the editor of the *Frankfurter Allgemeine Zeitung* – it would seem to be a random, an arbitrary constellation that no novelist would think up. *Dein Name* was the attempt to write that novel.

*

Joseph Breitbach certainly needed no one to preserve his name when he founded this award. But he wanted, I imagine, to let us take part in the life he led, in his intellectual as well as his material wealth. All those who knew him describe him as having a rare generosity. How grateful then we must be who did not know him, and who receive his generosity year after year. How grateful I am to be honoured in the name of Joseph Breitbach.

At the Public Commemoration of the Victims of the Paris Attacks

Appellhofplatz, Cologne, 14 January 2015

Dear fellow citizens, dear friends,

A week ago today, twelve people were murdered in Paris for exercising their right to free speech. Two people were murdered for being police officers, ordinary patrol officers doing their job. A day later, four people were murdered – the attacker himself gave this explanation on the telephone – for being Jews. This took place in the middle of Europe, in the middle of the French capital, not far from the Bastille where, in 1789, the citizens mounted barricades against the rule of a despot, for the reign of freedom, equality and brotherhood. It is that revolution which marks the beginning of our freedom as well.

It took years, decades, in fact almost two centuries – Europe, and France too, took roundabout paths and terrible wrong turns – before people could – no, I will not say *enjoy* equal rights, because Europe has not yet been made a reality, but *claim* and *uphold* equal rights, regardless of their sex, their origins, their religion, their sexual orientation. But liberty and equality are not all the legacy of the French Revolution. Recent days have reminded us that, in all questions of political rights and legal provisions, we must always keep in mind the aspect of fraternity, of empathy, of standing up for the weak, welcoming the stranger, defending the victim of persecution. That was the crucial civilizing breakthrough that was, not achieved, to be sure, but begun in 1789: the translation into social reality of the biblical commandment to love one's neighbour. Not we the French versus we the Germans, not we the white people above black people, not we natives above foreigners, not men above women, not we the nobility and we the commoners, not we the capitalists and we the workers, not we Christians, we Jews and we Muslims, not we Europeans, we Asians and we Africans – no: we human beings.

The terrorists want to drive a wedge between us; they want to force us to divide ourselves into Europeans and Arabs, Westerners and Asians, believers and unbelievers. They almost succeeded after the 11th of September 2001, when terror was answered with wars, with torture, with the undermining of the rule of law. The inevitable consequences were still more violence and counter-violence, still more prejudice and still more hatred, still more attacks and tens of thousands, hundreds of thousands more deaths. Today our answer to terror must be a different one, must be an enlightening one in the best sense of the word: not less freedom, but more! Not exclusion, but equality, now more than ever! And, most of all: not animosity, but brotherhood!

And in fact, dear fellow citizens, dear friends: we have seen the pictures of the past week, the pictures of the demonstrations on Sunday in Paris and yesterday evening in Berlin, Madrid and London, even in Beirut and Hebron; we have seen worldwide mourning and a worldwide solidarity. *Charlie Hebdo* appeared today with a circulation of 3 million copies, published simultaneously in almost thirty countries. The vast majority, the overwhelming majority of people, across all boundaries of religion, nation and ethnicity, have placed what we hold in common above what divides us. No, we Europeans do not all agree. Yes, we have our conflicts, differences and contradictions. And it is true that not all of us would laugh at jokes about a minority, whether it is Jews in Germany, Muslims in France or, say, Christians in Iran. Some of us may also feel offended by the cartoons that were published in *Charlie Hebdo*. But we all agree – we were never more in agreement than in these days – that we never again want to address these conflicts, differences and contradictions on our continent by violence.

And so I see again, this evening in this square, which was once one of the darkest places in our city, before the doors of the EL-DE building, once the seat of the Gestapo in Cologne and the embodiment of a nationalist terror regime, and yes, dear neighbours, dear friends, I am glad, irrepressibly glad, to see you all standing together. I see you together – no matter your religion, party or union, no matter what your background is, the colour of your skin, your sex, whether you are black or white, whether you are gay or lesbian or heterosexual, whether you are politically left or right, whether your party is liberal or conservative or Green or Red, whether you are poor or rich, whether you live in Marienburg or Mülheim, whether you listen to opera or watch comedies, whether you believe in God or FC Cologne or, like me, in God *and* FC Cologne – I see you all resolutely united in commemoration of the victims of Paris. Together we bear witness to our grief, together we bear witness to our horror, together we bear witness to our sympathy with the families of the victims – and we resolutely oppose all those who would abuse the murders of seventeen innocent people to inflame us against a certain segment of the population. We oppose the Le Pens in France and the Gaulands in Germany, we oppose the Islamophobia of Pegida and ProKöln, we oppose the Salafists and the right-wing radicals, the hate preachers in the mosques and the hate preachers on the talk shows. We oppose those who pretend to be rescuers of the West, but who betray everything that makes the West lovable and liveable. We oppose those who wreak havoc over a few cartoons and cannot see that they are the ones – they themselves! – who are making Islam into a caricature of itself.

We oppose them, yes – and we should have opposed them much sooner. For the past week has shown us not only an incredible solidarity – it has also reminded us all that liberty, equality, fraternity cannot be taken for granted, nor can they be had for nothing; that we have to stand up for them again and again; we have to fight for them and, if necessary, defend them with our lives. The struggle against oppression and violence is being fought not only in Kobane or Aleppo, not only on the 11th of September 2001 in New York or on the 7th of January 2015 in Paris. We must stand up for the ideals of justice, peace and tolerance every day, in our day-to-day lives, among our own acquaintances, at work or at school, in our parties, unions, clubs and religious congregations, and also – and many of us do not appreciate this enough – at the polls, especially at the elections of our European community. The past week has reminded us that Europe is at risk of being ground between the mutually escalating hatreds of nationalists on one side and religious extremists on the other. It has reminded us of the conflicts and wars taking place, not in times past or on far-away continents, but right at Europe's door. Just two, three hours from here by air, dozens, hundreds of people are dying every day, and if they are not torn apart by bullets or bombs, then they die fleeing, they drown in the Mediterranean, dozens, hundreds of people every day.

We should not stand by, and we cannot, because no matter what happens in the Middle East, it will affect us: our security, our prosperity, and the peace of our society. For decades we have supported the bloodiest dictatorships there, and even participated directly in the overthrow of democratic, secular governments. We looked on with almost no reaction as the Palestinians were robbed of their land and their future, settlement by settlement. But most of all, we have – yes, I say we, even though most of us protested against the Iraq war in 2003; after all, the war was fought by the leading nation of the West, in the name of Western values, and from German airfields – most of all, we have brought lawlessness and violence upon a whole country while claiming, or perhaps in fact believing, that we were liberating the Iraqis. The Paris attacks are, not least, a consequence of this war, which gave the al-Qaeda terror network a staging area in Europe's immediate vicinity such as Osama bin Laden could not have hoped for in his wildest dreams. And the attacks are at the same time a consequence of our failure in Syria, where we did not support peaceful demonstrators who were being shot down and sometimes gassed by a brutal regime, where we stood by passively, or perhaps even in perfidious scheming, as our own closest allies, Saudi Arabia and other Gulf states, were financing and arming the jihadists, including the so-called Islamic State, whom the attackers claimed to represent.

I say this not to downplay the Muslims' own responsibility: after all, Saudi Arabia and the Gulf states are also Muslim countries, and so are all the dictatorships that reign in the Islamic world. I say it to point out that terror does not simply happen in a vacuum but grows on a social, political and intellectual soil. Those who would defeat terror must have, yes, police, intelligence services, courts. Some of us who grew up, as I did, with the peace movement have taken a long time to realize that a security infrastructure is necessary – and to recognize the courage of our soldiers and police. And yet the only way we will defeat terror is by taking away the social, political and intellectual soil on which it grows. It is in the nature of the problem that those in whose name the violence is committed have a particular responsibility to bear.

When war and destruction had been wrought upon half the world in the name of Germany, it was in part the Germans in exile, who had themselves fought against the Nazis, who were especially called upon to explain a different Germany, the better Germany.

So permit me, dear fellow citizens, dear friends, permit me therefore at this point to address a word especially to the Muslims among you, my brothers and sisters in faith.

It is not enough to say that violence has nothing to do with Islam. The moment terrorists claim to be acting in the name of Islam, their terror has something to do with Islam. We must engage with the doctrine that is inciting people to hate one another, and murdering and oppressing people of other religions, all over the world today. In recent months, jihadists have expelled, raped, murdered hundreds of thousands of Christians, Yazidis and dissenters of all kinds. Just a few weeks ago, in Pakistan, they attacked a school and shot 141 people, most of them children. And the same day as jihadists attacked the offices of *Charlie Hebdo* in Paris, jihadists in Nigeria razed a whole village and massacred many hundreds, possibly two thousand civilians – in the name of Islam, my brothers and sisters. And whether those villagers were Muslims or Christians doesn't interest me in the least; I don't even want to mention that here – they were people: peaceful, defenceless human beings; they too were our brothers and sisters.

Islam has known waves of violence and barbarity again and again; there was the invasion of the Mongols and there was the invasion of the Crusaders. But this violence and this barbarity – they come from our own midst; they are neither Mossad's nor the CIA's doing. It is up to us – not just up to the organizations, no; it is up to every one of us – to tear off the mask that is distorting our religion. It is our responsibility and our job to make sure that Islam is associated no longer with terror and violence but once more with freedom and justice; no longer bigotry and dogma but reason and tolerance; no longer oppression and punishment but humour and culture. But most of all it is up to us to reassert the highest commandment of Islam: compassion. 'Yet if thou stretchest out thy hand against me, to slay me, I will not stretch out my hand against thee, to slay thee': most people today will think that is from the Sermon on the Mount, but it is our own Quran, surah 5, verse 28.[3]

Don't look the other way when your children, your siblings or your friends from one day to the next start holding up the Quran, saying it must be interpreted only strictly literally, and setting themselves up as moralizers and judges who think they know better: talk with them, show them the 1,400-year-old tradition of Islamic scholarship, beginning with the Prophet himself, who never understood the Quran only literally and always accepted more than one interpretation. Tell them that the emulation of the Prophet consists not in wearing certain clothes or a certain beard, but in using the faculty of reason, in seeking knowledge even in far-off countries, and in doing acts of charity. Explain to them that jihad, in all the interpretative traditions of Islam, can only be a clearly defined, temporally limited, defensive struggle, and never the murder of defenceless people. Remind them that the true jihad is not a struggle against unbelievers but the believer's inner struggle. In your mosques and schools and families, do not ignore the verses in the Quran which seem to advocate violence, but talk about them, discuss them, and embed them in their historical context. Intervene when people speak contemptuously of members of other religions, and especially, as happens increasingly often among our youth, especially of Jews. 'A person is either your brother in faith or your brother in humanity': thus said ʿAli ibn Abi Talib, the fourth Caliph and the first Imam, who unites the Sunnis and the Shiites as no other successor of the Prophet. That, precisely that, is at the same time the humanistic core which is common to the Eastern and the Western religions, and which was secularized in the French Revolution as the principle of equality.

Dear neighbours, dear friends, let us – no matter whether we are believers or not, men or women, black or white, native or foreign – let us never hesitate to mount the barricades again to demonstrate our liberty, our equality and, in so doing, our fraternity. The seventeen people who, a week ago in Paris, were murdered as journalists, as police officers, as Jews, live in our memory and our prayers as human beings. They are witnesses that the struggle which began in Paris in 1789 – the struggle for brotherhood – still goes on: *Alle Menschen werden Brüder*, 'All people shall be brothers.'

On Receiving the Peace Prize of the German Publishers' Association

St Paul's Church, Frankfurt am Main, 18 October 2015

Dear Mr Mayor, dear Mr Riethmüller, dear Mr Miller, excellencies and honourable guests, ladies and gentlemen,

On the day I received the news of the Peace Prize of the German Publishers' Association, the same day, Jacques Mourad was kidnapped in Syria. Two armed men entered the Mar Elian monastery on the outskirts of the town of Qaryatain and demanded to see Father Jacques. They found him no doubt in his bare little office, which was also his sitting room and his bedroom, seized him and took him away. On the 21st of May 2015, Jacques Mourad became a hostage of the so-called Islamic State.

I met Father Jacques in the autumn of 2012, when I was travelling as a reporter in Syria – the country was already shaken by war. He was the pastor of the Catholic community of Qaryatain, and at the same time belonged to the order of Mar Musa, founded in the early 1980s in a dilapidated early Christian monastery. Mar Musa is a special Christian community, perhaps a unique one, for it has dedicated itself to engagement with Islam and love for the Muslims.

As conscientiously as the nuns and monks observe the commandments and rituals of their own Catholic church, they are equally earnest in their study of Islam and take part in Muslim traditions even to the point of fasting during Ramadan. That sounds mad, preposterous: Christians who, in their own words, have fallen in love with Islam. And yet, a short time ago, such a Christian–Muslim love was a reality in Syria, and in the hearts of many Syrians it still is. By the work of their hands, the kindness of their hearts and the prayers of their souls, the nuns and monks of Mar Musa created a place that I found utopian, and they – they would say, not that it anticipated a reconciliation to come, but that it presaged, presupposed, nothing less than eschatological reconciliation: a stone monastery from the seventh century amid the overwhelming solitude of the Syrian desert mountains, visited by Christians from all over the world, yet where still more numerous Arab Muslims knocked on the door, dozens, hundreds day after day, to meet their Christian brothers and sisters, to talk with them, to sing, to sit in silence, and also to pray, in a pictureless corner of the church, after their own Islamic rite.

When I visited Father Jacques in 2012, the founder of the community, the Italian Jesuit Paolo Dall'Oglio, had recently been expelled from the country. Father Paolo had been too vocal in his criticism of the Assad government, which answered the Syrian people's call for freedom and democracy – nine months of peaceful demands – with arrests and torture, with clubs and assault rifles, and ultimately with horrible massacres and even poison gas, until the country finally sank into civil war. But Father Paolo had also opposed the leadership of the established Syrian churches, which were silent in the face of the government's violence. In vain he had solicited support in Europe for the Syrian movement for democracy; in vain he had called on the United Nations to establish a no-fly zone or at least to send observers. In vain had he warned of a war of religion if the secular and moderate groups were left to fend for themselves while only the jihadists received aid from abroad. In vain he had tried to break through the wall of our apathy. In summer of 2013, the founder of the community of Mar Musa returned to Syria in secret to plead for some Muslim friends who were in the hands of the 'Islamic State', and he was kidnapped by the 'Islamic State' himself. No trace has been seen of Father Paolo Dall'Oglio since the 28th of July 2013.

Father Jacques, who now bore sole responsibility for the monastery Mar Elian, is by nature a very different person: not a gifted speaker, not a charismatic leader, not a fiery Italian but, like so many of the Syrians I met, a proud, deliberate, extremely polite man, quite tall, his face broad, his short hair still black. Naturally I did not get to know him well: I attended the Mass which, as in all Eastern churches, consisted of enchantingly beautiful singing, and I observed how attentively he chatted with the faithful and the local dignitaries during the midday meal that followed. When he had taken leave of all the guests, he took me to his tiny room for a half-hour interview, placing a chair next to the narrow bed that he sat on.

It was not only his words that amazed me – how fearlessly he criticized the government; how openly he also talked about the increasing harshness in his own Christian congregation. His appearance impressed me more deeply still: a quiet, very conscientious, introspective and ascetic servant of God – that is how I perceived him – but one who now, since God had placed the care of the beleaguered Christians in Qaryatain and the leadership of the monastic community on his shoulders, exercised this public duty too with all his strength. He spoke softly and slowly, his eyes usually closed, as if he were consciously slowing his pulse and using the interview as a pause for breath between two more strenuous obligations. At the same time, his words were very considered, his sentences polished, and what he said was so clear, and so politically strident, that I asked him repeatedly whether it was not too dangerous to quote him verbatim. Then he opened his warm, dark eyes and nodded wearily, yes, I could print all of it, otherwise he wouldn't have said it; the world must know what is happening in Syria.

That weariness: that too was a strong impression, perhaps my strongest, of Father Jacques – it was the weariness of a man who had not merely realized but embraced the fact that rest might come only in the next life: the weariness of a doctor or a firefighter, pacing himself when need is most dire. And Father Jacques, as a priest in the midst of war, was a doctor and a firefighter too, not only to the souls of the fearful but also to the bodies of the needy, regardless of their faith, to whom he offered in his church food, sanctuary, clothes, shelter and, most of all, attention. To the last, the community of Mar Musa in their monastery sheltered and cared for many hundreds if not thousands of refugees, the vast majority of them Muslims. And not only that – Father Jacques was able to maintain peace, at least in Qaryatain, including peace between the religions. It is mainly thanks to him, the quiet, serious Father Jacques, that the different groups and militias, some supporting the government, some opposed to it, agreed to ban all heavy weapons from the town. And he, the priest who criticized his church, was able to persuade almost all the Christians in his parish to remain there. 'We Christians belong to this country, even if the fundamentalists don't like to hear it, neither here nor in Europe,' Father Jacques told me. 'Arab culture is our culture!'

The appeals of some Western politicians to grant asylum specifically to Arab Christians left a bitter taste in his mouth. The same West that cares nothing for the millions of Syrians, across all religions, who demonstrated peacefully for democracy and human rights, the same West that ruined Iraq and supplied Assad with his poison gas, the same West that maintains an alliance with Saudi Arabia, the primary sponsor of the jihadists – that same West now cares about Arab Christians? That must be a joke, said Father Jacques with a straight face. And he continued, his eyes closed: 'These politicians with their irresponsible statements are fostering precisely that sectarianism that threatens us Christians.'

The responsibility that Father Jacques bore, ever uncomplaining, continued to grow. The foreign members of the community had to leave Syria and found refuge in northern Iraq. Only the seven Syrian monks and nuns remained, dividing themselves between the two monasteries Mar Musa and Mar Elian. The fronts were constantly shifting, so that Qaryatain was ruled sometimes by the state, sometimes by opposition militias. The monks and nuns had to come to terms with both sides, and, like all the inhabitants, they had to survive the air strikes when the town happened to be in the hands of the opposition. But the 'Islamic State' continued to advance deeper into Syrian territory. 'The menace of IS, this cult of terrorists who project an appalling image of Islam, has arrived in our area,' Father Jacques wrote to a French friend a few days before his kidnapping. He continued:

> It is hard to decide what to do. Should we abandon our houses? That's a hard decision to make. It is terrible to realize that we have been abandoned – especially that we've been abandoned by the Christian world, which has decided not to get involved to keep the danger away from their territory. We mean nothing to them.[4]

In these few lines of a simple e-mail, written in haste surely, two phrases stand out that are characteristic of Father Jacques and, at the same time, a standard of intellectual integrity. In the first sentence, he writes, 'The menace of IS, this cult of terrorists who project an appalling image of Islam. . . .' The other sentence, about the Christian world: 'We mean nothing to them.' He defended the others' community and criticized his own. When the group which invokes the name of Islam and pretends to apply the law of the Quran becomes an immediate physical threat to Jacques Mourad and his congregation, a few days before his own kidnapping, Father Jacques still points out that these terrorists distort the true face of Islam. I would disagree with any Muslim who has nothing to say in the face of the 'Islamic State' except the empty phrase that violence has nothing to do with Islam. But a Christian, a Christian priest who must reckon with being expelled, demeaned, kidnapped or killed by people of another faith, and yet insists on defending that other faith – such a man of God shows a magnanimity that I have never seen except in hagiography.

A person like me cannot defend Islam in that way. He must not. The love of one's own – one's own culture or one's own country, and likewise one's own person – proves itself in self-criticism. The love of the other – another person, another culture, and even another religion – can be much more rhapsodic; it can be unreserved. True, to love another is impossible without the love of oneself. But to fall in love, as Father Paolo and Father Jacques are in love with Islam – that kind of infatuation can only be felt for another. Self-love, on the other hand, if it is to escape the danger of narcissism, of self-glorification, of self-indulgence, must be a wrangling, doubting, always questioning love. How true that is of Islam today! A Muslim who does not wrangle with it, doesn't doubt of it, doesn't critically question it – doesn't love Islam.

*

The problem is not just the terrible news and the still more terrible images from Syria and Iraq, where the Quran must be displayed at every atrocity and 'Allahu akbar' is cried at every beheading. In so many other countries of the Muslim world, perhaps in most of them, state authorities, state-aligned institutions, theological schools or insurgent groups invoke religion while they oppress their own peoples, deny women equal rights, persecute, expel, massacre dissidents, people of different beliefs, people who lead their lives differently. In the name of Islam, women are being stoned in Afghanistan, whole classes of schoolchildren murdered in Pakistan, hundreds of girls enslaved in Nigeria, Christians beheaded in Libya, bloggers shot in Bangladesh, bombs set off in marketplaces in Somalia, Sufis and musicians killed in Mali, critics of the regime crucified in Saudi Arabia, the most important works of contemporary literature prohibited in Iran, Shiites oppressed in Bahrain, violence fomented between Sunnis and Shiites in Yemen.

Certainly, the vast majority of Muslims reject terror, violence and oppression. That is not just a phrase; it is exactly what I have experienced in my travels: those who cannot take freedom for granted know its value best. All of the mass uprisings of recent years in the Islamic world have been uprisings for democracy and human rights: not only the attempted, although in most cases failed, revolutions in almost all Arab countries but also the protest movements in Turkey, in Iran, in Pakistan and, not least, the rebellion at the polls in the last Indonesian presidential election. The streams of refugees also indicate where many Muslims hope to find a better life than in their countries of origin: not in religious dictatorships, by any means. And the accounts that reach us from Mosul and Raqqa do not report enthusiasm among the population, but panic and desperation. All of the recognized theological authorities of the Islamic world have rejected the IS's claim to speak for Islam and have demonstrated in detail how its practice and ideology run counter to the Quran and the basic doctrines of Islamic theology. And let us not forget that it is Muslims themselves who are fighting on the front lines against the 'Islamic State': Kurds, Shiites, and also Sunni tribes and the soldiers of the Iraqi army.

All this needs to be said if we are not to fall for the deception propounded in unison by both Islamists and Islam critics: that Islam is waging a war against the West. In fact, Islam is waging a war against itself; that is, the Islamic world is being shaken by an inner conflict whose effects on the political and ethnic maps are almost as momentous as the dislocations of the First World War. The multi-ethnic, multi-religious and multicultural Orient whose magnificent medieval literature I studied and learned to love as an endangered, never whole, but vital reality during long sojourns in Cairo and Beirut, as a child during summer holidays in Isfahan, and as a reporter in the monastery of Mar Musa – that Orient will no more continue in existence than the world of yesterday that Stefan Zweig looked back on in wistful grief in the 1920s.

Was has happened? The 'Islamic State' did not just start today, nor did it start with the civil wars in Iraq and Syria. Its methods may meet with rejection, but its ideology is the Wahhabism whose influence extends to the remotest corners of the Islamic world today and is attracting mainly young people in Europe in the form of Salafism. When you know that the schoolbooks and lesson plans of the 'Islamic State' are 95 per cent identical with the schoolbooks and lesson plans of Saudi Arabia, then you also know that it is not only in Iraq and in Syria that the world is strictly divided into what is prohibited and what is permitted – and humanity into the faithful and the unbelievers. Over decades a philosophy has spread – in mosques, in books, on television, sponsored by billions in oil money – a philosophy in which all people of other beliefs are declared heretics, to be demeaned, terrorized, despised and insulted. If you publicly degrade other people systematically, day after day, it is only logical – as we well know from our own German history – that you ultimately declare their lives worthless. That a religious fascism of this kind has become thinkable, that the IS attracts so many fighters and still more sympathizers, that it has been able to overrun whole countries and capture major cities almost without a fight – that is not the beginning but the endpoint, for the moment, of a long decline: a decline which, significantly, is in part a decline of religious philosophy.

*

I began reading Middle Eastern Studies in 1988; my topics were the Quran and poetry. I think everyone who studies this subject in its classical form reaches a point where they can no longer reconcile the past with the present. And they become hopeless – hopelessly sentimental. Of course, the past was not simply a peaceful, colourful patchwork. But, as a philologist, I was dealing mainly with the writings of the mystics, the philosophers, the rhetoricians, as well as the theologians. And I – no, we students could only, can only gasp at the originality, the intellectual breadth, the aesthetic force and the human greatness we encountered in the spirituality of Ibn Arabi, the poetry of Rumi, the history of Ibn Khaldun, the poetic theology of Abd al-Qahir al-Jurjani, the philosophy of Averroes, the travel descriptions of Ibn Battuta, and even in the stories of the *Thousand and One Nights*, which are secular, yes, secular and erotic, and feminist too by the way, and at the same time permeated on every page by the spirit and the verses of the Quran. Those texts were not newspaper reports; no, the social reality of this advanced civilization, like every reality, looked greyer and more violent. And yet these records say something about what was once not only thinkable, but taken for granted, within Islam. There is nothing, absolutely nothing within the religious culture of modern Islam that would be even remotely comparable, that could exert a similar fascination, that might have such depth as the writings I encountered in my studies. And I have said nothing yet of Islamic architecture, Islamic art, Islamic musicology – they no longer exist.

I would like to illustrate for you the loss of creativity and freedom by an example from my own field. Once upon a time it was not only thinkable, but taken for granted, that the Quran is a poetic text which can be grasped only by the means and methods of poetics, no differently than a poem. It was not only thinkable, but taken for granted, that a theologian was at the same time a literary scholar and a connoisseur of poetry, and in many cases a poet himself. In our time, my own teacher in Cairo, Nasr Hamid Abu Zayd, was charged with heresy, driven from his professorship, and even involuntarily divorced because he conceived Quran studies as a literary discipline. In other words, an approach to the Quran which was once taken for granted, and for which Abu Zayd was able to cite the most important scholars of classical Islamic theology, is no longer recognized today even as thinkable. Such an approach to the Quran, even though it is the traditional approach, is persecuted and punished as heresy. And yet the Quran is a text which not only rhymes, but which speaks in disturbing, ambiguous, enigmatic images; furthermore, it is not a book but a recitation, the score of a chant that moves its Arabic listeners by its rhythm, onomatopoeia and melody. Islamic theology not only took note of the Quran's aesthetic qualities but also pronounced the beauty of its language the confirming miracle of Islam. But today we can observe, everywhere in the Islamic world, what happens when you disregard the linguistic structure of a text, cease to understand it or even to perceive it adequately. The Quran is degraded to a handbook in which you can look up this or that keyword using a search engine. The verbal force of the Quran becomes political dynamite.

We often read that Islam must pass through the fire of the Enlightenment, or that modernism must overcome tradition. But that is perhaps too simplistic, since Islam's past was so much more Enlightened, and the traditional literature often seems more modern than the present-day theological discourse. After all, Goethe and Proust, Lessing and Joyce were not out of their minds when they were fascinated by Islamic culture. They saw in its books and monuments something that we no longer perceive so easily, we who are so often brutally confronted with Islam's present. Perhaps the problem of Islam is not so much its tradition as the almost total break with that tradition, the loss of cultural memory, the amnesia of a civilization.

All the peoples of the Middle East have undergone a brutal modernization, commanded from the top down, at the hands of colonialism and secularist dictatorships. To take the headscarf as an illustrative example: Iranian women did not gradually abandon the headscarf; soldiers swarmed out in the streets at the shah's orders in 1936 to tear it from their heads by force. In contrast to Europe, where modernism could be experienced, in spite of all its crimes and relapses, as a process of emancipation, and where it took place over many decades and centuries, in the Middle East it was essentially an experience of violence. Modernism was associated not with freedom but with exploitation and despotism. Imagine an Italian president who drove his car into St Peter's, jumped on the altar in his dirty boots, and struck the pope in the face with his riding crop: then you would have a rough idea what it meant when Reza Shah marched in his riding boots through the holy shrine of Qom in 1928 and replied to the imam's request that he take off his shoes like every other worshipper by striking the imam in the face with his whip. And you would find comparable occurrences and pivotal moments in many other countries of the Middle East which did not slowly let go of the past, but demolished their past and tried to erase it from memory.

One might have thought that at least the religious fundamentalists, who gained influence everywhere in the Islamic world after the defeat of nationalism, would appreciate their own culture. However, the opposite is the case: in advocating a return to a supposed beginning, they not only neglected tradition but resolutely fought against it. If we are surprised at the iconoclasm of the 'Islamic State', it is only because we failed to notice that there are practically no ancient monuments left standing in Saudi Arabia. In Mecca, the Wahhabis have destroyed the tombs and mosques of the Prophet's closest followers – even the birthplace of the Prophet himself. The historic mosque of the Prophet in Medina has been replaced with a gigantic new building, and where, up until a few years ago, the house still stood in which Muhammad lived with his wife Khadija, there stands today a public toilet.

*

Besides the Quran, my studies were concentrated mainly on Islamic mysticism, Sufism. Mysticism sounds like a marginal phenomenon, something esoteric, a kind of underground culture. In regard to Islam, nothing could be further from the truth. Even into the twentieth century, Sufism formed the basis of popular piety almost everywhere in the Islamic world. In Asian Islam, it still does today. Furthermore, the Islamic high culture, especially poetry, the fine arts and architecture, were permeated by the spirit of mysticism. As the most common form of devotion, Sufism was the ethical and aesthetic counterweight to the orthodoxy of the legal scholars. By emphasizing above all God's mercy, looking beyond every letter of the Quran, always seeking beauty in the religion, recognizing the truth in other faiths as well, and explicitly adopting Christianity's commandment to love one's enemy, Sufism infused Islamic societies with values, stories and sounds that could not have been derived from a merely literalist piety. As the lived Islam, Sufism did not disempower the Islam of laws but complemented it in daily life, made it softer, more ambivalent, more permeable, more tolerant, and, most of all, made it a sensory experience through music, dance, poetry.

Of all this, hardly anything is left. Wherever the Islamists gained a foothold, starting as early as the nineteenth century in what is now Saudi Arabia and continuing to the present day in Mali, they have put an end to the Sufi festivals, prohibited the mystical texts, destroyed the tombs of the saints, cut the long hair of the Sufi leaders, or killed them outright. But not only the Islamists. The reformers and proponents of religious Enlightenment in the nineteenth and early twentieth centuries also considered the traditions and mores of popular Islam to be backward and antiquated. It was not they who took the Sufi writings seriously: it was Western scholars, Orientalists such as the recipient of the 1995 Peace Prize, Annemarie Schimmel, who published the manuscripts and thus saved them from destruction. And even today, only very few Muslim intellectuals take an interest in the richness that lies in their own tradition. The destroyed, neglected, littered city centres with their dilapidated monuments everywhere in the Islamic world symbolize the deterioration of the Islamic intellect just as clearly as the world's biggest shopping mall does, which has been built in Mecca right next to the Kaaba. You have to imagine it – you can see it in photographs: the holiest shrine of Islam, that so simple and splendid monument, in which the Prophet himself prayed, is literally towered over by Gucci and Apple. Perhaps we should have followed less the Islam of our grand muftis and more the Islam of our grandmothers.

Certainly, in some countries people have begun restoring houses and mosques, but only after Western art historians or Westernized Muslims like myself come along and recognize the value of the tradition. And, sadly, we came a century too late, when the buildings were already ruined, the building techniques forgotten, and the books erased from memory. But at least we thought we had time to study the things thoroughly. As a reader, I now feel like an archaeologist in a war zone, gathering up the relics quickly, and not always sensibly, so that future generations will at least be able to see them in a museum. Certainly, Muslim countries are still producing outstanding works, as the biennials and film festivals show, and as this year's book fair too has shown once more. But this culture no longer has much to do with Islam. There is no Islamic culture any more – at least, none of greatness. What is whizzing past our ears and at our heads now is the debris of a tremendous intellectual implosion.

*

Is there hope? Father Paolo, the founder of the community of Mar Musa, teaches: as long as we draw breath, there is hope. Hope is the central theme of his writings. On the day after the kidnapping of his student and deputy, the Muslims of Qaryatain came in droves, unasked, into the church to pray for their Father Jacques. That must give us too hope that love works across the boundaries of religions, ethnic groups and cultures. The shock produced by the news and the pictures of the 'Islamic State' is tremendous, and it has unleashed opposing forces. Finally, a resistance is forming within the Islamic orthodoxy as well, against the violence in the name of religion. And for a few years now we have seen, perhaps less in the Arabian heartland of Islam than on its periphery, in Asia, in South Africa, in Iran, in Turkey and, not least, among the Muslims in the West, a new religious philosophy developing. Europe too reinvented itself after the two world wars. And perhaps I should mention, in view of the carelessness, the indifference and the blatant disregard which not just our politicians, no: which we as society have displayed in the past few years towards the European project of unity, the most politically valuable thing this continent has ever brought forth – perhaps I should mention at this point how often in my travels people have talked to me about Europe: as a model, indeed almost as a utopia. Those who have forgotten why Europe is necessary need only look in the emaciated, exhausted, terrified faces of the refugees who have left everything behind, abandoned all they had, risked their lives for the promise that Europe still is.

This brings me back to Father Jacques's second sentence that I found remarkable, his statement about the Christian world: 'We mean nothing to them.' As a Muslim, it is not for me to accuse the Christians of the world of not caring – if not for the Syrian or Iraqi peoples, then at least for their own brothers and sisters in faith. And yet that is what I too often think when I experience the indifference of our public sphere to the disaster of apocalyptic proportions in that East that we try to keep far away by means of barbed-wire fences, warships, stereotypes and mental blinkers. Just a three-hour flight from Frankfurt Airport, whole ethnic groups are being exterminated or expelled, girls enslaved, many of humanity's major cultural monuments blown up; cultures are dying out and, with the cultures, an ancient ethnic, religious and linguistic diversity which, unlike Europe's, had been more or less preserved into the twenty-first century – but we come together and stand up only when one of the bombshells of this war hits us, as one did on the 7th and 8th of January in Paris, or when the people fleeing this war knock on our gates.

It is good that this time, in contrast to the aftermath of the 11th of September 2001, our societies have responded to terror by upholding our freedom. It is exhilarating to see how many people in Europe, and especially in Germany, are taking a stand for refugees. But all too often this protest and this solidarity still remain unpolitical. Our society is not carrying on a broad discussion about the causes of terror and flight, and about the extent to which our own politicians may even be exacerbating the disaster going on just outside our borders. We are not asking why, of all countries, our closest partner in the Middle East is Saudi Arabia. We are not learning from our mistakes if we roll out the red carpet for a dictator such as General El-Sisi. Or we are learning the wrong lessons if the conclusion we draw from the disastrous wars in Iraq and in Libya is that we should take better care not to get involved when genocides are committed. Nothing occurs to us that might prevent the murders that the Syrian regime has been committing against its own people for the last four years. And we have resigned ourselves to the existence of a new, religious fascism whose territory is about as big as Great Britain and reaches from the borders of Iran almost to the Mediterranean Sea. Not that there are easy answers to the challenge of how to liberate a metropolis such as Mosul – but we aren't even asking ourselves the question seriously. An organization such as the 'Islamic State' with an estimated 30,000 fighters is not invincible for the world community – it must not be. 'Today they are in our country,' said the Catholic bishop of Mosul, Yohanna Petros Mouche, when he asked the global powers to help expel the IS from Iraq. 'Today they are in our country. Tomorrow they will be in yours.'[5]

I hate to imagine what it will take for us to admit that the bishop of Mosul is right. For it is part of the logic of the

'Islamic State's' propaganda that its images ignite higher and higher levels of horror in order to penetrate our consciousness. When we ceased to cry out over individual Christian hostages praying the rosary before they were beheaded, the IS began decapitating entire groups of Christians. When we banned the beheadings from our screens, the IS torched the paintings from the national museum in Mosul. When we had grown used to demolished statues, IS started razing whole ancient cities such as Nimrod and Nineveh. When we had stopped worrying about the expulsion of the Yazidis, the news of mass rapes briefly shook us awake. When we thought the terror was limited to Iraq and Syria, we received the snuff videos from Libya and Egypt. When we had grown accustomed to the decapitations and the crucifixions, the victims were first beheaded and then crucified, as in Libya recently. Palmyra is not being blown up all at once, but building by building, at intervals of weeks, in order to generate new reports each time. This will not stop. The IS will continue escalating the horror until we see, hear and feel in our day-to-day European life that this horror will not end by itself. Paris will have been only the beginning, and Lyon will not be the last beheading. And, the longer we wait, the fewer options we will have. In other words, it is already much too late.

*

Can the recipient of a peace prize call for war? I am not calling for war. I am only pointing out that there is a war, and that we, as its nearest neighbours, must react to it – militarily perhaps, yes, but most of all diplomatically and as a civil society, and much more resolutely than we have up to now. For this war can no longer be ended in Syria and in Iraq alone. It can only be ended by the powers that stand behind the opposing armies and militias: Iran, Turkey, the Gulf states, Russia, and also the West. And only when our societies stop accepting the madness will our governments take action. We will probably make mistakes no matter what we do now. But the biggest mistake we can make is to go on doing nothing, or so little, against the two mass murders taking place on our European doorstep: that of the 'Islamic State' and that of the Assad regime.

'I've just come back from Aleppo,' Father Jacques continued in the e-mail he wrote a few days before his kidnapping on the 21st of May,

> that city that sleeps on the river of pride, in the centre of the Middle East. Now it is like a woman consumed by cancer. Everyone is starting to flee Aleppo, especially the poor Christians. And these massacres are striking not just the Christians, but the whole Syrian people. Our vocation is difficult to fulfil, especially in these days when Father Paolo has disappeared, the teacher and founder of the 21st-century idea of dialogue.
>
> In these days we experience that dialogue as a communal suffering. We are sad at this unjust world which bears a share of the responsibility for the victims of this war, this world of dollars and euros in the service of their own peoples, their own security, while the rest of the world is dying of hunger, disease and war. It seems as though their only goal is to find regions where they can make war and increase their sales of weapons and aircraft. What is the word for these governments that could end the massacres, but instead do nothing, nothing?
>
> I am not pessimistic in my faith, but at the state of the world.
>
> The question we are asking ourselves is this: Do we have the right to live, or not? The answer is already there, because this war is an answer as clear as sunlight. So the real dialogue we are living today is the dialogue of compassion.

Courage, my dear, I am with you and embrace you, Jacques.[6]

Two months after the kidnapping of Father Jacques, on the 28th of July 2015, the 'Islamic State' captured the town of Qaryatain. Most of the inhabitants were able to flee at the last minute, but two hundred Christians were kidnapped. Another month later, on the 21st of August, the monastery of Mar Elian was levelled by bulldozers. Pictures that the IS posted on the internet show that not one of the 1,700-year-old stones has been left standing. Another two weeks later, on the 3rd of September, photos appeared on a website belonging to the 'Islamic State' that show some of the Christians from Qaryatain sitting in the front rows of chairs in the auditorium of a school or a community centre, their heads shorn, some of them emaciated, their faces a blank – all of them marked by their captivity. Father Jacques too is visible in the photos, in plain clothes, also emaciated and with his head shaven, the shock clearly visible in his eyes. He holds his hand in front of his mouth, as if unwilling to believe what he is seeing. On the stage of the auditorium sits a broad-shouldered, long-bearded man in combat fatigues signing a treaty. It is what is known as a dhimmi contract, subjecting the Christians to Muslim rule. They are not allowed to build churches or monasteries or to have a cross or a Bible on their person. Their priests are not allowed to wear clerical garments. Muslims must not hear the Christians' prayers, read their scriptures, or enter their churches. The Christians are not allowed to bear arms and must unconditionally obey the instructions of the 'Islamic State'. They must cower, submit in silence to any injustice, and pay a tax, the *jizya*, to be allowed to live. This treaty is sickening to read. It quite explicitly divides God's creatures into first- and second-class persons and leaves no doubt that there is also a third class, whose lives are worth even less.

It is a calm but thoroughly depressed, helpless glance that Father Jacques casts at us in the photo while holding his hand in front of his mouth. He had been ready to accept his own martyrdom. But for his congregation to be taken prisoner, the children he has baptized, the lovers he has married, the old people whom he has promised the last rites – that must be driving him insane, the deliberate, inwardly steadfast, God-fearing Father Jacques. It was for his sake that the captives stayed in Qaryatain instead of leaving Syria as so many other Christians had done. Father Jacques must be thinking he bears the guilt for their captivity. But God, I know, God will judge him otherwise.

*

Is there hope? Yes, there is hope; there is always hope. I had already written this speech when the news reached me on Tuesday, five days ago: Father Jacques Mourad is free. Residents of the town of Qaryatain helped him escape from his cell, disguised him and, with the help of Bedouins, got him out of the 'Islamic State's' territory. In the meantime he has returned to his brothers and sisters of the community of Mar Musa. Evidently many people were involved in his liberation, all of them Muslims, and every single one of them risked his or her life for a Christian priest. Love has worked across the boundaries of religions, ethnic groups and cultures. As splendid, as literally wonderful as this news is, yet the concern is greater, and gravest is that of Father Jacques himself. For the lives of the two hundred other Christians of Qaryatain may be in still greater danger after his escape. And there is still no trace of his teacher Father Paolo, the founder of the Christian community that loves Islam. There is hope as long as we breathe.

The recipient of a peace prize must not call for war. But he may call to prayer. Ladies and gentlemen, I would like to make an unusual request of you – although, in a church, it is not as unusual as all that. I would like to ask you, at the end of my speech, not to applaud, but to pray for Father Paolo and the two hundred kidnapped Christians of Qaryatain, the children whom Father Jacques baptized, the lovers he married, the old people whom he promised the last rites. And if you are not religious, then join your wishes to those of the captives and Father Jacques, who blames himself because only he has been freed. For what are prayers except wishes that we address to God? I believe in wishes, and that they affect our world, with or without God. Without wishes, human beings would never have raised up the stones that they so readily demolish in war. And so I beg you, ladies and gentlemen, pray for Jacques Mourad, pray for Paolo Dall'Oglio, pray for the Christians of Qaryatain, pray or wish for the liberation of all the hostages and the freedom of Syria and Iraq. I invite you to stand up to do so, so that we can hold up the picture of our brotherhood against the snuff videos of the terrorists.

* * *

I thank you.

Eulogy for Rupert Neudeck

Church of the Apostles, Cologne, 14 June 2016

Your Eminence, dear Neudeck family, esteemed mourners,

Last Wednesday I watched television for an hour, perhaps a bit less: the end of *Mainz Report*, then the news magazine. The first announcer apologized for yet another story of refugees drowning in the Mediterranean Sea, saying we were probably numbed by now after having heard the same news and seen the same pictures over and over again. Then I saw a stout, blond-bearded man on a cargo ship who seemed to be cradling a brown-skinned infant in his arms. The baby looked so peaceful, eyes closed, mouth open, as if it was sleeping. The crewman had found it in the sea, almost at the surface, but completely covered by water, amid dozens, hundreds of other bodies.

In the next segment, a Syrian, visibly from a poor background, told how he had lost his son in the wreck. He had been able to grab his wife and his daughter at the last minute before the boat capsized, but his son wasn't there, his son had suddenly disappeared. What was the sense in living, the man sobbed, and his wife beside him, his wife couldn't say a word for weeping. Their daughter, nine or ten years old, watched her parents in silence.

Then the news magazine: a reporter had accompanied the Doctors Without Borders on their sea rescue mission for ten days; pictures of overfilled rubber boats; a hundred, two hundred refugees crammed together on the open sea. If we hadn't found them, 99 per cent of them would be dead, the Ukrainian captain said blandly. The Doctors Without Borders had chartered his ship, although sea rescue is not a medical operation – but if no one else is doing it . . .?

Five years ago he had left his home, a black African man said in English, a small child in his arms, beside him his young, incredibly pleasant-looking wife; five years, the last two years in Libya, where it was so unbearable that in the end the sea voyage was no longer so terrifying, even with the risk of death. Since they had boarded their boat, the reporter's voice-over explained, more than a thousand other refugees had lost their lives – more than a thousand had drowned in less than ten days in the Mediterranean Sea.

That was my evening in front of the television set last Wednesday: all the suffering that had come to public awareness last autumn – briefly, before being resolutely banned again after the closing of the Balkan route – was brought to my living room again in less than an hour.

And then? With a queasy feeling, I then went to brush my teeth. What does my queasy feeling have to do with Rupert Neudeck? you ask. I believe it marks exactly what distinguishes him from me, the difference between him and ordinary people.

Certainly, we can change the channel when the news shows, yet again, people drowned in the Mediterranean Sea or starved in Africa or butchered in Syria. We can let the pictures roll off us, or we can plead our fears: Good Lord, if they all want to come here . . . and some of them are sure to be terrorists! We can blame the drowned people, the starved people, and even the butchered people for their own fates; we can cite their culture, their religion; lately we can again invoke their race as the reason why they are incapable of prosperity, freedom, peace. But that is not how most of us react, we ordinary people, when we see on television the picture of a drowned person, a starved person, a butchered person; and if the victim is a child, even the cynical, the fearful and the racist find it hard to suppress their empathy. Then even they concede that such pictures are unpleasant, unbearable in fact, but this time, they say, we have to endure them.

Endure them: that is a very revealing word which was recently used in the public discourse. We have to endure our lack of empathy – that's not easy, because it is not at all in keeping with our nature, it doesn't conform to our God-given faculties, or to the nurture we received from our parents, much less to the civilization we grew up in. Empathy is the natural reaction, the human reflex; not ruthlessness. Reaching out our hand to a person in need is not something we have to learn; it is something we have unlearned in the course of our lives: yes, even we ordinary people have had to unlearn it in order to go on living our ordinary lives. If we let all the suffering that we see around us get through to us, unfiltered, we would break down.

Perhaps we send the Doctors Without Borders a little money the next day; perhaps we vote for a party that at least doesn't advocate shooting at refugees; perhaps we help out locally in a welcoming initiative, collect clothes, give language lessons, appeal for understanding. But we don't do what our queasy feeling actually tells us to do, which is what my daughter would have felt, if she had happened to be up so late last Wednesday when *Mainz Report* and the news magazine were on – what she would have not only felt but also said out loud, because it comes from the original human instinct which a child has not yet repressed as well as we have: we do not drop everything, take the next plane to Lampedusa, empty our bank account or chain ourselves to the chancellor's doorknob to make – yes, it sounds childish, but that is what children are, in their unreasonable wisdom – to make the world better. No, reasonable people like us go to bed and put out the light.

I imagine that Rupert Neudeck also had a queasy feeling in 1979 when he saw the pictures of the Vietnamese fleeing on the open sea in small boats. The difference I mentioned occurred at this exact point: Rupert Neudeck listened to his feeling. He did not put out the light and go to sleep. 'Cap Anamur, that was such a radical action,' he said thirty-five years later about what happened the next morning: 'I had to leap, and I had no idea where I would end up.'[7] As we all know, Rupert Neudeck ended up, along with you, Christel Neudeck, and the many other allies he won with his childish enthusiasm, saving 10,395 people in the South China Sea. And afterwards he went on to live the life of a person who lives for others, in 1991 in Angola, in 1995 in Sarajevo, in 2001 in Afghanistan, in 2011 in Syria, in 2014 in Iraq, to mention only a few of the places where he persisted, against all reason, when there was no other helper for miles around.

I said: the life of a person who lives for others. Doesn't that sound odd in our time, when individual fulfilment seems to be the supreme commandment, while sacrifice, asceticism, devotion are almost indecent? Psychologists and advertising professionals, I assume, would urgently advise against living for others. But they're wrong! Feeding children, caring for the sick is the most obvious thing in the world to do, Rupert once said about his life lived for others, the simplest thing, and the most beautiful. It gave him tremendous joy, he added. People, and especially the journalists, always wanted to hear that his work was hard, that he constantly had to pull up his socks, force himself to carry on, and the like. No, said Rupert, the work makes him happy, and that's exactly why he does it. It's much more exhausting to do the opposite, he said, to be harsh instead of friendly.[8]

I think each of us knows from our own experience how much good it does us when we are good to other people. And each of us sees on television how grim those people look who plead for harshness, how ugly for example those politicians' stiff features are when they say we just have to endure seeing pictures of drowned children. I feel sorry for them, these politicians, because after all they are people too, and with their harshness they harm themselves, because they cripple their own personality, which is, deep down, a friendly one. I can't imagine that they learned such harshness from their parents, and they certainly didn't learn ruthlessness from Christianity, which they occasionally invoke, or from German or Western culture, which they pretend to defend. If German culture or Western culture or any culture at all teaches anything, it is generosity; it is hospitality.

And yet we don't help, we ordinary people, we don't help in every need, or every needy person, and we certainly have reasons not to do so. If we fed all those who are hungry, we would soon have no bread left ourselves. Our hearts are great, but our means are limited is the translation in today's political language. I do not mean to criticize that kind of realism; that's not for me to do because in my personal life I live the same way; I can't do otherwise if I want to go on living my ordinary life. While the principle behind this is pragmatic, it is also a very old one. For the religions don't require that we give all we have, but only a certain part – of our wealth, our strength, our benevolence. 'God does not burden any soul with more than it can bear,' says the Quran, Surah 2, verse 286.[9]

And yet this verse can only be true because some individuals can bear more than we can. There is too much suffering in the world; our civilizations would collapse if each of us bore only his or her share of compassion. Some people have always been needed who give everything, who help as many people as they possibly can without asking what will be left for themselves. Such people used to be called saints, and, wherever they have been written about in the history of religions, they have a noticeably childlike aura; they are a little bit like children. Why is that? I think it is because they retain an impulse which each of us knows, which each of us often obeys but often doesn't: the impulse to reach out our hand to someone who needs our help – the most human impulse of all. 'Except ye become as little children, ye shall not enter into the kingdom of heaven,' says the Gospel of Matthew, 18:3. That was Rupert Neudeck's favourite verse.

Now he, I am quite certain, has entered into the kingdom of Heaven. We, however – we are left behind without him. Each of us feels – it's a feeling that has been imparted to me in all the conversations and phone calls since his death – that we needed him, not only personally, as a husband, as a father, as a friend, but also because, without him, something is lacking in our community, in the Germany and the Europe of 2016: his voice in the time of returning nationalism, his action in the time of the refugees' emergency, his reconciliation in the time of terror, his philanthropy that exceeded the ordinary measure. What can we do? I think, dear mourners, the only thing is for each of us, every single one of us, to carry a little more than we did before. None of us can do it alone, and a queasy feeling is no longer enough.

Eulogy for Jaki Liebezeit

Melaten Cemetery, Cologne, 6 February 2017

Dear Birgit Berger, dear Marlon Geuer, dear mourners,

For more than twenty years I lived three floors above Jaki Liebezeit. We did not see each other often, and it took me a long time to realize that he was *that* Jaki Liebezeit, the drummer from that band whose records my older brothers had played. But we saw one another regularly – never in the morning, never in the evening; it was almost always about four in the afternoon, when I came home from the kindergarten or the school with my elder daughter, later with my younger daughter; or else about six, when I went back to the office, or left the house in my jogging clothes – then I met him, yes, in the courtyard, in the passageway where the bicycles are parked, or on the pavement in front of the door to the courtyard. My neon yellow shirt, and still more my shorts, felt still more ridiculous when Jaki's eyes met mine, although he always kept a straight face. He was sparing with his facial expressions in general, and with words too of course.

Nonetheless, we talked whenever we met, greeted each other and asked how are you, exchanged a few words, the friendly words of twenty years. And the amazing thing, the incredible thing, was that he said little, and yet I understood a great deal. This, to be exact: the words, gestures, suggestive facial expressions, tonal variations, rising intonations, falling intonations – this unbelievably reduced, altogether parsimonious set of expressions was in his case inversely proportional to the wealth of meanings. I think anyone who has heard him play the drums, especially in recent years, will agree with me that it was the same in his music: such austere instrumentation, such a richness of meanings.

I know he liked me, otherwise he wouldn't have stopped every time we met and looked at me; I felt that deeply. At the same time there was always a surprise, a mild jeer in his eyes, because, although I too worked hard, as Jaki deduced from the sheer number of my books, I also pursued so many other activities. Just my jogging, or my frequent visitors in front of his window looking for the door to our courtyard building, my holidays, or when he saw me running to the train station with my trolley suitcase. Jaki travelled occasionally too, to concerts or studios, but that was different; those were interludes, or perhaps encores, in which what he was already doing day in and day out became public for the duration of a recording session or a brief tour. When I left on a trip, it must have seemed to him, I was interrupting my work, I was leaving my desk – at least when I was just running to the train station with my suitcase: then it must have been an appearance, a reading; nothing essential to my writing. When he left on a trip – and that was much less often – he was still working, just at some other location. That, I imagined, must be a boon.

Did we ever talk about it? No. I mentioned that we didn't talk very much. And yet I formed an image of him, and he no doubt of me. And these images of each other, images drawn by a neighbour with the same few strokes repeated many times over the years, were more accurate than if we had exchanged many words or met in the pub of an evening. You couldn't meet with him anyway; in twenty years he never visited me once, nor I him, least of all in the evening, because in the evenings he was always drumming, every evening with the same friends, for more than twenty years, until early in the morning. And that must have been going on for twenty years or more before I moved in, every evening until early in the morning. That was something I gradually came to understand about him, without his having to say anything: that regularity, or, as the critics always called it, that repetition.

Three times I heard him drumming live: the first time was years ago at the Rhenania; the second, at a 'Conversation Concert', amazingly enough, in our literary salon; and then at his very last public performance, on the 8th of December 2016 at the Kolumba Museum. I am not a musician, but I am a traveller, and I didn't need to read any reviews to hear the origins of his drumming: the religious ritual in which, by the alternation of identical sequences with minimal, gradually increasing variations, the listener's consciousness is slowly coaxed, like a screw being slowly turned, out of its underpinning. Jaki talked about it at the Conversation Concert, the only time I heard him say more than a few words. Besides Jaki, the guests included my other two musician neighbours, Pi-hsien Chen and Manos Tsangaris; it was a regular house concert, and a fantastic ensemble, two drummers and a concert pianist who improvised, in alternation at first and then together, and later even played Scarlatti. Between pieces, we asked about the music, and the neighbours from our building, who were gathered in the audience, were amazed to hear Jaki give the longest answers, and not only intelligently, but practically with encyclopaedic knowledge.

Although I cannot quote him, I remember that he talked about his study of Middle Eastern and African music, which were much more important for his rhythms than jazz and rock. And he used a technical term, additive rhythm or something like that, because it is based on the repetition of fixed patterns. He also said, though – he who supposedly played with the precision of a machine – that not even a machine can repeat itself with perfect accuracy. Why is that? I asked, surprised. Because even the smallest differences in the room's atmospheric conditions, or physical processes in the brain, change the sound. So the repetition isn't really a repetition; it just sounds like it to our ears. Other people attain the same trance by praying a hundred and twenty rosaries; the basic principle of always-the-same and always-different is the same in both cases.

Ah, I think today, how long we could have talked when we met, four, five times a week in the courtyard or in front of the house, so many things interested both of us, actually, repetition and euphoria, ritual and the regions where I travelled. I had even written a whole book about rock music, although I never had the courage to toss it in his mailbox. But then I think: no, we did talk, or at least he spoke to me, otherwise than with words and otherwise than with gestures; simply by his presence, always the same, always different. He was there, day in and day out, my good neighbour; drew back the curtains to the courtyard at noon, did his errands in the afternoon or, in the early years, was with his son; went out to drum with his friends in the evening and came back early in the morning.

I pictured the monotony of his days in the most exciting colours. To me Jaki presented the ideal of an artist – someone who lives only for his art. In practice, it must have been different: he had a wife; he had a son (who did not live with him, it's true); he must have gone out to eat or done his cooking – Jaki at the stove too was something unimaginable and yet, presumably, real – shopping, administrative errands, doctor's appointments; presumably he also had a family somewhere, siblings, cousins, nieces and nephews, perhaps even family gatherings. I couldn't even be sure that Jaki didn't go on holidays just like the holidays in bourgeois lives. I don't know about all that, and I never asked. But he did have a slightly sardonic look as he smiled indulgently when we packed up our station wagon every summer in front of the house, and a few weeks later when we dragged the same far too copious luggage, groaning, up to the third floor.

He himself – and I am not just imagining this – he himself lived more than frugally. His life was, in the literal sense, radical: that is, at the root, at the base. Not radical as it is imagined in youth cultures or political movements: not radical in the sense of an extreme lifestyle – extreme clothes or extreme opinions – but radical in the sense that he concentrated on the essentials, the roots; thus radical in the sense of a reduction, material and otherwise. We guessed that Jaki couldn't be poor with the royalties of a legendary band whose music continued to inspire one generation after another, and with his studio sessions in New York, London, Istanbul; to be honest, I would guess that he was the wealthiest person in our building by far. But to judge by appearances, at least, no one among us lived more modestly than he: a tiny ground-floor apartment, the most inconspicuous clothing, the same haircut for twenty years, which he did himself in front of the mirror, a compact car that he parked at the garage across the street. Jaki didn't even have a health insurance policy, thinking security was nothing but ballast; nor did he have hobbies, wines or cigarettes. He once mentioned that he did drink a glass of Kölsch every few years: that would have been quite a party. Jaki didn't need all that, I could see every time I met him, when his surprised, pleasantly sardonic and at the same time indulgent eyes met mine. He didn't need a word to tell me a great deal four, five times a week. Jaki Liebezeit needed only music.

On the 20th Anniversary of the Founding of the Department of Jewish History and Culture

Great Hall, Ludwig Maximilian University, Munich, 6 July 2017[10]

Dear Professor Huber, dear Michael, dear Ms Knobloch, dear Dr Schuster, esteemed colleagues and students, ladies and gentlemen,

I would like to begin with an observation that I noted last summer after a journey through Eastern Europe. To visit Auschwitz, I had to register online in advance for a guided tour and choose a language: English, Polish, German, et cetera. At the memorial, the system was not much different from that of an airport: the visitors, most of them with backpacks, short trousers or other identifying marks of tourists, held up a barcode to check in, received a sticker indicating their tour language, and went through a security check fifteen minutes before the tour was to begin. In a narrow waiting room they spread out along insufficient benches until their respective groups were called. After I had held my ticket under another scanner, I found myself, from one step to the next, standing in the former concentration camp, facing the barracks, the guard towers, the fences that everyone has seen in photos, reports, documentaries.

The groups had already assembled and were waiting to be fetched by their guides. While the young Israelis were – or was I only imagining this? – somewhat louder and more self-assured, the Germans – no, I was not imagining it – huddled silently against the wall of the visitor centre. Suddenly the sticker I was holding in my hand was heavy – just a little piece of plastic film, actually. It was heavy. Instinctively, I took a deep breath before I stuck on my chest the sticker bearing a single word in black on white: *Deutsch*, 'German'. That was it, that act, the legend on my chest from then on like a confession: German. Yes, I was one of them, not by descent, blond hair, Aryan blood or any such nonsense, but simply by my language, and hence my culture. If there is a single moment when I became a German with no ifs or buts, it was not my birth in Germany, it was not my naturalization, it was not the first time I voted. It was certainly not a World Cup tournament. It was last summer, when I stuck the sticker on my chest, before me the barracks, behind me the visitor centre: 'German'. I went to my group and waited, also silent, for our guide. Each group in turn lined up for a bizarre photo in the gateway surmounted by the motto *Arbeit macht frei*. Only our group was ashamed.

Ladies and gentlemen, for as long as the Federal Republic of Germany has remembered Nazism, the war of aggression, the genocide against the Jews and the gassing, shooting, starving and expulsion of millions more people, for just as long has that remembrance been pronounced shameful, unhealthy or, at the very least, excessive. The history of the young state, which since 1990 has been the sole successor of the German Empire, is pervaded by the dialectic of commemorative culture and commemoration criticism in the form of recurring debates which always run the same course. It did not begin with the historians' dispute in 1986, nor did it end with Martin Walser's Peace Prize speech in 1998. As early as 1951, the implementing statute for Article 131 of the German constitution, which permitted the summary reinstatement of all civil servants of the Nazi state, including the officials of police, prosecutors and the courts, was justified by the need to 'draw a line' under the issue; the Frankfurt Auschwitz trial of 1963 was called 'fouling the nest' and 'poisoning the well'; Willy Brandt's kneeling at the site of the Warsaw Ghetto in 1970 was criticized by large parts of the press and the Bundestag as 'treason against the Fatherland'; in 1979, opponents tried to prevent the broadcast of the series *Holocaust* by bomb attacks; in 1983, a 'later birth' was acclaimed as a redeeming grace; and the 1986 performance of a Fassbinder play was greeted with calls for an 'end of the close season' for Jews. And when this year's drive to declare the past finally over and done with – the speech in Dresden by Björn Höcke, the Thuringian state chairman of the AfD – resulted in a consensus of indignation rather than controversy, it was not in opposition to his statements, but because of the openly ethnic-national context, the speaker's reputation and his party affiliation. Höcke's theme, the 'memorial of shame', referred to the same thing as Walser's 'constant presentation of our shame', however indignantly the audience who gave Walser a standing ovation in St Paul's Church may deny it. At the core of all the public debates over how to deal with the Nazi legacy is the question: When will Germany finally be a normal country again?

The debate will probably recur in rather shorter intervals in the years and decades to come, and it will grow still more acrimonious, or perhaps not more acrimonious but more ingenuous, which is still more momentous. Soon the diehards who deny the past will be superseded by perfectly normal, even liberal-minded young people who no longer understand what importance Hitler could possibly have for them. For, ladies and gentlemen, we stand today at a watershed, and one which has not yet entered the public awareness, in spite of all the efforts of scholars, organizations and cultural policy institutions: the last survivors of Auschwitz will very soon be dead. And it is not only the survivors who will fall silent, but all the eyewitnesses: victims, perpetrators, fellow travellers, bystanders, resisters. We have already seen in the decline of the European Union what it means when political responsibility passes to a generation who have no experience in their own biographies of the import and the necessity of European unity. And by now we are another generation further along: those growing up in Germany today do not, as a rule, have even grandparents who can still tell the story, or refuse to tell it, as the case may be – after all, silence itself can incite questions, as the history of another generation, the '68 generation, has shown.

Those growing up from now on will never hear the live broadcast of eyewitnesses speaking at a commemorative ceremony in the Bundestag; in their civics lessons they will never meet a person whose suffering, guilt, or strength for reconciliation is written in their eyes, chiselled in their voice or tattooed in their skin. They are not likely to be insulted or taunted as Nazis in neighbouring countries, as my classmates still were – a paradoxical consequence of Germany's successful reintegration. On their school trip to Berlin, their teachers will no doubt take them to the Memorial to the Murdered Jews of Europe, but they will play hide-and-seek in its aisles, unwrap their sandwiches on top of one of the stelae, and be sure to take a selfie. At best, they will make an honest effort to muster some dismay on remembering a certain film or a particularly impassioned lesson. But the Memorial to the Murdered Jews cannot offer an encounter, an incisive experience, much less a turning point in a young person's political socialization. Here is a good reason, or at least an understandable one, for the expressions of dissatisfaction with official commemorative culture. Cultural memory needs rituals, monuments, anniversaries, recurring images and, yes, commonplace phrases too, in order to take shape, to endure and to develop. By its nature, ceremonial commemoration tends to be repetitive and formulaic. It evokes a remembrance through symbols. Religious rituals of re-enactment are no different. To a person who did not grow up with the Gospel, whose archives do not contain the Christmas story, the Sermon on the Mount, the Crucifixion, the Resurrection, and the memory of their own first Communion – to such a person, the Eucharist remains an extraneous operation, one that has at most a curious aesthetic interest. A person whose individual life history is not interwoven with the history of Judaism, the rich and tender but also terrible and violent 3,000-year love story between God the Creator and His people – such a person will hardly notice the moment when the magbiah lifts up the Torah scroll.

There was an expectation that the Holocaust was something like a founding myth of the Federal Republic of Germany, to be constantly recalled to mind, beyond the generations involved, through rituals and places of remembrance. The Memorial to the Murdered Jews of Europe in Berlin is explicitly not aimed at evoking empathy – its intention is not for the visitor actually to feel an anguish which would correspond to the victims' mortal terror. In its suggestion of a labyrinth of tombstones, the memorial's evocation of the experiences of being pent up in ghettos, freight wagons, concentration camps and gas chambers, of abandonment and hopelessness, is a symbolic one. Rather than being reproduced in the greatest possible fidelity, as in a film or a theatrical re-enactment, a real situation is translated here into a symbolic figure. But we can observe at this very memorial, day in and day out, how difficult this symbolic shift is. The visitors, especially the younger ones, run between the stelae as if they were participating in a re-creation that was supposed to be shocking. But of course it isn't shocking. So they get out their sandwiches. To a person whose own biography lacks the reference points to which the formulas, gestures and symbols of cultural memory refer – to such a person, those formulas, gestures and symbols feel empty.

I would like to draw your attention to yet another difficulty involved in what we call commemorative culture: a person who is born in Germany, immigrates to Germany, travels through Germany – such a person can hardly understand the dimensions of the genocide against the Jews. In Germany, the Jews were a tiny minority, 1 per cent of the population when Hitler became chancellor of the Reich and a quarter of 1 per cent at the outbreak of the Second World War. Comparatively rare are the Germans who live in houses where Jews once lived, who walk through streets in which every shop and every craftsman's workshop had a Jewish owner, who live in neighbourhoods where every street once had its mikveh, its cheder or its synagogue, who live in towns where a majority of the people spoke Yiddish. The golden 'stumbling blocks' set in the pavements here and there reinforce the impression, at least in naive, childish, ignorant or spiteful minds, that they weren't that many after all. And they weren't: 165,000 Jewish victims among almost 80 million Germans are not 'many', when 70,000 Jews were murdered just in Vilnius, Lithuania – out of a total of 150,000 inhabitants. The Western integration of the young West Germany, forward-looking though it was, erased the Holocaust from people's geographical awareness. The real genocide against the Jews took place where you didn't look if you were born and raised in western Germany: it was perpetrated in the East, in Bełżec, Sobibór and Treblinka, in Auschwitz and Birkenau, in Majdanek and Chełmno, in Maly Trostenets, Bronna Góra, Babi Yar, and in many other places. As a young German, you learn the numbers, of course. But running into the ghosts of the murdered inhabitants at every turn is something else again. If there were stumbling blocks in the pavements in Vilnius, or in Minsk, Lviv, Odessa, Brest, Riga, they would not be isolated specks: half the cities would be paved in gold – like the New Jerusalem.

It is not only the passing years that are to blame for the remoteness of the Holocaust, however, nor the kilometres that lie between present-day Germany and the principal sites of the genocide. There is also a demographic development. More and more people live in Germany whose families have no biographical connection to Nazism. Their names don't resemble those of the perpetrators; their faces don't look like the ethnic nation that Hitler forged together; when they clear out their attics they don't find old medals or letters from the front – or, if they do, then from different wars entirely: their own wars. More than a few come from Turkey, a country that received many victims of persecution fleeing Hitler's Germany. Others are citizens of the Islamic Republic of Iran, a state where the Holocaust is ridiculed in cartoon contests. Or they grew up in countries, such as Syria for example, which have been enemies of the state of Israel for decades. Some are members of the nation that lives under Israeli occupation. Others still have grown accustomed to hearing sermons, in Germany or in their country of origin, in which Jews are called 'swine'. They attend schools where the word 'Jew' has once more become a schoolyard insult.

There is no need to treat immigrants or their children and grandchildren as a disruption of commemorative policy. The question how a past can remain present when the biographical links are lacking arises just the same, whether the links are gradually dissolving or whether they never existed. The question merely arises two, perhaps three generations earlier, and it takes a different form in the case of those who do not know even the rough outlines of what was brought forth from German soil between 1933 and 1945. In view of those differences, the many young people who have come to Germany as refugees in the past two years do merit particular attention. But the knowledge alone – that can be imparted remedially if necessary, through lesson plans, integration classes, museum visits, field trips, and finally through exams and assignments to be completed. What will be more difficult to impart to future Germans is the understanding of Auschwitz not just as a crime against humanity but as their own history; not just as the past but as Germany's responsibility.

Auschwitz is not a myth that might be brought to mind by sufficient symbols, gestures, rituals and monuments. A myth, in order to be held as true and to be carried forward from generation to generation, requires wishful thinking: you would like it to be true. That means that its realization depends, to put it in secular terms, on a collective autosuggestion. But no German *wants* Auschwitz to be true. Although catastrophes can become the founding myths of a community – in fact, catastrophes are more often preserved as figures of memory over centuries and millennia than are triumphal events: the expulsion from Jerusalem, the crucifixion of Christ or, for Shiites, the murder of Imam Hussein at Karbala – the identification that is ritually rehearsed and renewed is always with the victims, not the perpetrators.

It is hardly conceivable that Auschwitz could be erased from the cultural memory of the Jewish people. In Germany, however, people have not only conceived the idea, but publicly demanded to have done with this guilt-ridden past and go back to identifying more, or exclusively, with the positive historical events and persons, whichever those may have been. The effectiveness of identitarian wishful thinking is visible in the fact that even Goethe and Heine – to let these two poets stand for the glorified German heritage – are claimed in the name of national pride, although their work better exemplifies the demolition of national categories, and although both of them heaped biting criticism on Germany all their lives. The more remote Auschwitz becomes, the easier it will be once more for Germans to find their history edifying. And they will overlook the fact that there is a contemporary German identity and, yes, a strength and vitality precisely in Germany's brokenness. There is nothing more whole than a broken heart, Rabbi Nachman of Breslov teaches us.

That is one of my favourite sentences and the epigraph of one of my books. Naturally it refers to love: to the love of one's fellow human beings or of God; in either case, an individual situation. But it can also refer to a community: there is nothing more whole than a broken heart. If there was anything that is specific to the 'normative German culture' that some are calling for again in these days, it would not be human rights, equality, secularism, and so on, because these values are all European, if not universal: it would be the consciousness of Germany's guilt, which Germany has gradually learned and ritually rehearsed – but precisely this achievement, which neither France nor the United States but only the Federal Republic of Germany can claim, in addition to its good cars and source-separated recycling – precisely this is what the nationalists want to abolish. Conversely, though, a person who opposes an ethnic conception of the nation cannot hold a narrow notion of historical responsibility. A person who acquires German citizenship by naturalization must also bear the burden of being German. They will feel it in Auschwitz, if not before, when they stick the sticker on their chest.

No matter what other crimes have been committed that one might invoke in an attempt to relativize the Holocaust – whether during the Mongol invasions, the Reconquista, the conquest of the Americas, European colonialism; whether under Stalin, in Rwanda or today in the so-called Islamic State – the crime that Auschwitz stands for remains unique, not only in its scale and in its industrial execution. No, I will put it another way: the scale and the execution of the Holocaust are not even the real reason why our group could not take a happy group photo under the gateway at Auschwitz. Would we have been more at ease if, somewhere in the world, there had been a bigger genocide – a nuclear one, for example? No, the real reason is a different one, and it is written above that gate: Auschwitz is the evil that, as it happens, was proclaimed and believed, commanded and carried out, in German. I read in Primo Levi that it was a matter of survival for the prisoners to know German so that they could quickly obey the rules, the barked commands and the abstruse decrees. 'It is no exaggeration to say that it was their ignorance of these languages' – that is, German and Polish – 'which caused the very high mortality rate of the Greeks, the French and the Italians in the concentration camp,' Levi writes. 'And it was not easy to guess, for example that the hail of punches and kicks which had suddenly knocked you to the ground was due to the fact that the buttons on your jacket numbered four or six, instead of five, or that you had been seen in bed, in the middle of winter, with a hat on your head.'[11] Even today, a visitor to the former concentration camp can't help noticing that all the orders that were posted on the walls, all the duty rosters exhibited in the display cases, and even the instructions on the chemicals stacked in front of the gas chambers, are in German. Anyone who speaks this language, especially a writer who lives with it, makes his living by it, instinctively falls silent on reading the posters of the camp commandants:

Ihr seid hier in einem deutschen Konzentrationslager, 'You are in a German concentration camp. . . .' And understands why none of the present-day signposts is in German. A German in Auschwitz will never be an uninvolved visitor.

From Auschwitz, I travelled to Warsaw to see the monument to the ghetto uprising. As I walked into the square where a German chancellor instinctively fell to his knees, I wondered where the house had stood in which Marcel Reich-Ranicki had lived after his expulsion from Berlin, and where the bed had been in which he had recited German poems to his Tosia for hour after hour. Most often they were poems by, of course, Goethe and Heine, 'which enabled us to forget what was threatening us every day, what, amidst that barbarism, might be our fate at any moment,'[12] Reich-Ranicki's autobiography reads, whose title, *Mein Leben*, acquires the correct intonation only as the reader progresses through it: 'My *life*'. And where was the courtyard in which, in the afternoons, members of the ghetto orchestra rehearsed Beethoven's String Quartet no. 9 in C major, Opus 59 no. 3, whose opening measures would accompany, forty years later, the title and credits of Reich-Ranicki's television programme, *Das literarische Quartett*? 'It is difficult to imagine now the dedication with which these musicians rehearsed and the enthusiasm with which they performed. . . . Haydn and Mozart were played, Beethoven and Schubert, Weber and Mendelssohn-Bartholdy, Schumann and Brahms – in other words, predominantly German music, as throughout the world.'[13]

Perhaps because the photos of Brandt kneeling showed almost nothing of the surroundings – always cropped to the square framed by the soldiers and officials – I had always imagined that there must still be a ghetto, something from that time. But of course there is not a single historic building, not even one wall; I should have known it. 'The previously existing living quarters of 500,000 subhumans, absolutely unsuitable for habitation by Germans, must disappear from the scene,'[14] Himmler ordered after the Final Solution had been adopted in Berlin. There is no Warsaw Ghetto any more. The place where Marcel and Tosia whispered poems to each other, where the ghetto orchestra performed in the afternoons, is empty. But anyone who has read Marcel Reich-Ranicki's autobiography will never forget that there, precisely where the Monument to the Warsaw Ghetto Uprising stands today, a rather bored young man with an apparently brand-new riding crop usually stood in the spring of 1942, deciding who would go left and who right: left to the 'transfer depot', to the freight cars, to the gas chambers; right back to life, for the time being.

> If only because of their age – my mother was fifty-eight and my father sixty-two – my parents had received no 'life numbers' and they lacked the strength and wish to hide out somewhere. I showed them where they had to queue. My father looked at me helplessly, while my mother was surprisingly calm. She had dressed carefully: she wore a light-coloured raincoat which she had brought with her from Berlin. I knew that I was seeing them for the last time. I still see them: my helpless father and my mother in her smart trench-coat from a department store near the Berlin Gedächtniskirche. The last words Tosia heard from my mother were: 'Look after Marcel.'
> As the group in which they were standing approached the man with the riding crop he was evidently becoming impatient. He urged these no longer young people to get a move on. He was about to use his riding crop, but there was no need: my father and mother – I saw it from a distance – began, in their fear, to run as fast as they could, away from the smart German.[15]

Ladies and gentlemen, I confess that I couldn't stand Marcel Reich-Ranicki's reviews, that I found his way of judging literature outrageous – only either ruthless or gushing, thumbs up, thumbs down, up to and including physically tearing books apart in front of the camera – and I am glad my own works never ended up in the hands of such a great critic (that is truly the mercy of a late birth). For that reason – out of resentment, ultimately – I hadn't read his autobiography, although it had been widely reviewed as a major event in German literary history. But now I was travelling to Auschwitz, I was travelling to Warsaw, I wanted to see with my own eyes the empty place, and so I got *Mein Leben*, got everything Marcel Reich-Ranicki had ever written about Jews in German literature, the 'troublemakers' as he liked to call them, and was not only amazed at his wealth of experience, knowledge and wisdom; I was touched still more by the tenderness of Marcel Reich-Ranicki's prose.

His essays on German Jewish literature are among the most careful, the most scrupulous texts ever written on the subject, and his descriptions of the Warsaw Ghetto, in their resolute anti-sentimentality, will move the most hard-headed reader to tears. And I wondered: what is it that I, that millions of readers – the book was on the best-seller list of *Der Spiegel* for almost three years without a break – what is it that practically the entire literate population of Germany felt on reading it – is it guilt? Yes, guilt: because bearing the burden of history, falling to one's knees under its weight, is not a matter of personal guilt – Brandt had fought against Hitler – but a matter of responsibility for the country one happens to live in. Shame? It is also shame, certainly: shame at leading the good, safe and comfortable life that Germany denied the Jews. But is that all? Are guilt and shame the only feelings, or even just the predominant feelings, with which today's readers respond to Marcel Reich-Ranicki's descriptions of the Warsaw Ghetto? I don't think so. I at least was seized still more while reading *Mein Leben* by the impression of an immense loss, a loss that cannot be made up – a loss for us who are Germans today. Reich-Ranicki described how, as a Polish Jew, he grew up with German culture, the passion with which Lessing and Schiller, Beethoven and Bach were loved in his Jewish milieu, and German literature and music were revered almost as something sacred even in the Warsaw Ghetto. If the Germany of Goethe and Heine, that intellectual world in which such concepts as world literature, Enlightenment, Europe and cosmopolitanism had greater currency than patriotism, fatherland or pride – if that culture had a home anywhere in the early 1940s, it was certainly not in Berlin or Munich but in the ghetto of Warsaw, in the barracks of Auschwitz. Hence the Holocaust is for Germany not only a history of guilt. It is also a history of loss.

The Federal Republic of Germany, as the community under law that it is, will always be the successor of the German Empire: this shapes its politics, its international relations, its obligations. But guilt – if it is not couched in categories of blood and ethnic community – guilt is not arbitrarily inherited over generations: we have a personal relationship to what our parents, our grandparents did; but for their great-grandchildren, at the latest, the guilt becomes an abstract concept, taking the form, in the ideal case, of political responsibility and understanding. Loss, on the other hand, is something that we recognize more clearly from further away, across the distance of generations. Loss is something that can be realized hundreds of years, even three thousand years later.

To return to Auschwitz once more: we had a three-hour guided tour during which the horror escalated continuously, from the bunkhouses to the various sites of execution by hanging or firing squad, torture chambers, laboratories for experiments on humans, to the gas chambers, whose walls still show the scratches of fingernails today. When the gas chamber was opened again after twenty minutes, the guide explained through the wireless headsets that all the visitors were wearing, the bodies were often entangled – as if the living had embraced one another one last time, I thought. In fact, there must be nothing more lonely than the death struggle, even in that tangle, and the bodies must have lashed out uncontrollably in every direction in pain, panic and grief. But this too is only a surmise, for anyone who survived Auschwitz did not themselves look into that deepest darkness. Auschwitz has become synonymous with the Holocaust because it was not only a death factory but also a labour camp: 100,000 prisoners survived Auschwitz. In Treblinka, where 700,000 Jews were gassed to death, there were only fifty survivors. There were still fewer witnesses of Paneriai, and as a result most Germans don't know even the name of that Lithuanian town where the Wehrmacht and the SS shot more than 100,000 people.

Memorials, stumbling blocks, commemorative rituals can convey no idea of the darkness into which people can be pushed by ideologies. They can only remind us of it. But in order for a memory to be burnt into our hearts in the first place, so that the memorials, stumbling blocks, commemorative rituals can refer to it, it will be still more important for future generations to see with their own eyes the places where Germany crushed human dignity, to travel in those countries that Germany drowned in blood, to hear the witnesses who live on in their books. The more often the sigh heard in St Paul's Church is repeated – 'the Germans today are a perfectly normal people, a perfectly ordinary society'[16] – the more necessary is that concretization which is the duty of literature, art and, of course, historical research. Although it is impossible, every generation must try anew to look into the darkness: the Jewish workers who entered the chamber after each gassing waded through blood, urine and faeces. They pulled the corpses apart and laid them on their backs to remove the gold crowns from their teeth, which the German Reich saw as its property. Many jaws were clenched so tightly that opening their mouths was hard physical work, requiring tools – as if the last act of the dying had been to resolve to keep silent. What can a human being say, having seen this work of human beings? I stood there and felt – it was a physical experience – my own jaw clenching too.

The idea that no more poems could ever be written after Auschwitz has so often been misunderstood, ridiculed, dismissed; yet Adorno himself was a vigorous defender of avant-garde poetry after the war. In the gas chamber, the statement takes on a natural self-evidence, not as a proscription but as the expression of an immediate feeling: how can civilization go on at all after such a thing; what is the good of it? In Auschwitz, Germany mutilated itself; it demolished pillars of its culture; it murdered the most faithful keepers of its language. Auschwitz changed the language itself: it made it into an instrument, much more than it had been before the war, reducing the language, more rigorously than other modern languages, to its communicative function. There are forms of expression – a certain elevated tone, a singing voice – which have become impossible in German, which are received, since Auschwitz, as tendentious pathos.

Certainly, German poems continued to be written after the war. But German literature was never again what it had been before Auschwitz. It lost not only its status and its character with the expulsion and annihilation of the Jews. It was able to go on living only in fragmentation – indeed, in silence, in the pauses; this was most exactly audible in Paul Celan's poems. Immediately after the war, Celan was scoffed at; he was ridiculed in particular at his presentation to the

Gruppe 47. Today it ought to be plain that no poems more veracious, poignant and, yes, beautiful in their devastation could be written in the German language after Auschwitz than Celan's poetry of survival. No, the remembrance of Auschwitz is for the Germans not a 'means of intimidation or moral bludgeon that can be employed on any occasion, or even a compulsory exercise,'[17] as Martin Walser complained. It is a Kaddish, and also a mourner's Kaddish for German culture. There is in German post-war literature nothing more whole than Celan's broken verse.

It is revealing that Martin Walser introduced the revision of his Peace Prize speech with a literary discovery: his discovery of Yiddish literature. Had he – he who in the 1960s had been more unflinching than most others in examining Germany's recent history – had he in 1998 overlooked German pre-war literature? Marcel Reich-Ranicki himself, who was deeply hurt by Walser's speech, once pointed out that the foundations of modern literature were laid by Franz Kafka, the foundations of modern physics by Albert Einstein, the foundations of modern music by Gustav Mahler and Arnold Schoenberg, the foundations of modern sociology by Karl Marx, the foundations of modern psychology by Sigmund Freud. All of them were not only Jews: they were German-speaking Jews. Reich-Ranicki called that a 'mystery that I cannot explain'.[18] Neither the French-speaking Jews, nor the Italian, nor the Russian brought forth such creative minds. And, in that early phase of our modern world, rarely Germans who were only German. To name some different figures in connection with Nazism besides just numbers of victims – 165,000 Jews murdered in Germany, or 6 million in Europe – let us quantify the richness that Jews gave to Germany: although the proportion of Jews in the population of Germany and Austria did not exceed 1 per cent, about half of the most famous, the most highly acknowledged even today, and the most translated German authors of the first half of the twentieth century were Jews – 50 per cent. Nazism destroyed the most productive symbiosis in the history of German culture and at the same time erased a conception of Germany that transcends national categories: that Germany of Goethe and Heine as an intellectual world. Of course, there are no stylistic or formal traits that could be called characteristic of Jewish German writers. But there is a specific social situation which finds expression in their work: that of living as Jews in a non-Jewish society and, often enough, a hostile, excluding society. The 'wound of being torn out of the natural order',[19] as Margarete Susman has called it, makes the German literature of Jews particular and at the same time comparable to other, likewise individual forms of alienation. Marcel Reich-Ranicki quotes Susman's phrase and adds: 'For only when we explicitly emphasize the specific situation and the particularity of German writers of Jewish origin, only then do we make them understandable and contribute to their repatriation.'[20]

The fact that Marcel and Tosia Reich-Ranicki were two of the few inhabitants of the Warsaw Ghetto to survive, that they returned to Germany, that the young, enthusiastic Marcel, at first so lost in West Germany, became the Germans' best-known critic, their 'pope of literature' – this is one of the strange turns, almost implausible in its felicity, that the twentieth century has taken among all its disasters. And yet he was unforgiving, and Auschwitz must remain unforgiven. Marcel Reich-Ranicki once mentioned a man who repeatedly said to his face: 'You, Mr Reich-Ranicki, were in the Warsaw Ghetto, and I at that time was one of Hitler's fighter pilots. We will remember that to the end of our days, and it will always divide us.'[21] Reich-Ranicki called this man 'more honest than the professional philo-Semites; he is closer to me than those from whose pens the words "reconciliation" and "brotherhood" always flow so quickly.' If we are grateful that Reich-Ranicki returned to Germany, more grateful still for the poems that Paul Celan has left us, grateful for Nelly Sachs, Peter Weiss, Theodor W. Adorno, Ilse Aichinger and the others who salvaged the German language and German culture after Auschwitz, then we should also take seriously the Germany they stand for: not the German nation, but an intellectual world. 'You must not see me as a German,' said Marcel Reich-Ranicki in the interview I quoted a moment ago:

> Don't make a German of me. I am a citizen of the Federal Republic of Germany. Naturally, and I am happy to be one. I like this country, in spite of everything. I write in the German language, I am a critic of German literature, I belong to German literature and culture, but I am not a German and will never be one.[22]

There are many people living in Germany today who are not *only* German, who perhaps do not want to become German in the sense of an identification with the flag, cuisine and customs, who see their foreignness and differentness as something beautiful and natural, but who are just as naturally citizens of the Federal Republic, and happy to be so. They write in German; perhaps they are producers of German culture. But their ancestors were neither in the Warsaw Ghetto nor were they Hitler's fighter pilots. When they visit Auschwitz, they too will wear the word 'German' on their chests. Under the wrought-iron gate, if not before, they will see Auschwitz as their own history. Therein lies perhaps an opportunity for Germany not only to recognize its guilt in the genocide against the Jews but also to feel its loss. *Jā-ye shān khālist*, we say in Persian when someone is missed, missing at a feast, a funeral, or simply in one's life.

Literally translated, it means, 'Their place is empty', or perhaps 'Their place is saved.' *Jā-ye shān khālist*: let this speech by a German about Auschwitz be ended in Persian. *Jā-ye khāli-ye kalimihā dar Almān wa hameh jā-ye donyā ke koshtande-shān wa tard-e-shān kardand yā in rouzhā hatā badnām wa tahdid-e-shān ham mikonand har-che bishtar ehsās mishawad.*

I thank you for your attention; I congratulate the Department of Jewish History and Culture on the twentieth anniversary of its founding, and I hope for a future in which Germany will become more Jewish again.

On Receiving the State Prize of North Rhine-Westphalia

The Gürzenich, Cologne, 27 November 2017

Mr President of the Bundestag, Mr Minister-President, Madam Mayor, ladies and gentlemen,

At the high point of the protests against the Vietnam War, having become an acclaimed protest singer with his song about the four anti-war demonstrators who were shot and killed at Kent State University, Ohio, Neil Young toured the United States. One evening – it was during the presidential election campaign – he lay on the bed of a hotel room in the middle of nowhere and turned on the television set. Richard Nixon, the peace movement's *bête noire*, the war-mongering, power-mad American president, appeared on the news leaving a hospital and climbing, stony-faced, without a wave, into a limousine. The newsreader said that Richard Nixon had visited his father, who was on his deathbed. The same night, on his hotel bed, Neil Young wrote 'Campaigner', which is one of his most moving songs: a song *for* Richard Nixon. 'I am a lonely visitor,' it begins in the first person, as if Neil Young were singing about himself too, or only about himself: 'I am a lonely visitor; I came too late to cause a stir, though I campaigned all my life towards that goal'[23] – that is, I fought one battle after another my whole life long, although of course 'campaigned' also suggests the electoral campaign, and the song is about the president, after all. 'I hardly slept the night you wept / Our secret's safe and still well kept,' and then the two famous lines, nothing less than offensive in 1972, which Neil Young will repeat as a tiny refrain after the verses that follow: 'Where even Richard Nixon has got soul' – even the enemy, the liar, the dreadful American president; 'soul' with no article, in the sense of 'soulful' – 'Even Richard Nixon has got soul.'

Mr President of the Bundestag, Mr Minister-President, Madam Mayor, ladies and gentlemen, a person celebrating his fiftieth birthday, as I am today, may perhaps take the liberty of speaking in general terms, more general perhaps than is already customary in acceptance speeches and soapbox oratory. He may ask himself, and hence his listeners, the question: What is important in life? Really important, I mean. If we take just a few seconds to answer, we may observe how one object after another that preoccupies us day in and day out, that we think about, that we argue about with friends or in public debate, rolls up before our mind's eye and then falls away again. Even a football player will admit that football isn't really important, and even a speculator will be aware, in lucid moments, that there are more important things than money. Fashion, leisure, fun? Rubbish. A row with a co-worker, a promotion denied? In the case of writers, annoyance at a review? No, not really important. The day's headlines, that is, say, the failed negotiations to form a coalition government between Christian Democrats, Greens and Liberals? Politics directly affects our lives, of course, but here in Germany we get one cabinet or another; what is at stake is not – fortunately, since this means it is not a matter of war or peace, not a question of survival, as in other countries in the world, of freedom or servitude – what is at stake is not what our national anthem calls 'the guarantee of our happiness',[24] namely unity, justice and freedom.

Cheeky as I am, I can't help having my odd thoughts when important people appear on the news. I find it interesting to see, for example, their weary, haggard faces after hours and nights of negotiations, and how their mouths weigh every word in front of the microphones. I think, O God, those poor people, they've been struggling for weeks now, to the point of physical exhaustion, to negotiate an agreement, probably working through tantrums and nervous breakdowns that we, the television audience, will never know about, and in the end they have to face the people with empty hands. I imagine each of the politicians getting into a limousine after their final statements, and it's three o'clock on Monday morning. And at home their two daughters are asleep, and the politician, before grabbing a few hours' sleep, goes to their bedside to give them a kiss on the forehead; or else a marital dispute is smouldering which for whatever reason always flares up just on the last night of the cabinet negotiations – let's say their wife announces she's moving out – and, from one second to the next, the politician is catapulted into a situation that is of course much more important, the end of their long love, the break-up of their family, the question how, not the country, but very specifically their life and the lives of their children will go on. Perhaps the politician in the back seat of their official car has found, among their many e-mails, the message from their sister containing data of a different kind from that of the current opinion surveys, namely blood pressure, oxygen saturation, prothrombin time, CO_2, haemoglobin, heart rate, and the next morning the politician visits his father in the early morning hours – I am a lonely visitor – disinfects his hands outside a frosted glass door, puts on a green gown, rubber gloves, mask, cap, and steps into real life, intensive life – I came too late to cause a stir – before driving on to his party's headquarters, where he will look into the cameras again: Our secret's safe and still well kept.

Anyone who had a heart in their chest and not a clump of dirt, fellow party members, members of the other parties, even most journalists, would understand that something like this – the dying father, a divorce, even just the children's peaceful sleep – moves a person more, agitates a person more deeply than all the things we talk about all day long. We wouldn't stop arguing for our political causes or personal goals; of course we would go on, and why not? But even our political adversary would realize for a moment, or perhaps a few hours, that what is going on here, now in the conference room, in a little while in front of the cameras, is not, any more than what is going on at this podium where I am standing before you, the most important thing in life. Then what is? No, not for Germany, not for Europe, but for every single one of us?

The answer is so banal, and so obvious, that I hardly want to say it, because it comes down to the usual desires: health; family; work; a partner who is dependable and reciprocates our love; not money, but a livelihood that allows us to live in dignity; friends. In some countries, the most important things are simpler still: clean water, enough food, a roof over one's head and heat in winter; peace, a state that, if it doesn't protect one, at least leaves one in peace. Some would also mention God, who is closer to them than their own heartbeat; the next life; other people, or the same people, would also say music or literature. But even faith and art are not universally urgent, not in the same way as a loaf of bread, dying, or a marriage breaking up; they are essential only to some of us. What is universal is always simple, concrete, physically tangible: that which seems to go without saying.

In sermons, it can easily sound preachy for that reason, but the essence of great literature has always been about nothing else: about birth and death, love and betrayal, pain and hunger; or it demonstrates how unimportant most other things are. And precisely in those countries and those times in which the basic needs go unmet because of war, terror and economic distress, great literature reminds us that nothing about our existence, not even the breath we draw, can be taken for granted. 'Little suspecting what would betide, I left the house . . .' is the prototype of Romantic literature at least, if not all literature. Literature is always the intrusion of reality into our sleepwalking lives.

I travel a great deal, as you may know, and I often go to areas dominated by war, terror and distress. Just recently, I travelled for *Der Spiegel* through Eastern Europe to Iran and stood on three fronts in succession: in eastern Ukraine, in northern Georgia and in Nagorno-Karabakh. As a reporter, never having held a weapon in your hand, you wear a helmet and a heavy armoured vest, and you look, well, not military, but a little uptight. And yet not much happens in a trench if there doesn't happen to be a battle raging or one of the frequent minor skirmishes. You crouch alongside the soldiers who, in addition to their vest and helmet, also carry an assault rifle; you take care not to leave the cover of the sandbags and earthworks, and you have plenty of time. Yes, you have time. Soldiers are often bored, especially in wartime. You get to talking, no, not just about the military situation, but about all kinds of things: about the weather, about the bought and sold World Cup in Qatar, about Led Zeppelin. And, for whatever reason, I have fallen into the habit of asking, in the trenches, what the soldiers – who almost everywhere are young people, eighteen, twenty, twenty-five years old – what the most important thing in life is: What are your goals, your hopes, your plans for when the war is over? And this is the truth: no matter what war I happen to be visiting, on both sides of the front I hear the same things, the usual things, the simplest things: health, family, a good job, friends. Then I ask the recruits – on the front lines it's mostly recruits, who don't have a choice – whether they honestly believe that the recruits in the trenches opposite, 300 or 800 yards away and just as young as them, wish for different things than they do. And, to my amazement, the recruits serving in the war often answer yes. Yes, the other side, the enemy, are blind; they are filled with hate; they want nothing more than to destroy our country. They are not like us. And every time, when the conversation dies down, I mumble in silence a song.

> Hospitals have made him cry
> But there's always a freeway in his eye
> Though his beach just got too crowded for a stroll.
> Roads stretch out like healthy veins
> And wild gift horses strain the reins
> Where even Richard Nixon has got soul,
> Even Richard Nixon has got soul.

I too have a sick father who cannot be here today; I will just mention that. And that is not all that is more important in life than success. And before me, in the front row – I would like to mention this too, which is often bashfully passed over in acceptance speeches and soapbox oratory – before me sit the mayor of my home town and the president of the Bundestag, both of whom have come within a hair's breadth of being murdered and have lost their good health in the course of public service. Not only in war, not only in dictatorships: in our so sheltered Germany too, politics can be a matter of life and death, and we must be grateful for representatives who will never forget for a second what is important. It is not a small thing, but heroic, that they have not despaired but continued to serve without complaining.

As a young person, I faced the state that honours me today, well, not as an enemy, but as a protester against the nuclear arms race, seeing that state as something hostile, as an adversary at least, confronting me in the form of rather uptight police officers. Even then – hard to believe more than half my life has passed since then – my laudator already bore political responsibility. And not only that, he belonged and belongs to a party that I, in my youthful self-indulgence, thought of as evil incarnate. Certainly the Christian Democrats have changed since then, since Alfred Dregger and Friedrich Zimmermann, may their souls rest in peace; and a Federal Republic of Germany which recognizes immigrants as citizens, which is phasing out atomic energy, which admits refugees, in spite of all the disputes about how and how many, which no longer discriminates against homosexuals, is easier for me to identify with. But of course the state has not become another; it is I who, over the years, have become another, today if not before, somehow a grown-up person after all, with nuanced views which sometimes have to be weighed against one another to be sure; with revoltingly conservative if not reactionary notions on child-raising in particular – I'll just say the word internet, the word me-ism – may God help my daughters; and with a deep appreciation of our commonwealth. Unfortunately, however, politics is a bit like love: you only start to fight for something when you realize you could lose it. And then it is often too late.

The majority of British citizens, and young British citizens especially, only realized the value of Europe when the referendum on Brexit had already been lost because of their lack of interest. The discontent in rural regions and the impoverished industrial centres of the US was only taken seriously after it had carried Donald Trump to the presidency. When the world began to worry about climate change, the necessary climate protection goals had already become unrealistic. The war at Europe's doorstep, in Syria and in Iraq, was ignored for five years until its bombs exploded in Berlin and Brussels and its refugees marched along the motorway to Germany. And, as for Europe, it is in any case high time to overcome the paralysis, the national egotisms, and hence it is a disaster in itself, if I may mention it here, that Germany has not given any answer to Emmanuel Macron's proposals and, because the exploratory talks for a coalition government have failed, will not in the foreseeable future. Europe cannot work without a common financial policy, without an adjustment of standards of living, and without a democratic legitimation, any more than Germany can work without fiscal equalization between its states. And keeping a United States of Europe at least in mind as a goal is not a wild-eyed utopia but – have we forgotten this? – a mandate of our constitution.

Our commonwealth is far from perfect: that is true of the European Union just as it is true of Germany, and how much more of my beloved Cologne, whose disasters are legion, from bridges to theatres, from the collapsed Hall of Records to New Year's Eve of 2015, from the European Capital of Culture bid to the fairgrounds development. Nevertheless, a functioning Europe, a European Germany and a flourishing Cologne are worth fighting for, protesting for and, yes, sacrificing for. In times of Islamist terror, right-wing disparagement of the state, and dramatic conflicts on Europe's southern and eastern borders, democracy will probably depend once more on people making sacrifices or bearing witness with their blood. But even when, and especially when, opposition threatens to break out in hostility, the song says once more: Even Richard Nixon has got soul.

If there is one thing that constitutes a constitutional democracy, it is this: that the state accords rights even to those who fight it: the right to bodily integrity, the right to legal counsel; the rights to property, free expression, privacy; the right to a fair and public trial. A few days ago, after 523 days of proceedings and the testimony of six hundred witnesses, the International Criminal Court issued its well-reasoned judgement of the war criminal Ratko Mladić: justice is exactly that; not a secret summary court and an execution during a military action or a drone attack. A constitutional democracy accords protection, permanent or provisional, to foreigners who are denied their fundamental rights in their country of origin. Behind this universalism – *every* person's dignity is inviolable – is an ideal that first came into the world with the prophets of Israel: the equality of all people before God. That is a characteristic of the monotheistic religions which is not found even in ancient Greece, although it is called the cradle of democracy. In the polis, the freedom of male citizens was founded precisely on the bondage of the slaves who did their work for them.

The secularized idea of the equality of all people is the core idea of the European Enlightenment, even if it took a hundred, two hundred years before slavery was actually abolished in its core countries, colonialism overcome – and even if social equality in the sense of equal opportunity is all too often an unattained ideal today. Nevertheless, in times of terror, right-wing populism, and the wars to the south and east of Europe, we must remember that even an adversary, or simply a stranger, may come out of a hospital where his father is on his deathbed. The purpose of literature in particular is not to judge the other, even the convicted extremist or barbarian. Its purpose is to understand: that is, to try to see the world with the other's eyes. And, ideally, our own eyes are changed by the attempt. Such empathy isn't always achieved; or, if it is achieved, it may be morally dubious – in the case, let us say, of mass murderers, torturers or sadists.

But the ideal that lies in the attempt is nothing less than that propounded, over and above the idea of equality, by Jesus: Love your enemies.

In one of the wars I travelled to, in Nagorno-Karabakh, I met a priest who had served at the front. I did not succeed in coaxing one word of empathy out of him for the people who had lost their home, simple shepherds and peasants who happened to have the wrong language, the wrong blood. Home? asked the priest. Yes, home, I said; a place is home to a person if they were born and raised there, no matter who lived here two hundred or two thousand years ago. The priest didn't want to talk about individual persons, though; he spoke of the expelled people only collectively, as a group that had expelled and massacred his people. I tried the idea of loving one's enemy, which is actually the distinguishing feature of Christianity: what had that meant at the front? As if he was in the pulpit, the priest raised his voice and explained solemnly that a Christian must never begin a war.

'All right,' I said, 'but once you are at war – does loving your enemy have any meaning then?'

'We had to defend our country against the enemy.'

'But did you love the enemy?'

'There is a rule,' said the priest slowly, and leaned his upper body backwards as he stood, as if to get more breathing room: 'The enemy has to leave at least a chance for you to love him. But the Turks don't. They have been brought up to hate us, to kill us. They don't leave us any chance to love them.'

'That's too easy!' I exclaimed, not very reverently. 'If the enemy gave you a chance to love him, he wouldn't be your enemy. The special thing about Christ is that he says thou shalt love not just thy neighbour, but thy enemy. In other words, love him who hates you or wants to harm you, or in some way rejects you. That's who you're supposed to love. Is that possible?'

'Yes, if we were to live with them in peace, the different religions I mean, then we could love them. But in wartime it doesn't work.'

'Why not?'

'You can't kill a person you love.'

'And what was it like for you when you were at the front?'

'If you say to yourself, in the moment you're aiming at someone, that you love them, then you can't pull the trigger; you just can't. That's how it was for me. That's how it is in war.'

Maybe fate will one day lead us, or more likely our children or our grandchildren, into the trenches again, not just with a vest and a helmet, but with a rifle too: Little suspecting what will betide, they leave the house . . . I hope not, and at present I see no indication, but for a young peace protester it is part of growing older that he no longer feels, in every case and at all times, that war is wrong. Fascism couldn't have been defeated without war, nor could the 'Islamic State' in Iraq. And should the Ukrainians – to take one of the wars I visited on my most recent trip – should the Ukrainians have simply resigned themselves to the fact that Russia actually occupies parts of their country? What country would have been next? What was wrong in all three cases was the policies, including Western policy, that made the war necessary in the first place. May our children or grandchildren, if policy should plunge them into the abyss, nonetheless be aware – their grandparents and great-grandparents rarely were – that the recruits in the trenches opposite, 300 or 800 yards away and just as young as they, have the same hopes, the usual ones, the simplest ones.

But it doesn't have to be a war, an attack, that makes us realize what is important in life. Reality can come crashing down on a person in other ways: illness, parents, heartbreak, the birth of a child; it happens to every one of us, and to everyone it is a matter of life and death, even if the stroke of fate, seen from a distance, is just the usual distress. Nonetheless, we still follow what is happening around us, at work, in the street, on the news – of course we follow it. We are not paralysed with shock for weeks and months. That too is something I have learned in wars – in fact, it is what interests me about war: when the state of emergency becomes normal; writing against the readers' tendency to accept it as normal. Our father, our mother ought not to die; our family ought to stay together. But sooner or later our parents do die; some families do split up. It happens. Sometimes the son dies before the mother: that is the worst thing, as the Gospel knows. Common sense tells us that we can't change it. The religions say we must accept it, that it must be so that not our will, but a higher will, be done. That what we find bad, unjust and cruel is, essentially, good – that it must be. But literature, if it doesn't rebel, which is rarely good for it, must at least note the loss, and feels the enemy's loss as well. Even . . . has got soul.

I thank my state for the State Award and you, ladies and gentlemen, for your attention.

Eulogy for Djavad Kermani

Melaten Cemetery, Cologne, 8 December 2017

Mādar-e aziz, dear family, dear mourners,

The story our father told that impressed me most as a child is one of powerlessness. Our father was a strong person – everyone who lived or worked with him daily knows that – and my mother experienced it most frequently, and sometimes unhappily; he defined himself, so to speak, by his strength, by his will to attain, to impose, to achieve what he set his mind on, often for himself, but more often for the good of others: for his family, for the benefit of the needy. As a child I always experienced that enormous strength in part as something physical – yes, why deny it? as something masculine. His face dissolving into a thousand wrinkles and turning red when he tried to open a long-stored jar of Mother's jam which my older brothers, of legal age in fact, had already given up on, and after a few seconds during which I watched him breathlessly, he casually laid the lid on the kitchen table as if he had just pulled apart a Velcro strip. Or in the garden, when, dripping with sweat, he wanted to finish a task he had set himself, repairing some pump or painting the last of the shutters, although our mother had already called him to lunch repeatedly in a piercing voice, 'Djavaaaaad', and we sons, unruffled, cleaned our plates so that we could dash back to our rooms – while our father was still fighting with a heavy wooden door that, for whatever reason, wouldn't go on its hinges.

It goes without saying that the door was hanging snugly in its frame in the afternoon when we played football in the yard; at most there were still some wood shavings on the floor for one of us brothers to sweep up. It likewise goes without saying that 'one of us' was always some other one, which reliably enraged our father. Yes, he could get angry, absolutely furious; his grandchildren never saw him that way, and his great-grandchildren saw only the kind old man; our father could shake the walls with his shouting: then his strength scared me. But he could also be unbelievably tender towards me: he could weep, he could melt in sympathy.

But the story our father told which I remember best, and which he probably passed on to his great-grandchildren too – this story is about something else entirely, because then he was a child himself. A father is at the same time a son; this is something a son can only appreciate when he sees his father helpless in the face of death, and returns his tenderness. The child who would become our father lived with his parents, his four sisters and other relatives in the house near Shah Square at the Kermani junction, *chahārrāh-e Kermāni*, named after his ancestor who had been Isfahan's highest cleric, and he had a lamb. Yes, a lamb. In those days the houses in Iran all had courtyards that were like little paradise gardens, with a fountain in the middle that reflected the sky and fruit trees that gave cool shade, quinces, pomegranates, the best cherries in the world. Among the little people, which included my grandparents by this time – that is, in houses where the four sides of the courtyard were divided between several families – the courtyard was also a vegetable garden, a chicken run, and what have you. And our father, this late arrival, pampered by everyone, this little boy among the many girls and women, had taken a fancy to the lamb that also lived in the courtyard, and the lamb apparently to him. For everywhere our father went, in the square, through the bazaar, even in the schoolroom, if we may believe our father, who, in addition to everything else, was a storyteller, the lamb followed him, even into the schoolroom.

All right, our father couldn't take his lamb everywhere, apparently not into the schoolroom, or at least not every morning, for one day he came out of school at noon and his lamb was gone. Someone had taken it to the butcher's. Our father claimed – as I say, he was a great storyteller – our father claimed he ran right across the great square, into the bazaar, through half Isfahan, howling and sobbing to save the lamb that had become his friend. He didn't find it, of course, and none of the grown-ups understood his tears when he came back to the courtyard, understood the snot running from his nose, heard his heart pounding, paid his accusing look any mind. It was just a lamb, said the grown-ups, waving it off, a lamb such as we eat at every holiday. No one gave any thought to the fact that, to a child, a lamb can be more than just livestock: it can be a friend, a child of God like every other creature, a son, like our father himself.

I shouldn't read too much psychology into this episode, and yet it is striking that this of all experiences was the formative childhood memory, the one most often retold, and doubtless embellished, of a man who amazed his contemporaries by his unbending will, his absolutely uncompromising obstinacy, his persuasiveness. Our father, who could move mountains, knew very well – the experience had been burnt deep into his soul – that a human being is actually powerless; that nothing is under his control. This realization emerged in a way that was positively saintly during the last months of his life, only the accusatory attitude had long ago, many years ago, been supplanted by gratitude – so many years and decades ago that none of the grandchildren believes us sons when we say their grandfather was capable of anger, absolute fury. For, to our father, the masters of the universe were no longer the other adults, parents, uncles, teachers and statesmen: to him, the Master of the universe was God alone – His will be done – Who deals justice where it is concealed from mortals.

That trust – whatever happens is good; God be praised in every moment – that is what all of us, no doubt his great-grandchildren too, the little children, admired, or at least sensed, in him when, from early August on, we went one after another to his sickbed. In four months of misery, of agony, of the exposure that such infirmity inevitably brings with it, of hopes disappointed time after time – in four months he did not complain once, in spite of torments like Job's, not to the nurses, not to the doctors, not to his sons, daughters-in-law or grandchildren; only sometimes, in secret, moaning helplessly, to his wife. Always, at every welcome and every leave-taking, truly every day that he was conscious, he smiled gratefully, as peacefully as a man blessed. What a long way from the child who, bawling his eyes out, entered the courtyard of his parents' house with an accusatory glare; how many years, experiences, realizations, moments of happiness, strokes of fate, successes and failures, from Isfahan to Cologne.

As I mentioned, our father came from modest circumstances; his family was respected because of his clerical ancestors but had come down somewhat in the world, and much though he loved his parents, who must have been kind, gentle people, he wanted to get out of those circumstances as fast as possible. He managed to get admitted to medical school, which was no mean feat for a child of the old city centre, and he managed to catch – by claiming he had his degree before he actually did – the beautiful, rather pert daughter of an upper-class family. Whether by luck or otherwise, his prospective father-in-law turned out to be an eminently republican bourgeois who attached more importance to the suitor's piety and decency, and also his professional ambition, than to his social background.

How our father nonetheless had to strut, almost like a rogue, with a borrowed suit, a borrowed car, a sham degree and a new house bought with every last rial of his credit, to win over his mother-in-law, his saucy sisters-in-law and of course his bride herself – our mother has described that delightfully in her memoirs, the funniest episode perhaps that of the used Cadillac convertible that our father bought on credit, dead cheap, paying the deposit from his first paycheque, only to discover that the chassis was too long for his little yard – no matter how he pulled in, the bright red rear end always protruded into the street. Nor could our father park his convertible in the street, because the convertible had no roof – not even a convertible hood. Ah! that's why it was so cheap, our father realized too late.

Yes, our father was a show-off, an overachiever, a man determined to rise in the world, but not only for his own sake. Our mother had hardly had time to grow accustomed to the living conditions in the new residential neighbourhood – modest by her standards, but proper and also exciting for a young woman – when, just like that, he took her with him to the countryside. Certainly he wanted to do something meaningful, to treat the neediest people. But perhaps he secretly wanted to get away from his wife's condescending relatives. In his euphoria he probably didn't even notice that our mother was aghast when he showed her into their new home, in a dusty village street in the middle of nowhere, or that she probably cursed him when he left her alone in the shabby room on the very first morning to drive over the mountains in his jeep. But when he came home in the evening, fainting with exhaustion, and the next evening too, and then when, because our father rarely accepted money, first the neighbours and then the other villagers and finally people from the countryside all around started arriving on the doorstep to heap gifts on the young couple from the city – chickens, rice, flour, sugar and fruit – then our mother conceived a fondness in her heart for the show-off. And when she witnessed herself how, when a neighbour's boy was choking on a nut, he cut open the boy's throat, just like that, although sweating with apprehension, surrounded by the boy's screaming parents, his frightened siblings, the deathly pale neighbours, when our mother cheered in chorus with all the villagers because the nut popped out of the boy's throat and the wound was so small that our father was able to staunch the bleeding, so that the child, a simple peasant boy with holes in his trousers and no shoes, was soon smiling again and cavorting in the village street the next day – then our mother knew there was something special about this man, and no matter how often she was cross with him, how loudly she scolded him, in the end she always forgave him, for he rarely did anything for himself, and he did a great deal for this world.

Of course, in the long run, the village was not enough for him: Isfahan was not enough, even Tehran was not a sufficient prospect for the future; and so he travelled to the land of the Franks, *Farangestān*, as Europe was known in Iran, only to discover that his degree meant nothing to the stringent Germans – not that he could be deterred from his plans by another course of study. Nonetheless, he told our mother, whom he missed, that everything was marvellous in Germany, big house and lots of money, so that she sold all their possessions and, against her parents' will, boarded an aeroplane with the children. And thus began our story in Germany, with a young Iranian who financed his medical studies by working night shifts and, from the little money he earned, even provided for his parents in the old country, learned German from the dictionary, starting with the word *Aal*, 'eel', and, when asked about the state of the cadaver in the packed auditorium, for lack of German skills could only stammer: '*Guten Tag*'; with a pretty Iranian wife from an affluent family who felt betrayed again, as before in the village, soon with three little children in eighteen square metres in a tower block in Erlangen. Thus began the history that is gathered today in this mourning hall, the history of a medical career, of a love that weathered all storms, of four sons who all became doctors, although the youngest only a doctor of philosophy; and not only his sons, as the obituaries indicated, which read like the programme of an academic symposium; with daughters-in-law, grandchildren and even great-grandchildren, his family numbering twenty-nine by now. It is also the history of big business deals, since even the medical profession was not enough for our father: of precious carpets, of trade with far-off continents, of a political errancy after the revolution in Iran, and an aid organization that built schools and shelters in Isfahan, translated the *Nahj al-Balāgha* into German, the second most important book to Shiites after the Quran; provided for earthquake victims, helped refugees, and is managed today by his eldest son and his daughter-in-law. It is our history, which we owe to the man beside me and the woman before me, our parents, who came to Germany in 1957, now sixty years ago. 'Unbelievable', our mother murmured as we left the hospital room on one of those days, back in Barcelona or here in Cologne, 'unbelievable, *bāvarkardani nist*', and she sounded almost scandalized: 'Your father achieved everything he set out to achieve in life, everything.'

I am our father's youngest son, separated by some years from the other three: almost eight years from Omid, twelve from Khalil. Of his sons I must have seen him least, lived with him least, not only because my lifetime so far is shorter. When I was little, our father was already a senior physician, later a businessman, and he worked from early till late. When I think back today what my father gave me most of all at that age, it was, yes, my religious upbringing. That was not easy, because of course I was just as obstinate as he and, if he felt something was important, I sometimes looked right past him on principle. He had no success with the rituals, the prayers, the Quran readings, or not until decades later. But he taught me, and at a very young age, the religious attitude: compassion for others and trust in God for oneself. Whatever happens is good; God be praised in every moment.

Everyone who visited him in recent months was able to observe that, even in the most extreme dependency and distress, indeed up to the very last night of his life, he turned his palms towards Heaven and said, murmured, whispered: '*Khodāyā shokr*', thanks be to God. And when he was too weak to speak, he still formed a single, soundless word with his lips: '*Shokr*', Thanks. Shrugged his shoulders and smiled at us wearily.

Mādar-e aziz, dear family, dear mourners, this *shokr* is not just any word. It is Arabic – that is, the language of Islam. Unbelievers are called in the Quran *kuffār*. Do you know what the literal meaning of the word is? It means 'ingrates'. In Islam, belief is essentially gratitude. *Shokr*. The unbelievers are they who stand before the signs of God, the '*āyāt*, before the sun and moon, before humankind made of a clay like the potter's, before the revelations of the prophets from Abraham on, before the bliss of love, and of lust too by the way, and not least before the beauty of nature, but who are deaf, blind and mute, or, more exactly, who act as if deaf, blind and mute, for it is up to each person whether they look, listen and bear witness to their Creator: *fa-bi'ayyi 'alā'i rabbikumā tukazzibān* – 'Which of your Lord's bounties will you deny?'[25]

In recent months – may I say this even though it is presumptuous? – it was I who came the closest to him: the youngest, the most remote of his sons, and the only one to have taken a different path in life than the one our father desired and planned. One reason was simply that the two hospitals in which our father lay happened to be, by chance or otherwise, in my immediate neighbourhood. As I mentioned, my brothers had seen more of our father and had the more formative experiences with him, and by that I mean not only childhood experiences but also later situations, up to and including his illnesses and afflictions. Each of them has treated our father and saved his life at least once, and my brother Hamid several times. That is, after all, another thing around which legends grew during his lifetime, at which the doctors shook their heads more incredulously each time: how often our father slipped out of death's clutches. Heart attack, two dramatic cardiac operations, artificial ventilation over weeks, later chronic respiratory insufficiency, after his prostate cancer a bladder carcinoma too, and, every time, our father came back, was miraculously wheeled out of every intensive care unit alive, woke up from every coma, although more infirm, his respiratory volume smaller, his bones more weary, but each time more grateful than he had been before. *Shokr.*

In the end it was I, for the first time, who stood most often at his hospital bed. Again he fooled the doctors, who had given up hope three times in just these four months, and survived his sixth bout of pneumonia at the age of ninety; came back four times from intensive care to the regular ward. He loved life, which to him was a boon, a bounty. He didn't want to die. Even in the first night, when I arrived in Barcelona with Hamid and the doctors shook their heads pessimistically, I observed how, under the mask, he concentrated on every breath, arduous though it was to breathe, little oxygen though he got through his lungs. Yet his breathing never stopped, not that night, not in the many nights that followed. He wanted to live. He fooled the doctors, his colleagues; he triumphed over them by his tenacity and his irrepressible willpower, but he knew with every breath he took that he would never triumph over God. In the end, a human being, even our big, strong father, is powerless, and nothing is under his control.

And yet he had a last wish, which he pleaded before his Lord with healthy self-confidence. He said: God, make me just well enough that I can get up one more time, go home, and walk across the road by myself to the Rhine, just to the riverbank, not along the embankment as I used to do, that would be too much, I don't need that; just the few yards to the bank, once at least, on my own two feet, even with the stupid walker if I must, so that I don't forget how beautiful the world is. Or else, God, let me die, take me back. But please, God, don't leave me halfway. I don't want to be a burden to my wife, any more than I am already, and I don't want to go to a nursing home. That was our father's wish, and he told it to me and to others. He was not a fawning servant of God but conscious to his last breath of his own dignity as a *khalīfa*, a viceroy of God on Earth. It is not only God who has rights in Islam: human beings have them too.

When it started to become apparent, three weeks ago today, that, no matter how strong-willed he was, he would never stand on his own feet again, that his body was depleted, lungs, heart, kidneys deteriorated by secretions, his resistance exhausted, his soul too exhausted, his so unwavering soul prostrated to the ground, we planned everything for him – transitional care, remodelling, domestic help, nursing, caregivers several times a day, an Afghan couple supporting him. But he, our father, had made a different plan with his Creator. Before God's will was done with him for the last time, his death had become his own will too. Their will was done. In the night from Saturday to Sunday, he turned his hands again towards Heaven, and then he waved to us: that is my last image of him, his weary, friendly wave of parting.

When I came back to the room early in the morning, his body was still warm; his hands lay peacefully on his stomach, his eyelids spread kindly over his eyes like a blanket. His face, which still had colour, was almost free of wrinkles, miraculously decades younger. And he, our progenitor, had become a lamb, the innocent creature that, in the land of the Franks, is God's son, God's lamb, to whom death brings eternal resurrection. *Shokr.*

Eulogy for Karl Schlamminger

North Cemetery, Munich, 21 December 2017

Dear Turan, dear Saam, dear relatives, friends and colleagues of Karl,

I see an image of Karl – perhaps I should say a dream, for I see him in motion, in different settings; I see Karl in the dream scene of a life, a scene with a unique congruity. And yet, by conventional patterns, nothing about this life fits together: a strong, broad-shouldered man with a tousled beard, speaking German with the colouring of Allgäu in Bavaria, and not only the colouring, but also the unhurried pace of the back country, where people place every word with deliberation and take as much time as they like for pauses between the words – a real man, if I may put it that way; a big strong Bavarian in an old mansion in pre-revolutionary Tehran, with fruit trees and the obligatory basin in the garden; at his side a genteel Iranian woman, beautiful and self-assured as a young queen, the director of a museum for precious vases and vessels; and, between the two lovers, the two most gracious children in the world. Servants appear too in the dream scene, but they seem almost to belong to the family, the interactions are so friendly, and there are friends, apparently countless, coming and going, artists, writers, musicians, scholars, some of them Iranian, but others German, French, Japanese, a thoroughly cosmopolitan world of the mind and the arts in the middle of Iran. And this Bavarian speaks in the most sensitive way, with deep knowledge, about Iranian culture and the aesthetic traditions of Islam, praising the wisdom of the old building arts and demonstrating the logic of the ornaments which only seem to be haphazard.

He has students too, this Bavarian, art students at the academy who evidently worship him and listen in amazement to his explanations of modern painting's non-European structures and the modernism of Persian architecture. And he has discussions not just with students – this Bavarian often travels from Tehran across country, through the desert and into the mountains, into the remotest Iranian villages, to listen in amazement himself as the people, simple people, as his parents in Kempten were, tell him about their rich customs and traditions. He laughs with the villagers, asks them impish or scholarly questions, drags everyone into a discussion. And yet his Persian – this is the funniest thing – of course his Persian too has the colouring and the unhurried pace of far-away Allgäu. Nothing fits together in this life: the term Middle East with the name Schlamminger; the muscular man with the almond-eyed Asian woman, the scholars from all continents in Tehran, the art professor in the village, the Bavarian conversational style in the Persian language – and yet everything is just as it should be; everything is in its proper place, a stroke of destiny too audacious for any human imagination. The scene is not a dream, as I know from many eyewitnesses, photos, films, and most of all from his own stories: it is the life Karl led with his family in Iran in the 1970s.

When I first met Karl and Nasrin almost twenty years ago, they had long since transposed their world of the mind and the arts from Tehran to Munich. They still had an elegant, generous house, although now a more recent building; the children had become artists themselves; writers, musicians, scholars still came and went, and even without servants there was wonderful, elaborate and refined cooking by Nasrin, and very simple cooking, but likewise with the best ingredients, by Karl. It was a house in which people not only lived but observed life and, most importantly, appreciated it: every beautiful detail as precious as an antique vase; every peculiarity worth conserving and conversing about. 'Sehr gut', said Karl when he ate something he liked, and when he closed a book he had enjoyed reading or saw a work of art that was felicitous, and that 'sehr gut', always preceded by a shorter or longer pause, a contemplation with squinting eyes before he pronounced it all the more resolutely, with an approving nod as if applying a seal, that 'sehr gut' was much more than just an aesthetic judgement: it was a judgement about life itself, which, for all its pain and frustration, contains so much joy and so many blessings even in the smallest things: not just 'gut', but 'sehr gut' – very good.

Coming from a family of physicians, I am the only one among my kin to have chosen the world of ideas and the arts as his path in life. Our house was not one in which people attended to the little things, fleeting things, or took more time than necessary for conversations or observations, much less for idleness; in our house, everyone was always busy with something. Perhaps that was one reason why I felt as comfortable at the Schlammingers' as if in a second home; they were soon friends, my first readers, and almost a kind of parallel parents to me, Nasrin kind and easily delighted, Karl critical, often painfully so.

I say that uneasily, because Karl's criticism referred often enough to my own books, and especially to my public appearances: to my rapid speech, which to him, the slow speaker who pronounced every word with deliberation, was a horror, unintelligible, and thus disrespectful to my listeners, insulting, nothing less than insolence, as Karl mercilessly spelled out to me more than once. But, as a recipient of Karl's criticism, I also know best that his constant fault-finding, his *granteln*, as I believe it's called in Bavaria, was always intended as a motivation to greater efforts to make a work of art, a recipe or, as the case might be, a text still better: not just good, but very good. It must always have been that way, even in the dream scene of a life, and he had learned it, he recalled, from his own teachers, the Benedictine Brother Gregory at school, the painter Johannes Itten and the philosopher Ernesto Grassi. Outside Tehran, in Shahrud, a little town Karl often visited, the craftsmen in the bazaar had a set expression for a pitcher or a brass plate was made especially lovingly and mindfully: such a piece was *eshlämmingeri*. *Eshlämmingeri*, pronounced with an approving nod, as if applying a seal: that is how I imagine it must have been; the Persian translation, no doubt, of Karl's '*sehr gut*': *esh-lämmingeri*.

Only there was something else as well that drew me to the Schlammingers, something besides the art of living: there was also a love – an infatuation in fact; after three, after four decades there was still an infatuation that I had never seen in any other marriage. The loves all around, the loves of many years, my own included, were either passionate or stale; they were faded or had blossomed anew; they had problems that led to separations or to a succession of new starts. No matter how well the lovers were suited to one another – same background, similar social status, related interests – there was always something that didn't add up, at least one thing, even if it was something as tiny as a discord in their expectations, that widened into ruptures, into tragic or just barely surmountable upheavals. Nasrin and Karl, on the other hand, as different as they were in their families of origin, their cultures and also their characters – she receptive, interpretative and always soothing, he creative, restless, challenging, to outline just these two poles – Nasrin and Karl seemed to me, in their so different natures, to be made for each other in a way I did not see in any other couple. The exterior was different: origins, qualities, social background. In their soul they were similar – no, united; they had become one: that is the feeling I had, the feeling many of us no doubt had. In an exemplary sense, in a way that also radiated upon the people around them, attracted people to them, Nasrin and Karl were *hamdam*. That was a favourite word of Karl's which also became one of mine: in Persian, it denotes a married couple or two people who share a long-lasting love and their day-to-day life with each other. Literally, *hamdam* means something like 'breathing the same'. Two are different, and so they should be, but the air they breathe is the same: *hamdam*. And the word *dam*, which in Persian means 'breath', both the breath of life and a 'waft' or 'sigh', always carries the connotation, like the Hindi *ātmā*, of 'soul'. Like air wafting into two different vessels, their one soul went into one and the other of them and back out again, in and back out at the same time.

Karl brought from Iran back to Germany the elementary form of his creation as a sculptor: the *muqarnas*. It is the basis of cupolas, and it is a way to shape a block by its own inner movement into an arch, into something completely different, its opposite; to shape the square into a circle. In one of his most important works, Karl made even a Christian cross out of the *muqarnas*: instead of two beams, the longer one vertical, the shorter horizontal, Karl took a single block and set it in such an oscillating motion that the square figure rose into a curvature, and not only a curvature, but two extremities that grew out of the curved block as organically as a person's arms grow out of their body. In Karl's cross I saw for the first time, in the symbol of threeness, the idea of oneness; in the Trinity, monotheism; and it is one of the most astounding arcs of his life, completed only at the end, that his last publicly exhibited sculpture, twenty, thirty metres high, applies a thoroughly Islamic formal principle to the Christian cross.

And so too in life, the life of Nasrin and Karl, all plurality sprang from a symbiotic unity, the unity of their souls which was set in oscillating motion. Many of you will know the story of their first touch; Karl told it often after Nasrin's death. It was in the 1960s at the Art Academy in Munich: they met there often; they took walks together; he never dared touch her, not after weeks, not after months, not even her hand. Then winter came; they were standing somewhere outdoors, everything was grey, hazy, perhaps evening was falling – I don't remember; they wanted to say good-bye, but couldn't part; they kept looking in each other's eyes. Snow began to fall, the first snow of the year. They went on standing there looking at each other while all around them everything turned white: the pavement, the quiet street, their shoulders, their hair. Finally, a snowflake alighted on Nasrin's eye, on her eyelash, to be precise. Karl raised his hand and moved his fingers to her eyelash to take away the snowflake, or to liquefy it; Nasrin could only half see. When he touched it, Nasrin broke out in tears and complained that he had ruined everything. But that wasn't true: fortunately Nasrin was mistaken, as cautious as she was; Karl in his presumption had not ruined everything, far from it. With a single movement of his hand, he, creative, restless, challenging, had set his seal upon her heart and his seal upon her arm, as the Song of Solomon says: 'for love is strong as death; jealousy is cruel as the grave: the coals thereof are coals of fire, which hath a most vehement flame. Many waters cannot quench love, neither can the floods drown it.' It was from this touch, from the snow melting between two fingertips, that all the rest arose; this stroke of fate: not only his love and his family, not only his bond to the Middle East, but also his art, in which the non-European structures of the modern era and the modernism of Persian architecture became one.

After Nasrin's death ten years ago, Karl's life was no longer complete. No one saw that more clearly, more realistically, than he himself. Between one breath and the next, he was left to inhale and exhale their shared soul by himself. His relation to his bisected existence was almost mathematical and kept him from feeling sorry for himself: a person who has been given such a love as he had, such an extraordinary symbiosis, pays a price so much higher for its loss. And a person whose life has been one of such great abundance feels it all the more keenly when everything that makes it worth living gradually runs out. That's just the way it is; Karl never complained to his friends about the way things go but went on cooking for them his simple dishes with the best ingredients as long as he could. '*Sehr gut*', he said then, still '*sehr gut*' after a short pause or a longer one, a contemplation with squinting eyes, very good, and that was a judgement not only of a dish, a book or a work of art: it was always a judgement of life itself, which, for all the losses, all the afflictions of the soul and the growing infirmities of age, offers such pleasures, not only the little blessings but right up to the end the big ones too, a finished work, joy in the children and grandchildren, the community of friends: *sehr gut*.

And when that was no longer possible because the physical afflictions and limitations threatened to take the last remaining pleasures too, Karl gradually prepared himself for death.

I must not beat around the bush; that would not suit Karl: all the years since Nasrin's death were hard, his last months a torment, and the two weeks after his operation a battle that one would not wish on one's enemies, much less one's father and grandfather, a sculptor, a friend who made so much that was good – no, very good – in the world. But – and this is important perhaps for his peace, and certainly for ours – at the very end, when only Saam and Turan remained in his room hour after hour, in the end, it was in the warm reflection of the next world that Karl willingly left his life. *Dāram miram?* he asked at first: 'Am I going now?' and then, some time later, almost as his last words: 'I want to know now what happens next.' To his last breath, Karl Schlamminger remained creative, restless, challenging.

And God saw that it was good, says the Bible, on the evening of the third, fourth, fifth day. But on the evening of the sixth day, after God had completed the Creation which challenges mankind to love, to discern, and to do good works – after the sixth day, it no longer says just 'good', in Hebrew *tov*. It says, *ve hine tov me'od*, 'And behold, it was very good.' The rabbinical scholars have thought a great deal about why the word *tov*, 'good', is augmented on the sixth day by the word *me'od*: 'very good'. One scholar of the twelfth century from Narbonne, Rabbi David ben Yosef Kimhi, gives it an interpretation based on the consonance of *me'od*, 'very', and *m'ōt*, 'death'. In his interpretation, 'good' refers to the Creation, the third, fourth, fifth day. But the Creator, finally finding rest, pointed in *tov me'od*, 'very good', to death, to dying, without which life would not be complete. This is how I imagine it, as Turan and Saam intimated: not just good but, after a short or long pause, a contemplation with squinting eyes: *sehr gut*.

On the 70th Birthday of FC Cologne

MTC Hall, Cologne, 17 November 2018

Dear Mr President, ladies and gentlemen, dear sports fans,

Permit me to begin with a question that reaches beyond FC Cologne: Why do we love football? Football, more than any other institution – most closely comparable to theatre in antiquity or to religion over many centuries – football is still able today to create a public space for moving experiences: breathtaking suspense, grief, anger, malice, dread, rapture, shame, fellowship, gratitude, pride. Where else in modern society would grown-up people fling themselves rejoicing into each other's arms, or jump up on their seats screaming, shout the most offensive curses, weep uninhibitedly like children, break out in an anxious sweat, tremble with joy, stammer stupidly in happiness or desperation? Where else but on the pitch, or in the stadium, do we still go through all of life's highs and lows, triumphs and defeats, promotions and relegations, collectively and not just as individuals?

Its self-image notwithstanding, FC Cologne is not the greatest football club in the world, second only to Real Madrid, or to no one. We have not captured the most titles; we do not have anywhere near the most money; no child in

Mali or in China runs around wearing an unlicensed counterfeit of our jersey. At most, we are still in competition for a top spot as the team most often relegated. But, in the seventy years of its existence, FC Cologne has given us, as no other football club in the Rhineland at least – my dear guests from Gladbach, Düsseldorf, and especially you there, the claque from the Bayer works over in Leverkusen – and probably in the world – to maintain the modesty for which we are widely celebrated – FC Cologne has given us what constitutes the essence of football, what we love football for: emotional community – even if it is often a community of suffering. Unimaginable drama, fantastical characters, feats of genius, but also excruciating defeats and, yes, madness bordering on the pathological. Rises and falls as high and as low as in any human life. And even birth, death and resurrection, as in the religions. All this has been given us by FC Cologne in its seventy years of existence: damnation and redemption, Hell and Paradise.

At the time I first fell in thrall to the FC, in southern Westphalia in 1972 at the age of four, when Welz was playing keeper, Kapellmann, Cullmann, Weber and Konopka defending, in midfield Overath, Simmet and Heinz Flohe – much too soon sold away, so soon disastrously injured, much too soon deceased – and Löhr forward – I can still hear the names as they were broadcast on the radio, and I can still see the red jersey on the television screen, with its striking white sleeves – when I neither stuck with Dortmund or Schalke like the grown-ups around me nor defected to the more successful Bayern or Gladbach like the other boys in my kindergarten, our club's most glorious era was already in the past. But when I recall today what really impressed me as a child about that legendary prehistory, it was not the serial championships, unchallenged, light-footed and confident. Impressed on my memory as a hereditary myth is of course

– and you, dear sports fans, will no doubt say the same – the Drama of Rotterdam.

It was not the coin toss alone. It was the fourth scheduled leg, after two ties and a cancellation fifteen minutes before starting time: Wolfgang Weber had continued playing in spite of a broken leg and the FC had made up a 0–2 deficit; Hannes Löhr had been laid low by an unpunished punch from the Liverpool captain; just before the whistle Hornig had shot a clean goal which the referee, for reasons still undiscovered, did not allow; the pouring rain had turned the grass into a bog; total exhaustion was apparent in the faces, including those of the spectators, the officials, the referees; and then the coin – no author could have written such a story; only football writes tragedies such as this – then the coin, on the referee's first toss, landed edgewise in the mud, although listing heavily towards Cologne, whereupon the Liverpudlian captain – yes, that rogue! – quickly urged the referee to repeat the toss, so that our fate fell only on the second stroke. No question which side a child will take on hearing such a story: real heroes, in football as in literature, can only be tragic. Victory and defeat are forgotten with the very next match, or the next championship at the latest, but this – the bravery of Bull Weber and the inexorability of chance – burns its mark into the psyche for a lifetime, even if we younger ones have only had the story told to us. Besides, the FC had Hennes the Billy Goat as its mascot, and no plush toy with a person inside has a chance in a child's heart against a real live goat.

The rest of the story down to the present I have seen with my own eyes: the final against Günter Netzer, admittedly magnificent himself; the double championship of the Bundesliga and the DFB in '78, the cup victories, and the fiasco in the rematch against Nottingham, the duels against the Bavarians in the 1980s, Christoph Daum defeating Uli

Hoeness in the TV studio but not in the league tables; the millions received for Hässler's transfer to Juventus, mysteriously gone a year later; Erich Rutemöller's order to Frank Ordenewitz – 'Mach et, Otze!' – to commit a foul and risk suspension; and the unremitting decline in the 1990s, the fans' shameful whistling at Kevin Pezzoni, the thunderous salute to the players at the last – and bitterest – relegation; Podolski fleeing in tears to the dressing room; and, behold, suddenly we knuckle down after all, make the promotion, qualify for Europe – only to put in the darkest streak in club history in the very next season and the most pointless relegation since the game was invented. So we find ourselves starting over yet again, dreaming, as most recently in the 90th minute against Schalke, of a final in Berlin, only our defence goes on dreaming just a minute too long. But then at Carnival time we pick up an 8-to-1 win. We're just one of Cologne's Carnival clubs after all, and that, as long as you don't happen to be the president, manager or coach, is really a wonderful thing.

And again: if I ask myself what caused this deep bond that has driven me, even in the middle of reporting on a war in Afghanistan, to seek out an internet café on Saturdays, sit down between two possible Taliban activists and catch up on the headlines of the Cologne *Stadtanzeiger*, this love – not only a childhood love, but often enough a childish love for the not always lovable FC Cologne – it is not only the victories; not even mostly the victories. The '78 Bundesliga championship, for example, would have been only half as glorious if we hadn't landed in fourth or fifth place year after year before that – and if, after the title seemed certain, Dortmund hadn't made a cliff-hanger of it with their 0–12 loss to Gladbach. And the years that followed, when we were really among the best again – I can remember my first matches at the stadium, when 12,000, 10,000, sometimes only 8,000 spectators in the old concrete bowl at Müngersdorf turned away in annoyance when we beat teams such as Stuttgart or Berlin with a mere 1–0. Although we have erased that from our memory, it was often rather dismal, in spite of good standings.

Thus it is paradoxical, yes, but at the same time no more illogical than human feelings, that the club's popularity and membership grew rapidly precisely in those years after the utterly unthinkable – the first relegation – had happened. Immunity to relegation, just like invulnerability in a person, is a very boring condition, and suddenly we noticed, the whole city noticed, that our FC needs us and we must not take it for granted. The celebration when we finally qualified for Europe, that incomparable, spontaneous, both light-hearted and peaceful mass hysteria, unimaginable anywhere else in Germany – we were celebrating our own loyalty, the fact that we had stood by you, FC Cologne, through every defeat.

Who else would we do that for? Who would we bear all the hidings for, the rebukes, all the gloom? Only for the very few people we love from the very bottom of our soul. And if we think what unites us with our own wife, our own husband, maybe with our siblings, at the outside, or a best friend, it is in the end not only, or not so much, the honeymoon, the exams passed, the money in the bank or the seventieth birthdays; it is the fact that we have muddled through a day-to-day life together, although it was often dull; that we had crises and found our way out of them; that we shared moments of bliss, such as the birth of a child, and also supported one another in moments of grief, as when, one after another, our parents died; that we have grown old together and yet still burn for one another as we did the first day; that we were proud of each other yet never ran away when the other was laughed at or got out of line. All this we have lived through with you, our first and only football club in the whole wide world: tears of happiness and tears of humiliation, all the outrages of fortune and the mercies of fate, passion and loyalty, betrayal and courage, life's great dramas and, at the same time, just a game. We thank you, FC, for the feelings that bring us together – '*et Jeföhl, dat verbingk*'.[26]

In Memory of Egon Ammann

Literarisches Colloquium, Berlin, 5 July 2019

Dear Marie-Luise, dear relatives, friends, colleagues and authors of Egon Ammann,

The last e-mail I received from Egon is dated the 1st of February 2017, six months before his death. By then his heart had been ailing for so long, and his blood was heavy in his veins, as we could hear in his voice, which was nonetheless always friendly, always cordial. He spent his days mostly watching television; he had bid his books farewell, having rented an old factory hall for them after he moved to Berlin; he had bid farewell to life itself – that is, to his life up to then, which had consisted of books – and was waiting, not in an ill humour by any means, to see what would happen next. I heard that his life with Marie-Luise was particularly affectionate; I could well believe it, but found it hard to imagine Egon in front of the television set before noon. It was hard to believe that Egon spent his days with anything else but books, yet he himself assured me on the telephone that, although his eyes could still read, he no longer had the strength. Books had given him so much, he been so enriched by reading, and now it was enough. Only in his Pessoa he still read a little every day, in his Isaak Babel or his Josef

Roth; he took note of new books – but nothing more; he no longer perused them. His conscience was not troubled about it. Egon was exactly the kind of passionate reader mentioned by Montaigne and Borges; 'obligatory reading' was to him a contradiction in terms. 'Should we ever speak of "obligatory pleasure"?'[27] Borges jibes, and Montaigne, four hundred years earlier, confesses that he follows his whims in choosing his reading: 'I do nothing without gaiety; continuation and too strong contention dazes, depresses and wearies my judgement.'[28]

But a reader by passion must – no, not contend, but be patient and indeed persevere, must receive and respond, feel, and actively touch too. And only when both sides give of themselves does that connection come about which we call love – even when it is between books and people – in which each contributes to the other's growth. It is not like watching television, in which the person only receives but doesn't add anything. A book can succeed only in a relationship, and a relationship doesn't exist, or is no better than barren, if only one of the two speaks. And just as an author can fall silent, so can a reader: that is the point where he no longer has anything to answer to a book. Egon knew as a reader so many authors who had exhausted themselves; as a publisher he had probably supervised a few; it was not an obligatory course of events, but it was a natural one, and not particularly tragic as long as the authors in question accepted it instead of torturing themselves with routine and wasting other people's time with books that were unnecessary. Now Egon had exhausted himself as a reader, it seemed to me.

Egon had been such a reader that I continued to send him my manuscripts long after he was no longer a publisher – including my last one, *Paris, So to Speak*. I guessed what his judgement would be depending on how short or long a time he took to send his answer, which was always encouraging, affectionate, but sufficiently plain, between the lines at the least. Now Egon didn't want to examine any more manuscripts, that much was clear; not mine, not anyone else's; and the loss, it seemed to me, the loss was not his; he had read more than enough for one lifetime; the loss was ours, for we would never find another reader like him. That made me sad, much sadder, I thought, than he was himself about his condition. He groaned about the pain and the shortness of breath, certainly; but apart from that he sounded as welcoming and cheerful as ever: he was worried, as he had always been, only about the world, which seemed to be going off the rails, as so many were saying, what with Trump and Brexit, the refugee crisis and the terrorist attacks. Of course I could feel that Egon, hardly reading any more, was preparing himself for death, but here too he hardly seemed concerned about himself but more about others, most of all about Marie-Luise, who would be left behind alone. A book can't last forever either, and you know as soon as you open it that it will progress towards its end. Why should life be any different? Only all books taken together yield a kind of eternity, just as a human being can last only as an element of humankind – as a cell, to be exact, that connects with another cell and so creates a third cell: trinity as a fundamental principle. As individuals, our existence is so fleeting that it is only detectable in a god's microscopic sight, but all existence taken together is as big as the universe itself. What the duration of a reading is to a book – beginning when a loving reader wakes it with a kiss – is to a person the brief pause after God has breathed the spirit into us and before He draws our soul back into His breast. Egon read his Joseph Roth right up to the end, his Isaak Babel, and his favourite, Fernando Pessoa, whom he had introduced to the Germans, no doubt including this poem, which he published in Ines Koebel's German translation:

I have in me like a haze,
Which holds and which is nothing,
A nostalgia for nothing at all,
The desire for something vague.

I'm wrapped by it
As by a fog, and I see
The final star shining
Above the stub in my ashtray.

I smoked my life. How uncertain
All I saw or read! All
The world is a great open book
That smiles at me in an unknown tongue.[29]

Dear Marie-Luise, dear relatives, friends, colleagues and authors of Egon Ammann, we have not gathered today to mourn, and so I will not look back on a life which is past. Thomas Hürlimann gave the eulogy, wonderfully, while I was absent for the only admissible reason: because I was standing at a sickbed, for the living always take precedence. Now both years of mourning are long past; we have all gone forward, returned to our day-to-day lives, which contain many joyful hours, I hope; the deceased would not wish it otherwise. The authors among us have all, as far as I can tell, found new publishers: the Ammann seal evidently guaranteed quality. But many of us feel – if we did not, we would not be here – we feel that Egon has not ceased to advise and support us. In my case, perhaps in the case of other authors as well, that means: Egon continues to read all my manuscripts. There is not one on which I haven't asked myself the question what he would think of it. And so I would like today, not to remember him as if I were standing beside a casket, but to reflect on what Egon still is to us: the ideal reader.

The world is a great open book
That smiles at me in an unknown tongue.

Every morning, if I am in Cologne and have no other obligations, I go to my office, where the walls are filled to the ceiling with books; sometimes I spend the night there too. Many of us who were Egon's relatives, friends or acquaintances may also have such a room, for a person who lives with books as he did is also surrounded by people who live with books – there is so much to talk about among readers! Egon himself, after he had retired from publishing, rented that factory hall, as he probably reported to all of you as enthusiastically as he did to me, outside or on the outskirts of Berlin, by a lake or on an island, as I seem to recall. Sometimes, he said to me two or three years before his death, sometimes he went out to that hall even though he had nothing in particular to do there, didn't need any specific book. He just wanted to be there, amidst all his books. I imagine how Egon then stood between the shelves in which his books stood in rows, he silent, they silent; complete silence in that no doubt high hall with no windows, skylights perhaps, and hearing the birds outside or a boat's horn from the lake. Then it was not a single book that he was visiting, it was books per se, from A as in Aeschylus to Z as in Zhuangzi, nothing less than a random, neither regionally nor temporally balanced, but all the more truthful history of humanity that he had compiled in the course of sixty, seventy years. Doesn't every reader collect stories which, taken all together, make up his or her own humanity?

Humanity, ah! – that big word again, much too big. There is no such thing as a humanity, for where would it live, what would it dream about, would it have enough bread, what would it whisper in its dying father's ear, and would it have to go to the toilet all at the same time? There is nothing but individual human beings, with whom we happen to share a part of our lives, or not. Books too have no meaning as a collective noun; and that is why libraries, for all their serenity, also emanate a mournful aura, especially when you are alone in one. For all these books do not speak by themselves; if no one reads them they are only paper, the authors buried alive in them; so it seems to me when I walk past my own shelves full of so many books that I haven't taken in my hands in years, if ever, so that I can't remember, or, worse still, will never know what they have to tell, and how. Then the spines of the books are transformed into so many tombstones, and I stand before the wall of graves as the only person who could reawaken the dead, those buried alive behind it. And, every time, I think I must read or reread all of them, every single book: each author has taken such pains, borne so many torments, doubts, deprivations; captured such a wealth of ideas, experiences, phantasies on a hundred or two hundred or a thousand pages.

And so I imagine that Egon too sometimes felt as if he was in a crypt when he stood in his factory hall. But then he would take a book from a shelf to open it at random or to find a passage that he had marked with a pencil many years ago. And if it was a good book – and I am certain that, in Egon's library, all the books were worth reading – he instantly had a whole destiny before his eyes: a boy deported beyond the Urals without his parents; a night in Buenos Aires in the summer of '73; or two lovers with all their illusions. From the first chance line, whether poetry or prose, a voice crept up within him, memories of the first reading returned, or of something similar or something exactly the same that he himself had lived through or wished he'd lived through or hoped he would never have to live through. As attentively as Egon read, he immediately noticed a peculiarity that he had not seen in any other author, even if it was only a deviation from the accustomed word order, an original metaphor or, on occasion, a wilfully lopsided one, a line that seemed very meaningful, although the reader did not understand it right away; a sentence that seemed to have no end, on this page or on the next. And in some books, he turned another page and another and another, still standing, in spite of his ailing heart, which had already been unreliable in Zurich, and said to himself, even if the book was long since familiar to him, that this sentence was truly astounding or that description extraordinarily haunting, mumbled it aloud to himself perhaps in his melodic Swiss-German voice, raising exactly one vowel in each word brashly aloft, although a German German-speaker never knows which vowel it's going to be or why. As if about a book, Pessoa wrote a poem about the lover he looks at, not to analyse her, but to disappear in her:

> So abstract is the idea of your being
> Which I get from gazing at you, that, on beguiling
> My eyes in yours, I lose sight of them,
> And nothing remains in my gaze, and so far distant
> Is your body from my vision,
> And the idea of your being remains so close
> To my thinking I'm gazing at you, and to my knowing
>   myself
> Knowing that you are, that, just to keep myself
> Conscious of you, I don't even feel myself.
> And thus, seeing you and ignoring myself, I belie
> The illusion of the sensation, and I dream,
> Not seeing you, seeing nothing, knowing nothing,
> That I see you, or that I am, I smile
> At the melancholy inner twilight,
> In which I feel I'm dreaming what I feel myself being.[30]

He would take the book with him to his reading chair, to his desk or to the bench outside, where he could see the lake and the birds and the boat whose horn greeted the two of them, Egon and his book, which he now opened at the beginning; and if it grew late over his reading, he would pocket the book to go back to Berlin, where Marie-Luise was waiting, but perhaps Marie-Luise was out, or already in bed, and in his library Egon had a mattress, as I do in my office, and a refrigerator with a little cheese in it, and bread and wine, which always reminded a man like him of Hölderlin's poem of that name – 'what are poets for in these meager times?'[31] – and he just stayed there overnight to finish the book.

So then wander defenseless
   Through life and fear nothing![32]

When he finally returned home the next day, he would tell Marie-Luise enthusiastically about the book that he had found or rediscovered, and no doubt read the most wondrous passages to her. And yet the real wonder was he himself, he as a reader, for with a single reading he had restored the continuum which consists of all books together. While the Torah and the Quran agree almost word for word that whoever saves one person's life saves all humanity, it is more certainly true of literature: whoever reads a book, whoever reads it with inspiration, thus adding to it his or her own life, to discern in the other himself, herself, sets the whole library aglow.

   Yes, this is all more a dream, I know, more than it can possibly be reality; I doubt in fact whether the factory hall was actually situated on an island, as I seem to remember hearing, for how then would Egon have got there in his beloved automobile? Though it may have been otherwise in reality with his daily drives to his library, I always imagine Egon as someone who liberates books from their mere material existence. Before his eyes, before the eyes of all readers, of whom

Egon is a paragon, a few sheets of printed and thus worthless paper metamorphose into a fullness of life more dense and more spiritual than is found anywhere outside, beyond the skylight, on the mainland, painful and beautiful. And to those who would inform me that, in reality, the hall stood in an industrial park, I pre-emptively object that, when Egon talked about his library, it sounded as though it was on an island, and the birds chirping and the boat's horn hooting were, for all I care, only – but why 'only'? – imaginary.

Many of us have such a room for our books, even if it is not a whole factory hall. The authors among us in particular are surely no less assiduous readers. All of us stand in front of our wall of potential relationships, all of us know the urge to read on the spot everything from Aeschylus to Zhuangzi, all the magnificent books that are already there or that could be added to the shelf. But then, as a rule, we do not take a book from the shelf, as Egon did, and then another, and read away impetuously until our eyes fall shut, and leave again early the next morning. And we certainly don't fill our days with manuscripts that have yet to be transformed into books, because if we did we wouldn't have any time to write ourselves. And what we read always has a direct or indirect influence on our own book. As obligatory as reading is for an author, our writing just as inevitably limits and determines our reading. 'After a matter of minutes, I would become the person writing, and the words on the page would be nowhere to be found':[33] thus Fernando Pessoa explained what happens to him while reading. For a publisher, as Egon was, it is different: to him, reading is an end in itself. He himself said so, as early as 1981 to Thomas Hürlimann, whom he sent the following very simple explanation after the founding of his publishing house: 'I simply had a love for books, and I had always lived this love as a reader, and then I wanted to tell those around me what I had read.'

What a fortunate choice! Not only for his authors, living or rediscovered; but for himself a fortunate choice right up to the end – or as long as he could still drive his car across the water, at least. Jorge Luis Borges counted reading as one of the forms of happiness.[34] Writing, or rather poetic creation, was in comparison a far lesser form of happiness. And what we call poetic creation consists in essence merely of readings: 'a mixture of forgetting and remembering what we have read'.[35] The author, we may suppose Borges means, is a second-rate reader, or a degenerative reader, inasmuch as he always reads in view of his own book instead of surrendering to what he reads without wanting anything. Egon, on the other hand, must have been a happy man.

Certainly Egon Ammann was also a son, he was a cousin, he was a friend, a lover, a husband and a father; he was a political mind and a manager and a representative of his industry; he loved not only literature but also driving; he loved company, wine and good food. To his authors, however, Egon was, first and last, their publisher. And what is a publisher, the ideal of a publisher, which only rarely comes so close to reality as in his case, an editor and patron in one, a friend and advisor, a propagandist and critic, an admirer and a teacher, a backer and a hustler? Publishing houses have not been around for very long – five hundred years perhaps. Beneath the job description of a publisher, however, although it is quite new in the history of literature and will pass away again with the growing concentration of the industry, there is something else, something elementary and much older, shining through. To the author, the publisher is the epitome of the reader, who has necessarily existed since the first book and will outlive the last independent publishing house. The publisher stands for all the readers a book may or may not find; the publisher reads with the abandon of a lover and at the same time appraises as neutrally as a judge; the publisher is subjective in the highest degree and at the same time represents the readership in general.

To the author, there is no one more mysterious than the reader. The publisher is a specific person, successful or struggling, generous, clever, cunning, cordial, whatever – there is no generic publisher. The reader, on the other hand, is never a single person. The author never knows who the reader is, not even when the author sees the reader at readings or receives letters from the reader. In the solitude that is necessary for writing, the author knows no readers, only a necessarily abstract, and also mostly anonymous, readership. The author wonders all the more who this invisible person is. For why should someone be interested in what the author dredges out of himself day in and day out? As if the author's mind was something special, meriting such communication devoid of all practical purpose or even logic. You have to pump up your puny ego tremendously to persist at your desk against the challenges of common sense. Yes, narcissism must be part of the job description for a person to exceed all sensible standards of self-restraint hour after hour, over weeks and years. There is no one there; only the great predecessors to the left and right on the shelf as mute witnesses rolling their eyes; the author calls out into empty space. If he were to address a specific person, he would fail to reach the reader in general. At best, he is gradually persuaded by sales figures, reviews, prizes or invitations that there really is somebody out there after all, perhaps even many people, to whom he apparently has something to say, otherwise they wouldn't underwrite his livelihood. But he never figures out who he is writing for.

Some authors may claim not to care who reads their texts, or whether anyone does at all. Even Pessoa, who was certainly no braggart, noted that he only wrote to distract himself from life, and only published his writing because that was one of the rules of the game; if all his papers should disappear overnight, so that no one would ever read what he wrote, it would not trouble him as keenly and maddeningly as one might suppose. But I don't believe the authors who say that; not even Fernando Pessoa; and I can cite him in evidence, for Pessoa contradicts himself in the very next sentence, saying, 'It is no different from the case of a mother who has lost her child: after a few months, she is the same as before.' What nonsense! No mother who has lost her child will ever be the same as she was before. Christianity itself issues from nothing else but pain over the murdered son. In other religions too, the believer can bear anything and rebels only when the child dies before the parent; then it is as if God had forsaken Christ on the Cross. When Pessoa compares the loss of his papers with the loss of a child, he sanctifies the reader instead of relativizing his importance.

Besides the fact that my non-fiction books have a different publisher, who likewise endows me with a first reader, it may have happened, or it may have been the usual case, that someone else had read a manuscript before I sent it to Egon – my wife or a good friend – but to me they were not readers properly speaking; they were part of the author: my wife, my best friend, were and are an extension of my own consciousness. I do not write for them; as a writer, one writes for no one in particular, much less for a target group or even for one's contemporaries. The publisher – the ideal of the publisher; for other writers an editor will have this function, or a professor in the Department of Literature, or a writers' group, if such a thing really exists – a publisher such as Egon is the first time and actually the only time the reader acquires a face, a voice, a character; the reader has moods, influences and of course weaknesses – those the author attributes to him whenever he feels unappreciated. For the publisher is not only the author's advocate; he is at the same time the reader's advocate: he stands on the threshold which a book crosses, or does not cross, into the public sphere. He reads therefore not only for himself but always thinks, from the first page on, of all the others, the unknown readers, too. The publisher is the gatekeeper who passes a manuscript on to that anonymous readership, or doesn't.

The relationship is nothing less than existential, if writing is one existence and publishing another; and, in the case of Egon and myself, it bore all the marks of a long love, from the initial infatuation to the day-to-day routine of a marriage, but also the unfaithfulness, the break-up, and the reconciliation in due time, before the two finally grow old together. The first time I heard his voice was about 2001 on my answering machine, and while the tape was still running on which he raved about my *Book of the Listeners Slain by Neil Young*, he had already got into his car in Zurich to come and visit me in Cologne. You may imagine how exalted a young author feels who has not yet published any work – at least no literary work – when a renowned publisher, after reading his manuscript, sets out immediately to get him under contract. That feeling – as silly as it sounds when I say it myself – that feeling that one's own manuscript, if only for the duration of the pause between one breath and the next, can become the most important thing there is for a reader, is what one needs, is what I needed in any case, in order to fend off the self-doubts hour after hour, over weeks and years, in the solitude of my office. Egon gave me that feeling from the first message on my answering machine, although he did not mention at the time that a publisher has more than one lover, and that raving about manuscripts is as much a part of his job description as narcissism is of ours.

Sliding towards the back of the catalogue, or seeing how the publisher promotes other authors, is not only a signal that one has moved from the assets to the liabilities in the balance sheet; with a publisher such as Egon, whose business ran on his enthusiasm, it always felt like watching a lover in a bar at night cosying up to someone else. At the same time, I could depend on him – and that is also a mark of love – to publish my books even if no one bought them; out of loyalty even, I suspect, if they were no longer necessary. His letters meant so much to me that I was shocked when, during my work on *Dein Name*, the samples of which he had replied to with full encouragement, he stopped answering for several years. I remember a visit to Zurich, when I crept around the publishing offices in Neptunstrasse like Hölderlin around Suzette's house in Frankfurt. And why? In the insane hope that he, who must have known I was in town, while the manuscript lay in his office, would wave me to him, would cry out, embracing me: Your manuscript is great! Finally his answer did come, cordial as ever, but by then he no longer had the publishing house. As the lover he still was, even in his betrayal, Egon had sensed perhaps that I must not quench my doubts if I wanted to progress further. But I am a lover too, and so perhaps I am only making excuses for his unfaithfulness.

The last e-mail he sent me, dated the 1st of February 2017, was not about any book. In the night when Donald Trump was elected, I had decided to do a series of political events in theatres and schools, on an emotional impulse that the advance of nationalism, the end of Europe, the dominance of IS in broad parts of Syria and Iraq, and the next war, whose battlefield already seemed to be Iran, must be preventable if everyone fights back with whatever means they have. And I thought: the means that I must resort to, if all the books haven't helped, must be public discussion. When the programme had been drawn up, fifteen events in eight days, I had long since begun to feel silly and regretted that I hadn't stuck to my desk or gone on a real trip instead of jetting from one podium to another, carried on reporting on the state of the world instead of joining in the production of opinions. Egon no longer read books, but he still received mail, and so he had received the announcement of the discussion series. Knowing me as well as he did, he apparently guessed that my courage had already left me again, for he congratulated me all the more enthusiastically on the 'magnificent enterprise, so important in this time, for the success of which I wish you luck with all my strength.' He no longer had any strength, I knew, and yet he gave it to me. He himself would not be able to come, not even to the event in Berlin. But he was sure he would be able to follow my activities in the press, and that was something. And because that sounded rather hopeless, he closed with an encouragement for good measure: 'Once more: hats off to you!' and signed himself: 'Always your partisan, Egon.' And there he was again, up to his very last e-mail with his own particular, raving tone, helping us over our despondency even after his death.

> Death is a bend in the road,
> To die is to slip out of view.
> If I listen, I hear your steps
> Existing as I exist.
>
> The earth is made of heaven.
> Error has no nest.
> No one has ever been lost.
> All is truth and way.[36]

Thank you, Egon, in my name and that of the other authors, always your partisans: *Tudo é verdade e caminho*.

Dinner Speech at the Investment Conference of Flossbach von Storch AG

Hotel Petersberg, Königswinter, 11 September 2019

Dear directors of Flossbach von Storch AG, dear investors, ladies and gentlemen,

Permit me to begin with a story, a story from long ago and far away. It is said to have happened in the late twelfth century in Nishapur, a city in the northeast of what is now Iran, that a tattered old fool walked into a chemist's. When I say a chemist's, ladies and gentlemen, of course you mustn't think of Boots or Superdrug, with shampoos and washing-up liquids. Chemists' shops at that time, especially along the Silk Road, were treasure chambers full of fragrant essences, sinfully expensive elixirs, vital medications, rare minerals and carefully mixed herbs from all over the world. And thus the chemists were no mere merchants, but at the same time apothecaries, physicians, alchemists and perfumiers, all in one, and they were respected and very well-to-do citizens of their town. And into one of these treasure chambers, the chemist's shop of Nishapur, there came a beggar, a vagrant, a madman – that was not plain on first glance – a man with long, matted hair in any case, a straggly white beard, and around his body only a rag. He stood in the middle of the shop, in which there were no other customers at that moment, and looked around him for a long time without saying a word. Gradually the chemist behind his counter grew uneasy, a quite young man, but for all his education a purposeful businessman who was afraid the old fool would upset his customers who might come in at any moment. Are you looking for something in particular? he asked the old man. But the old man only went on looking at the stuffed shelves with great big eyes, and remained mute. Finally the chemist asked him to leave.

'That is easily done, sir,' said the old man, breaking his silence; 'my baggage is light, for I own nothing but the rag I wear. But you, sir: what will you do with your sacks full of treasures when the time comes for you to go? How do you expect to take all that with you? I can vanish quickly and effortlessly from the bazaar of this ephemeral world; but you should think about what you are going to do with all these goods, and how you intend to carry them.'

The chemist assumed the old man was making fun of him, and so he returned the question with a sneer: 'And you? What do you need to do to leave this bazaar?'

'This,' said the old man, and he lay down on the floor of the shop and died.

The chemist to whom this is said to have happened was called Fariduddin Attar. After the old fool's voluntary death, he gave away his possessions, practised asceticism and devoted himself to meditation and studying the mystical literature. He wandered as far as India, central Asia, Egypt, and met the most important spiritual teachers of his time. When he had reached middle age, he began to write epic poems which today are among the most important works of Persian literature. All of them have long since been translated into all the Western languages; his most famous work, the *Conference of the Birds*, has been adapted for the stage again and again, once in a famous production by Peter Brook in Paris. The old fool's investment, one might say, paid off. While he himself would have had at best only a few more years to live, by his death he gave a gifted young man his start, a man whose name every Iranian now knows even eight hundred years later, and whose poetry has inspired countless generations of readers all over the world, and theatregoers too by now. And Attar himself could hardly have done anything better than the sheer folly of closing a successful business from one day to the next and wandering off without a penny. If Attar had stayed behind the counter of his shop, he would certainly have increased his wealth; perhaps he would have opened a branch or two, and in the best case would have become the richest chemist in Persia, or even the richest man in the world. But if Attar had become a tycoon, not even his name would have survived. He would have disappeared without a trace. What, then, constitutes a profitable investment?

Dear directors of Flossbach von Storch AG, don't worry, I am not going to recommend that your investors give away their possessions rather than trusting your institution to increase them. Spirituality, asceticism and altruism can work miracles in an individual, but as maxims for a society overall they would be disastrous: with just spirituality, asceticism and altruism, humanity would have died out long ago, if only because the survival instinct would have atrophied in a world of saints and poets, and probably the reproductive instinct too, to say nothing of innovation and pragmatism. An Attar, a Francis of Assisi or a Homer would never even have discovered fire! I myself am a person who, apart from the joys, hardships and obligations of a bourgeois day-to-day life, spends the whole day with intellectual matters – during office hours at least – with nothing but literature, religion, occasionally philosophy, a lot of useless stuff. But I can only do that because the people all around me, indeed almost the rest of humanity, are pursuing eminently useful occupations. They bake the bread that feeds me; they build the walls that shelter me from the cold; they research the medicines that cure me; they cut the trees from which the books in my library are made; they put a pen in my hand for me to write with – and so on and so forth. Yes, some of these people around me even buy my books or invite me to give readings and lectures, and so finance the life which I devote to intellectual things – that is, almost by definition, superfluous things. Thus I cannot advise anyone against increasing their possessions, since I profit from that indirectly in the form of sales, fees, prizes and, not least, the subsidies paid to the artists' health insurance and pension fund by the state, hence society at large. Art per se, along with religion and all forms of play, presupposes the principle of utility even as it rejects it.

But, inversely, a utilitarianism void of meaning, a pure striving for material profit, would also have robbed humanity of its survival – if only because the reproductive instinct alone would not have motivated it to the efforts, exertions, torments that it takes to raise generation after generation without protective fur, without sharp claws, without strong muscles, with a fragile psyche and, compared with animals, with a sadly inferior immune system. To do that requires love, which is at least as foolish as art, just as it is love that brings two people so close together that they become good parents – as evolution pragmatically requires, of course. What, then, to pose the question once more, makes a good investment? It can hardly be purely material profit.

Ladies and gentlemen, eighteen years ago today, nineteen young men also sacrificed themselves for a payoff that they can only have thought of as heavenly: the hijackers of the 11th of September 2001. But while some of us would place

Fariduddin Attar's old fool somewhere among the holy men, all of us consider those attackers criminals. In their own view, they were no such thing; subjectively, and in the eyes of their ideological comrades, the nineteen young Arabs performed a heroic act in the skies over America when, equipped with nothing but box cutters and pepper spray, they inflicted on the imperialist superpower perhaps the most painful defeat in its history, more humiliating than Pearl Harbor, because they struck at the most central location imaginable. Yet the difference from the old man's death in Nishapur is obvious: while the old man gave up only his own life, the attackers of New York and Washington took three thousand people with them to their deaths. If we consider the wars that have subsequently broken out, the Afghanistan war, the Iraq war, and ultimately the wars in Libya, in Syria, and the long, apparently unstoppable progress of the so-called Islamic State – if we consider that America's counter-strikes have ignited the conflagration which the terrorists evidently wanted to cause, the attacks of the 11th of September indirectly cost the lives of hundreds of thousands if not millions of people. The violent regime changes in the Middle East have created huge lawless zones on the very borders of Europe, where terror organizations have been able to establish themselves unhindered; their advances have in turn driven a wave of refugees towards Europe and also brought the jihadists' terror into our cities, and, with the refugees and with the terror, nationalism has grown stronger in Europe – just as it had earlier in the USA – and that nationalism in turn combats the project of European unity. The indirect effects of the 11th of September continue as far as Brexit and Donald Trump, and so one might conclude that, in a ghastly way, Osama bin Laden, by means of a single terror attack and with just nineteen fearless young men, came close to achieving his strategic goals, namely the rupture of the transatlantic alliance and the fragmentation of the West as a community of values. It is no coincidence in any case that Germany and France, the two countries that resolutely opposed the Iraq war and its lies in 2003, continue to be governed by the political centre, at least for the time being, while the two countries that occupied Iraq under false pretences and in violation of international law, the United States and Great Britain, are led today by right-wing populists who are given to a more than creative attitude towards the truth and contempt for the parliamentary system. Were the attacks of the 11th of September thus a profitable endeavour?

Politically, it is too soon to tell, and the answer is by no means unambiguous: on the one hand, the image of radical Islam among Muslims has deteriorated severely since then, and the movement has recently suffered heavy military defeats, including the killing of Osama bin Laden and the expulsion of the 'Islamic State' at least from all the cities of Syria and Iraq. On the other hand, it is not at all clear yet how the West will overcome its current crisis: will the self-regulating mechanisms of liberal democracy be effective? Will the European Union and the transatlantic alliance consolidate? Or will one country after another choose an authoritarian nationalism which abrogates the separation of powers, subjugates the media and thus gradually abolishes democracy by democratic means – as in Hungary and Poland, Russia and Turkey, the Philippines and Brazil – or, after the economically very successful example of China, does without the detour via democracy.

Morally, however, I repeat, and I hope you will agree, ladies and gentlemen, morally the answer is quite clear to the question which sacrifice – and every investment is a sacrifice; one gives up some of one's possessions to receive something greater in return – which sacrifice was profitable. It was certainly not the mass murder. Only how can I, how can we be so sure that the 11th of September was a crime and not a legitimate act of resistance? It is often said that what one side calls terrorists are the other side's partisans. People always tend to justify the violence of their own kin, nation or religion as a reaction whose cause is a threat by the other, the foreigner; likewise a marital crisis is practically never caused by oneself, but always by the other, if only by the other's coldness driving me, alas, to be unfaithful. There are good reasons why judges no longer decide guilt and innocence in divorce cases, at least in Germany. Where international politics is concerned, we can point to The Hague as a neutral jurisdiction, except that the International Court of Justice is not recognized even by the United States, much less by jihadists. How then can we be so sure that the old fool's sacrifice is profitable, while that of the 9/11 attackers is reprehensible?

To people of faith, God would be the judge, and His judgement could be deduced from the holy scriptures, although with very contradictory results. But, to unbelievers, God has also given a hint, in the Bible and His other revelations, as to who on Earth is able to distinguish good from evil intuitively, without studying the divine commandments: our children. Theirs is the kingdom of heaven, says Matthew 19:14. Jesus did not glorify children: he thought them capable of evil, and was himself far from being an endearing son, at least according to the apocryphal Infancy Gospel of Thomas. But, as other prophets, saints and founders of religions do, and as we as parents also do, in a way, when we look into the mysterious eyes of our newborn children, Jesus ascribed to children a purity and an impartiality – in a marked contrast to the later Christian doctrine of original sin – which allowed them an unobstructed, non-rational access to knowledge. The Talmud recounts in several passages that a wise man who does not understand something asks a child what verse he has just learned in school. Although the child is so much more ignorant than the wise man, by his spontaneous answer he always provides the crucial hint. And if we now imagine we could place the yields of the two investments side by side, that of the old fool and that of the suicide attackers of 9/11, in front of your child, or my child, or any child on Earth, as long as he or she has not been brainwashed: on this side, a fantastic work of world literature, with stories of sparrows and hoopoes, kings and beggars, lovers and fools, which have found their way via the tea houses and marketplaces into folk and fairy tales, and not only those of the Middle East, but as far away as India and central Asia, and via Andalusia into our own bedtime stories. And on the other side? A series of wars, massacres, attacks that seem to have no end even eighteen years later, whoever carries them out and for whatever reason – a child, unlike a political scientist, isn't interested in that when he or she looks at the television and sees starving babies, desperate mothers, bodies torn apart by bombs, no matter what colour the skin. The child's heart fears not for the well-fed officials behind the microphones but for the families sheltering in tents in the freezing cold, or fleeing across the Mediterranean Sea in little boats. Because a child perceives distress more accurately than we adults, including the distress of others, of foreigners; because the child does not shield his or her psyche from the images with rational explanations – 'a just war', 'local solutions', 'we can't accommodate all of them that labour and are heavy laden', et cetera.

It is certain that a child considers poetry a greater return on investment than violence, and therefore we too can be certain and need neither God nor philosophy for this; the natural, innate human sense of right and wrong is sufficient. This standard – how does a work measure up in the eyes of an innocent child? – is probably what comes closest to the Last Judgement, which may or may not exist. And this standard, ladies and gentlemen – can we, when we die, justify our works to our children, our own and the children and the children's children of this world? – this standard would be better suited than any index and any rating to decide what is a profitable investment.

I admitted earlier that humankind would not have survived with spirituality, asceticism and altruism alone. One reason why capitalism has proved superior to communism is that it is based on self-interest, which is more pronounced in human beings than public spirit. But utilitarianism alone, I also noted earlier, would have robbed us all the more of everything on Earth worth living for. It would not have needed Karl Marx to expose as false and naive Adam Smith's claim that the pursuit of individual gain which is promoted in capitalism would be guided to the benefit of society as if 'by an invisible hand'.[37] Fully 2,500 years earlier, one of the seven sages of antiquity, Pittacus of Mytilene, had summarized the whole essence of monetary economics in one of his laconic aphorisms – in just five words, to be exact: 'Desire of gain' – and Pittacus meant monetary gain – 'is insatiable.'[38] But the world's resources are not infinite, and that is quite obviously the problem which confronts humankind today: the pursuit of gain which capitalism has unleashed and even sanctified is faced with an Earth whose circumference is all of 40,000 kilometres. Marx, by the way, whom even capitalists have found well worth studying, had the far-sighted realization, not just of the exploitation of labour in the monetary economy, but also the inevitable destruction of the environment: 'Capitalist production', he wrote at the end of the fifteenth chapter of *Capital*, 'therefore only develops the techniques and the degree of combination of the social process of production by simultaneously undermining the original sources of all wealth – the soil and the worker.'[39] In other words, the production of wealth in capitalism destroys its own prerequisites: ever-compliant labour and the exploitable natural world. By its tendency to treat all the expressions of life, up to and including love, play and nature, as commodities to be monetized, capitalism deforms the human personality, which has never found sufficient meaning in gain and consumption. And, at the same time, capitalism destroys the soil, which in this context in Marx explicitly includes water and air.

The conflict between the insatiable pursuit of gain and finite resources has always propelled peoples, but has also erupted in wars and conquests, although they are ostensibly fought in the name of a nation, race or religion. But when humanity finally learns by experience that the water we drink, the grain we eat, the oil that warms us, the shade that cools us and the air we breathe are running out, the migrations will swell dramatically, and the wars for resources will escalate. We have already heard of oil wars, and that the desertification of fertile land in the southern hemisphere, whose causes are found mainly in the northern hemisphere, forces millions of people to flee year after year. But who is aware that even the now forty-year-old war in Afghanistan is also a war for the increasingly scarce water of the Hindu Kush? That the revolution in Syria was preceded by a critical drought which exacerbated the distress of the mostly Sunni rural population? Or that a cut-throat competition is raging south of the Sahara between China, Europe and the United States for access to minerals, rare earths, diamonds and other resources that we need for modern industrial products?

The pure monetary economy against which Karl Marx was writing would have collapsed from its internal conflicts within a few decades. Capitalism was able to survive, and ultimately to prevail over Marxist doctrine, only by abandoning its own logic of competition time after time and adopting the arguments of its enemy, from Bismarck's social welfare legislation to the New Deal to the social market economy and its particularly successful variant, Rhine capitalism, which brought the West Germans great prosperity along with an unprecedented degree of social security. Yet the triumph over socialism which the capitalist model celebrated in 1989 at the fall of the Iron Curtain also seemed retroactively to justify its unchaining by Thatcher and Reagan, which harks back to capitalism's beginnings and is associated with the inaccurate term neoliberalism. Because people certainly do not become more free, in the sense intended by liberalism, through the privatization of state functions or the deregulation of the financial industry; reforms of the free-market economy, whether justified or not, must not be confused with an increase in individual freedom, especially when they bring with them a dramatically increasing inequality in the distribution of wealth – to the point where the eight richest people in the world today own as much as the nearly 4 billion poorest.

What is more, we in the wealthy industrialized nations may associate privatization with cheaper phone rates or more customer-friendly service, but, in poorer countries, privatization all too often means that millions of people lose access to such basic services as water, electricity and health care. The free market economy, and with it the liberal democracies, and not least the European Union, will be able to prevail only if they maintain the social balance, or restore it in Southern Europe, for example, where youth unemployment is as much as 50 per cent. Otherwise our countries will be ploughed under one after another by left-wing or right-wing populism, which is deploying the supposedly autochthonous population today – like the exploited working class in the nineteenth century – against the 'cosmopolitan elites'.

And that, ladies and gentlemen, is not the only challenge, or even the greatest challenge, confronting the free-market order: it must become not only more socially just but at the same time more ecological, and unfortunately the one task can conflict with the other, as exemplified by the Yellow Vest protests in France against the introduction of a fuel tax. Karl Marx did not foresee that: workers and the Earth, humankind and the environment, not only simultaneously exploited but at the same time in conflict with each other. Nonetheless, there is a future for capitalism, and with it liberal democracy and perhaps even humankind as a whole, only if the monetary economy succeeds yet again in outsmarting its own free-market logic and treats the world's natural resources as a good which belongs to all people and has to be paid for accordingly. After all, there exist at present only two realistic models for stopping climate change and the total destruction of the environment: the eco-authoritarianism towards which China may be heading or a capitalism that dyes itself green to the marrow. And there is some probability that the competition of the systems would once more be won by the market economy if it is permeated this time not just with social checks and balances but with radical ecological incentives as well. Because, to preserve the Earth, it is too late for mere appeals to conscience. And the prohibitions which would be necessary from the scientific point of view are too drastic and socially unacceptable to win majorities in free elections. To remodel societies ecologically, it would thus be more effective to utilize that pursuit of gain which Pittacus declared insatiable 2,500 years ago than to rely on comprehension or coercion. But that might mean that capitalism definitively takes leave of its own logic, which it has so often violated, and for good reasons. For rewards would now go not just to growth but also, where necessary, to abstinence.

Ladies and gentlemen, would I entrust my money, if I had enough of it to be accepted as an investor, to Flossbach von Storch AG? A delicate question, I know: after all, a guest doesn't want to be uncourteous towards his hosts. But the fact is that Mr von Storch has sent me the company's capital market reports of recent years with the express invitation to peruse them with a critical eye. So I did that, and immersed myself for a few hours in a world that is truly foreign to me. What did I find there? Well, I was surprised, first of all, to see that the authors of the reports are not merely market observers and financial analysts but politically thinking people who express distinct, sometimes contentious opinions, and who display their determination even in their language: in other words – and to a writer this criterion is not unimportant – they are good writers. I have not seen the like in my bank's reports, which land directly in the recycling bin twice a year because they consist only of melodious phrases, incomprehensible figures and hardly verifiable graphs. And I was also impressed to see that Flossbach von Storch AG actually sends members of its staff to the countries where it makes investments – that is, the company researches its market not only at the computer screen but also in conferences and in the streets. I am no expert, but I can't imagine that this is something to be taken for granted among financial institutions when even the newspapers are reducing their networks of correspondents, which are their most important asset.

In more than a few passages of the capital market reports of Flossbach von Storch AG, a sympathy is discernible for positions of economic liberalism which were advocated by the founders of the party AfD, up until those founders resigned in 2015: positions opposed to state intervention, opposed to zero interest rates, and opposed to a supposedly excessive welfare state. In spite of the economic ignorance which I confess, such a Ludwig Erhardian laissez-faire does not seem to me to be the appropriate answer for the European common market, which benefits no other member as much as Germany: if there is a European Union at all, it must be understood as a commonwealth in which uniform social standards apply and governments are legitimized by general elections. Indeed, Ludwig Erhard as West Germany's first minister of the economy and second chancellor would certainly not have led the country to general prosperity without the interstate fiscal adjustments and the constitutional goal of establishing 'equivalent living conditions',[40] without cooperative industrial relations, without majority rule in the Bundestag as the supreme legislative body instead of a federal council passing only unanimous resolutions. I have the impression, by the way, that the authors at Flossbach von Storch AG are not always justified in citing Ludwig Erhard, who after all is also a paragon to Sahra Wagenknecht, the former whip of Die Linke in the Bundestag: she too could be wrong, but it does suggest that Erhard, the architect of the post-war boom, was not a pure free-marketeer. Be that as it may, however, it is not only legitimate to advocate a resolutely liberal economic and regulatory policy; I also find that such a position, Euro-critical though it may be, has been noticeably missing from the spectrum of German political parties since 2015. And, after all, such a position alone would be no reason to doubt that Flossbach von Storch AG is capable of good or ethical business management, especially as the company sharply dissociates itself from the AfD of today, and that too is part of the remarkable clarity of its capital market reports. For a party whose chairman considers the Nazi period a 'bird dropping'[41] in German history, ladies and gentlemen, is not an electoral option to any German patriot.

What bothers me about the reports is something else, and this is probably inevitable for a person who spends all day dealing with so-called intellectual matters – literature, religion and occasionally philosophy. Although it may be inherent in the market analysis genre, I found the narrow focus on economic growth troubling. The authors scoff at so-called sustainability ratings, and their reasons for their criticism of banks and funds that put on a green veneer are both plausible and sobering. But what the authors offer as an alternative to green labelling is all too general. Ultimately, they reduce sustainability to long-term success, which is only possible, they say, when a company takes ecological and social parameters into account. Although the authors at Flossbach von Storch AG are right to advocate a broader perspective on sustainability than that of good intentions, it is no less important, especially for a financial institution, to re-examine the ideology of growth itself. As I said, if capitalism had not entertained self-doubts time after time, it would never have lasted beyond the nineteenth century.

I would like to give an example, since I am not quite as purely cerebral as I have pretended to be up to now. After all, I do get away from my books from time to time, and then I am a traveller, a reporter, a war correspondent. And therefore I can assure you with some credibility that the capital market reports of Flossbach von Storch AG, and probably of most financial institutions in the world, do not sufficiently consider the political, social and ecological consequences of a policy which banks on sheer economic growth, comforting itself with globalization's usual success stories – a billion people rescued from dire poverty in the last thirty years, et cetera. The most obvious illustration of the shallowness of simple market assessments would be the Brussels bailout measures in answer to the debt crisis in the Eurozone, which have the authors audibly tearing their hair because their business sense cannot comprehend them – yet without such emergency measures, Europe as a political union, and as the civilizational project of the Enlightenment, might well have disintegrated in that dramatic situation. But permit me to offer an example which has received less public attention, although it may be more important for the future of the planet than the development of the European Union: India.

The world's biggest democracy has developed under Prime Minister Narendra Modi into one of its fastest-growing economies, the capital market report rejoices. The report does not mention who bears the cost of that growth: namely the environment, as multinational businesses are released from the last restrictions on the appropriation and exploitation of land. Or the rural population, who are beset by an unprecedented wave of suicides: 600 million of India's 1 billion inhabitants make their living in agriculture. Six hundred million people are not included in the praise of India's growing prosperity. Nor does the capital market report mention the Hindu nationalist government's severe, potentially deadly attacks on the secular state, its subjugation of the major media, its far-reaching discrimination of Muslims, Christians and casteless people. An analysis of India's national economy cannot be complete without mentioning such names as Gauri Lankesh, Narendra Dabholkar, M. M. Kalburgi and Govind Pansare. Who are they? They are critics of the government who have recently been murdered by contract killers. Nor is there any mention that the governing 'Indian People's Party', the BJP, is the political wing of the 'National Volunteer Organization', the RSS, which claims inspiration from Hitler and Mussolini. Not a word about the fact that the nuclear power India still has not signed the Non-Proliferation Treaty; not a word about the wilful escalation in relations with the nuclear power Pakistan, which is thus one of the most dangerous conflicts in the world. The capital market report admits only that India's official gross domestic product does not completely reflect reality because the greater part of the Indian population is employed in the informal sector. With what rights, under what conditions? Again, not a word. Instead, the report advises – meaning:

instead of glancing at the people and their rights – we should pay attention to the development of specific companies; this provides 'a picture of structurally positive trends' in India.

Almost all of my Indian fellow writers, ladies and gentlemen, who are certainly not purely cerebral but paint a much more accurate, comprehensive and in-depth picture of the reality of Indian society, would see the matter very differently. To Arundhati Roy, the most famous and, admittedly, one of the most critical among them, the world's biggest democracy is on the brink of fascism. We are not obliged to adopt her view, but anyone who espouses taking long-term stability, the political conditions and the ecological and social consequences of economic performance into account in assessing markets cannot simply ignore whatever doesn't fit the success story. Or should we also rejoice at the fact that every farmer's suicide – more than 12,000 per year – lowers the poverty rate a little further?

To come back again to the attacks which took place eighteen years ago today: 9/11 not only had devastating consequences; it also had preventable causes in a foreign policy which did not rely on sustainability, to use that evidently worn-out word. And what I will now summarize for you very briefly is not a conspiracy theory, but has become general knowledge in Middle Eastern studies just as the history of the free market is in economics. Since 1979, the United States, in pursuit of a collaboration with Saudi Arabia, has in many countries, consistently and against all the warnings of its own Middle East experts, directly promoted Wahhabism, whose militant variant is jihadism, going so far as to train and help finance the Afghan Taliban, among whom Osama bin Laden found refuge. Why? One reason was in order to embroil the Soviet Union, which had occupied Afghanistan in 1979, in a guerrilla war; but another – and this is once again a primary strategic interest of the US since the election of Donald Trump – another reason was that Sunni extremism seemed the most effective means to oppose the Shiite extremism of the Iranians after the pro-American monarchy in Tehran had been swept aside and the American embassy occupied, also in 1979. Both strategies are perfectly plausible *realpolitik* for the time in which they originated, and indeed hardly any doubt was cast on them in the broader public sphere – on the contrary, the Afghan mujahidin were almost always portrayed in the media as gutsy resistance fighters. Nonetheless, both strategies have caused immense damage, not least for the United States itself, if we consider 9/11 and the wars and disasters that followed in turn from it. Never in the last seventy years has America had less influence in the Middle East than today, while the Islamic Republic of Iran, which was not involved for once in 9/11, has been able to increase its influence: witness Iraq; witness Afghanistan; witness Syria, Yemen, Lebanon; witness the Gaza Strip.

And that is not the end of the story, or rather not the beginning: why was the secular dictatorship of the shah swept away in 1979 in the first place? The anti-American revolution in Iran would have made no sense, and probably never would have broken out, if the United States hadn't abolished Iran's earlier secular democracy by means of a CIA-sponsored coup in 1953. The leader of the democratic government, Prime Minister Mohammed Mosaddegh, who, by the way, was a glowing admirer of the United States, had dared, after extensive study of Theodore Roosevelt's anticolonial speeches, to nationalize Iranian oil, which up to then had belonged to the British Petroleum Company, BP. In 1953, any capital market report would have congratulated the American government on its overthrow of the Mosaddegh government. But all Iranian writers, even the most purely cerebral among them, immediately guessed at the time the disaster that the coup would bring. Numbers, ladies and gentlemen, tell us nothing if we do not see the reality behind them. And money, dear investors, destroys us too in the end if it is not earned in an ethical way.

The foreign policy of the United States has by no means always been dictated by short-term interests: it has also stood for one of the most visionary political achievements of the twentieth century, the reintegration of Germany in the community of nations. We need only imagine that there had never been a Marshall Plan, no reconstruction, no rule of law, no civic education; instead, imagine America had recklessly exploited Germany's resources, as it did Iraq's in 2003, looted its national museums and archaeological sites, run torture prisons like Abu Ghraib, dismantled the civil administration and met the population with unveiled contempt: can we honestly believe West Germany would have developed into a stable democracy and the USA's closest ally, whose loyalty we can only hope will survive Donald Trump's term of office? Standing by the detested Germans, believing in German democracy before anyone in the world thought it possible, was less popular in the United States at the end of the war than the Morgenthau Plan, for example, which called for a permanent deindustrialization of Germany. Fortunately for us, at that time politicians prevailed in Washington who could see further ahead than the next election or the next tax cut. Yes, altruism alone may be an adequate foundation for a religion, but not for a state. But the so-called *realpolitik* that is always held up to dreamers and visionaries reliably leads to real disasters and could hardly be more detrimental to our own interests. This insight is certainly applicable to business as well, ladies and gentlemen. A tunnel vision focused on short-term profits – without considering the effects on the overall society, and not just at home but all over the world – will lead, if not into court, as in the recent banking and diesel scandals, then to an erosion of the political and ecological systems in which profits are possible in the first place.

What, then, is a profitable investment? Dear Directors of Flossbach von Storch AG, dear investors, ladies and gentlemen, do not look only at share indexes, fund performance and gross domestic product: look in your child's eyes. I would entrust my money to a bank that calculates profits for the lifetime of our children and our children's children rather than just for the annual financial statement. For even the greatest fortune dissolves into thin air the moment we leave the bazaar of this mortal world, if not before. And whether or not we believe in another world, our death will be harder the more we must worry about our children, and thus about the Earth we leave for them. Ladies and gentlemen, before I sit down at the table and you start asking me where I invest my money, I prefer to admit straight away that I do not conform to all I have been preaching. Thus I too am faced with the task of using my few precious possessions in such a way that I leave some good behind on Earth. But I have vaunted my lack of business sense often enough now that I may permit myself to close by asking Flossbach von Storch AG to think more comprehensively than other financial institutions about what a good investment is. I will be happy to advise you, dear directors, if you are looking for literature that will reward you for every minute you spend reading it, but, for the management of its assets, society must look to the expertise, the ethics and the passion of your staff. And if you have persuasive reasons to mistrust the usual sustainability ratings, then develop better and verifiable criteria. It would make a difference.

I told you at the outset the story of Fariduddin Attar's initiation. There is also a legend about the great poet's death. He was a hundred and ten years old, the story goes, when the Mongols invaded Nishapur in 1227. Just as an enemy soldier was about to cut Attar's head off, another Mongol came along who felt sorry for the venerable old man. He offered his comrade a thousand dirhams to let Attar go. The soldier wanted to accept the money, but Attar, longing for death and his return to God, advised him to wait for a better offer; perhaps the life of a poet would fetch more than just a thousand dirhams. After a while, another Mongol came along. The soldier asked him what he would offer for this old man.

'A sack of straw,' replied the other Mongol.

Attar laughed and said, 'Take that offer! A sack of straw – that's my worth exactly.'

The first Mongol, angry that he had been cheated out of a thousand dirhams, drew his sword and beheaded the poet whose name, eight hundred years later, every Iranian knows, and whose work has inspired countless generations of readers all over the world, and now theatregoers too.

I thank you for your attention and wish you all a pleasant dinner.

Keynote Address to the Congress of the International Association for Analytical Psychology

Great Hall, University of Vienna, 26 August 2019

Dear analysts, ladies and gentlemen,

When Muhyi d-Din Ibn Arabi arrived in Mecca in July or August of the year 1202, he was thirty-seven years old and already one of the great mystical leaders of Islam. He was so self-assured as to consider himself one of the four cornerstones 'on which the structure of the universe and of mankind rests', and he was so respected that no one contradicted him. He had been little more than a child when Averroes, the most famous philosopher in the world at that time, had received him, and Averroes had paled, had trembled, had literally broken out in a sweat at the boldness of his young visitor's replies, at the self-assurance of his demeanour. While still a young man, Ibn Arabi had acquired all the accessible knowledge of the time, had learned a good deal of Islamic literature by heart, including the Quran, and, most importantly, had spent days, weeks, months in contemplation. After having been initiated in a dream by Sufism's three great spiritual teachers all together, Moses, Jesus and Muhammad – something which had never happened before – Ibn Arabi had left his home in Andalusia, where the Reconquista was in full swing, to preach in various cities of the Maghreb. He had studied with all the major mystics of the Islamic West and taken leave of them as their master. He had received such clear and spectacular visions as no one else since the Prophet Muhammad himself, so that the professional dream interpreters predicted he would reveal 'the highest mysteries, the particular properties of the stars and the letters, which will be given to no one else in his lifetime.' On his way to Mecca, the 'mother of all cities', he had stopped in Hebron, where Abraham and the other patriarchs are buried; he had prayed in Jerusalem, the city of David and the later prophets; he had meditated in Medina, where the last resting place of Muhammad lies, thus physically retracing the Prophet's celestial journey, which he had already experienced in inner contemplation. At night, having arrived at last at his destination, Ibn Arabi circled the 'heart of the world', the Kaaba:

> I felt a deep peace, a very delicate feeling, of which I was nonetheless perfectly conscious. I left the immediate area of the stone, which is paved with tiles, because the crowding there was too great, and continued circling further away, on the sand. Suddenly some verses entered my mind, which I recited so loudly that another person could have heard them if he were standing directly behind me:
>
> > Would that I were aware whether they knew what heart they possessed!
> > And would that my heart knew what mountain-pass they threaded!

Dost thou deem them safe or dost thou deem them
dead?
Lovers lose their way in love and become entangled.[42]

I had hardly recited these verses when I felt the touch of a hand softer than silk on my shoulder. I turned around and beheld a young woman, one of the princesses of Byzantium. Never had I seen a more beautiful face, never heard a gentler voice, never felt a more tender heart, never shared deeper thoughts, never listened to subtler parables. She surpassed all people of our time in wit and culture, in beauty and wisdom.

The meeting at the Kaaba with the sensually and intellectually attractive Nizam bint Makin ad-Din is the turning point in Ibn Arabi's life, and in his work. Thirteen years later he dedicated to her the *Interpreter of Desires*, *Tarjumān al-Ashwāq*, a volume of love poetry which was quite unusual even for him, explicitly erotic, and which is one of the most famous cycles of lyric poetry in Arabic literature today. In the preface to his poems, Ibn Arabi wrote about their addressee, 'Whenever I mention a name, I am always alluding to her, and whatever house I mention, I always mean her house.' On hearing names invoked, every Muslim thinks of the names of God; at the mention of a house, the house of God, the Kaaba. Ibn Arabi perceived in the young woman nothing less than the reality of God Himself. Thus it is far from coincidence that, soon after his encounter with Nizam, Ibn Arabi began writing the many volumes of his *Meccan Revelations*, *Al-Futūḥāt ul-Makkīya*, the most important and in any case the most influential work of Islamic mystical literature, if not all religious literature in the scope of Islamic culture. The *Revelations* contain the summa of Sufi knowledge and at the same time expose a fundamentally new, sensational approach to divine truth, which in Islam is supposed to be objectless, hence absolutely abstract, but in Sufism becomes perfectly concrete and perceptible anywhere, to anyone. Nizam – who in reality was not Byzantine, but Persian, the daughter of two highly educated and aristocratic pilgrims from Isfahan – Nizam bint Makin ad-Din was Ibn Arabi's Beatrice.

We are no longer accustomed to taking seriously the mystical references that Dante Alighieri attributed to his meeting with Beatrice. But there is no reason to doubt that, in his consuming love, he also had a deep religious experience. To Dante, Beatrice reflected the incarnation of God in Jesus Christ; moreover, her beauty was to him a medium through which God Himself appeared. As Nizam was to Ibn Arabi, Beatrice was to Dante earthly love and at the same time divine revelation, wellspring of inspiration and at the same time an object of longing, his muse and at the same time his addressee. When we consider that translations of Islamic journeys to Heaven, and perhaps even excerpts of the account Ibn Arabi had written of his dream vision, were very probably available to Dante when he began the *Divine Comedy*, the correspondence raises questions about the relation between East and West, questions which ought to be posed anew today in view of the growing, often antagonistic dichotomy. But the differences between the two poets are still more interesting than their similarities. For Dante was, yes, first and foremost a poet, not a Christian scholar, while Ibn Arabi, although, like many Islamic scholars, he often expressed himself in verse, was considered a religious authority, an outstanding scholar of the Quran, and the *Shaykh al-Akbar*, the undisputed 'Greatest Master' of Sufism. The title alone of his magnum opus points to its eminently religious orientation, since neither the place it names nor the genre it announces is meant metaphorically: the basis of the text consists of religious visions which were perceived by the author, and by most of his readers, as 'revelations', and which occurred nowhere else but in Mecca. In Christianity, Ibn Arabi would have to be compared with Meister Eckhart or Jacob Böhme rather than Dante or Hölderlin, except that mysticism has never been the main stream of Latin Christianity, whereas Sufism was the broadest religious movement in Islam even into the twentieth century. It not only permeated high culture – literature, music, architecture and art – but also ran deep in popular piety. The Sufi teachers were usually closer to the so-called simple people than the dogmaticians and legal scholars who became the focus of Western research on Islam, and, even in our time, thousands of people pray every day at the tomb of Ibn Arabi in Damascus; during the war, the crowds are said to have been even bigger, even though the shrine would have been a logical target of attacks by the 'Islamic State'.

The difference between Dante and Ibn Arabi, then, concerns their status within their respective religions – that is, their reception. The close structural similarity of all mystical traditions, and especially Christian and Islamic mysticism, has often been described: the progression of religious experience and its expressions, the universal character of the messages of salvation, the motif of the holy fool. But, once again, the differences interest me more than the similarities, and, most of all, the different relations to the material world. None of the well-known Christian mystics had a Nizam, a Beatrice. Erotic though the mystics' texts often appear – especially those of women, such as Teresa of Avila and Hildegard of Bingen – the relation of earthly love to divine love is one of analogy, not identity. And, in Christian mysticism, physical union is not the locus but the image of mystical annihilation; neither Teresa nor Hildegard can be assumed to have had a real lover who served as her medium of divine revelation. Nizam on the other hand is a real, historical person, and, in the same way as Ibn Arabi's love for her was intrinsic to his religious experience, other Islamic mystics too had altogether earthly lovers, some of them women, some men, who to them embodied God in the truest sense of the word. 'For one who loves religiously is mind without body, and one who loves naturally is body without mind,' say the *Meccan Revelations*, 'but spiritual love includes both the body *and* the mind.' Ibn Arabi even goes so far as to write that ignorance of sexuality is nothing less than a religious deficiency.

> When I first trod this path, I was in all God's creation one of the greatest loathers of women and of sexual intercourse. I remained in this condition for some eighteen years. This contempt left me when I learned of the saying handed down from the Prophet that God had made women worthy of His Prophet's love.

Since Ibn Arabi entered the mystical path in 1184 and arrived in Mecca eighteen years later, it is evident that he realized the importance of physical love only during the pilgrimage. It is unlikely, however, that he had a sexual relationship with the young Nizam; after all, she was the religious, highly educated daughter of two aristocratic and devout pilgrims from Isfahan, and Ibn Arabi was a regular visitor at their guesthouse. Besides the fact that Ibn Arabi himself later denied ever having been Nizam's lover, it is difficult for practical reasons to imagine a secret rendezvous between the two during the pilgrimage. Moreover, it is known that, during this first sojourn in Mecca, Ibn Arabi married another woman, Fatima bint Yunus Amir al-Haramayn. As her name implies, she belonged to one of the most venerable Arabian families – her father was the superintendent of the holy sites in Mecca and Medina, the *ḥaramayn* – who presumably would not have permitted even the suspicion of an extramarital relationship.

And yet not Fatima, but Nizam became the quintessential beloved in Ibn Arabi's work. The reason is surely related to the fact that, in premodern literature, love was associated with symptoms that we today would assign to infatuation: rapid heartbeat, loss of appetite, foolish and embarrassing behavior; whereas marriage was a pragmatic partnership and seldom the stuff of poetry. Not until the modern period did marriage for love become an ideal. This explains why Ibn Arabi was able to see the divine beauty in Nizam and yet marry Fatima, whom he mentions in his writings always lovingly, but rather as a companion on the mystical path.

In the preface which Ibn Arabi added to the *Interpreter of Desires* after it had been in circulation for several years, he writes that his love for Nizam was a purely spiritual one and, accordingly, that the physical images must not be taken literally. Rather, Nizam embodies 'a sublime and divine, essential and sacred wisdom [in the sense of the Greek *sophía*], which was visibly manifested to the author of this poem, and indeed with such sweetness that he was overcome with ecstasy and happiness, with tenderness and joy.' This has often been interpreted as a self-serving claim on Ibn Arabi's part in response to accusations that he had written pornographic poems. But that wouldn't mean his explanation was necessarily false. In his *Revelations*, Ibn Arabi explains how God reveals Himself first and foremost in sexuality, 'the most perfect union that exists in love'; yet further along the mystical path, knowledge is increasingly realized in the imagination, and thus transcends material experience. It would be in keeping with his teaching for Ibn Arabi to have had a love relationship with Nizam without ever touching her, not because he would have rejected physical love – that remains a step on the mystical path, discussed in detail in his theoretical writings – but because he, at the highest stage of his spiritual development, no longer needed it.

It is certainly not a mistake at this point – and I thank my good friend the philosopher Almut Shulamit Bruckstein for the suggestion – to remember Jewish conceptions of the bride as infinitely heightening the sexual desire of her earthly lover by messianically elevating its fulfilment. The consummation of love would be at the same time *tikkun olam* – the healing of the world. The bride – an expression which attests to the greatest familiarity – who is able to delay the actual union until the moment of *tikkun olam*, a moment which would be at the same time the healing of the soul – the bride is Nizam, who is called Shulamite in the Song of Solomon, the fairest among women, whose breasts are as clusters of the vine, and the smell of whose nose is like apples, and the roof of whose mouth is like the best wine, causing the lips of sleepers to speak: 'A garden inclosed[!] is my sister, my spouse; a spring shut up[!], a fountain sealed[!]'.

Today the Song of Solomon is modernized in audiobooks, celebrated at church conferences, interpreted in radio worship services; its open eroticism is closer to the spirit of our times than, say, the ban on contraception. It is often overlooked, however, that Solomon speaks of desire, not fulfilment: there is no sexual relation, to use the words of Lacan, whose thinking is not as mysterious as it is said to be once we know the mystical tradition from which he stems: 'Love makes up for the absence of the sexual relation.'[43]

Even the fact that Ibn Arabi calls Nizam a Byzantine, a Christian in other words, indicates the religious significance he attached to the meeting at the Kaaba. For, in Islamic mysticism, God's appearance in a human being is inevitably connected with the example of Jesus Christ; all theophany is attributed to the 'Christian sophia' or wisdom, *al-ḥikma al-'isawīya*. Nizam herself underscores the precedence of mystical knowledge – that is, experienced truth – over rational consideration in her accusatory words to Ibn Arabi:

My lord, how can you declaim: 'Would that I were aware whether they knew what heart they possessed'? I am surprised to hear such a thing from you, the greatest mystic of our time. Is not everything we possess also something which we know? Can there be such a thing as possession without knowledge? What I wish is the deeper consciousness that is made known through not-being and the path which consists of truthful speech. How can someone like you permit such thoughts?

As the young Nizam reprimands the great Ibn Arabi for the first line, she goes on to censure every line of his poem. For the questions that trouble him are still questions posed by his intellect. But mystical insights follow the laws of love, not logic. Only when it is indifferent to him whether he is dead or safe, because the one leads to the other, nothingness and perfection converge, only then will the mystic approach God. Through his meeting with a young girl, Ibn Arabi learns that he must leave behind the knowledge he has learned if he wants to understand the divine truth. When he shyly asks her name, she answers with another riddle: 'Solace of the Eyes' (*qurrat al-'ayn*). She is alluding to a saying of the Prophet that 'the solace of the eyes is granted in prayer,' but at the same time she is referring to her own beauty, of which she is apparently aware. Then the young woman takes her leave, leaving the greatest mystic of his time, and perhaps of all time, to gape after her like a child. Thirteen years later, Ibn Arabi writes in the *Interpreter of Desires*:

> Threefold is my beloved and yet one
> as the entities of God are only one.[44]

Nizam was a woman, and to Ibn Arabi she was connected with Christianity, which teaches the Trinity of God. These two facts have a deeper significance: although Ibn Arabi was born in patriarchal conditions, women were influential in his work – his teachers, his beloved Nizam, both his wives, his daughter, his students, most of whom were women. Against the orthodox mainstream, he emphatically declared women to be equal in religion and empowered to interpret the Quran, to lead the congregation in prayer, and to receive illumination from God. At the same time, Ibn Arabi found instruction and inspiration in Jesus Christ as he did in no other prophet. And these two facts are connected: for in his compassion, his beauty and his ability to raise the dead – that is, to give life – Jesus represents the female principle of God, which Ibn Arabi has emphasized as no other Islamic mystic. In the *Interpreter of Desires*, he writes about Nizam:

> When she kills with her glances, her speech restores to life,
>   as though she, in giving life thereby, were Jesus.
> The smooth surface of her legs is the Tora in brightness,
>   and I follow it and tread in its footsteps as though I were Moses.
> She is a bishopess, one of the daughters of Rome,
>   unadorned: thou seest in her a radiant Goodness.
> Wild is she, none can make her his friend; she has gotten in
>   her solitary chamber a mausoleum for remembrance.
> She has baffled everyone who is learned in our religion,
>   every student of the Psalms of David, every Jewish
>   doctor, every Christian priest.[45]

Dear analysts, as scholars if not followers of the teachings of C. G. Jung, your ears will be ringing by this point: here is the female principle that Jung called anima and considered fundamental to every psychic impulse; here too is the incarnation of God as a paradigm which is rooted in the human psyche as a relationship between the Self and the ego. In Ibn Arabi, anima is joined with the symbol of Christ: God appeared to him at the Kaaba, not in the generic form of a human being, but in the form of a woman and a Christian. The interweaving of woman and Incarnation is by no means alien to Christianity, as early representations attest in which the Redeemer bears disturbingly feminine features, and C. G. Jung in particular has pointed out Christ's androgyny, calling it 'the utmost concession the Church has made to the problem of opposites.' The idea that religious insight, like aesthetic insight for that matter, being non-discursive, cannot be directly named, and hence can be expressed only in veiled terms, in images, in parables, as paradox or by means of negation, is found in all the world's religious traditions, and especially the mystical traditions; it is best known perhaps in Taoist formulas such as 'The way that can be trod is not the true Way.' The Sufi literature is full of paradoxical expressions, such as black light or the colour of water, and Ibn Arabi himself calls God the 'totality of mutually contradictory names'. Consequently, in the *Interpreter of Desires* he praises the beautiful, godlike Nizam over and over again as the unity of opposites:

> The whiteness of her forehead is the sun's, the blackness
>   of the hair on her brow is the night's: most wondrous of
>   forms is she – a sun and a night together!
> Through her we are in daylight during the night and in a
>   night of hair at noon.[46]

'The union of opposites is not rationally possible,' Ibn Arabi himself commented on the image of the light-dark Nizam, and quoted the early Islamic mystic Abū Saʿīd al-Kharrāz, who said, when asked how he had recognized God:

> 'By His uniting two opposites, for "He is the First and the Last, and the Outward and the Inward",' and that always

simultaneously and equally, not alternately or under different aspects, as the scholastic would have it, employing his conceptual faculties and dividing Truth into categories.

Because the One and Eternal is necessarily revealed in the manifold, temporal, and also contradictory nature of human experience, writes Ibn Arabi in the *Meccan Revelations*, they err who recognize God only in a certain form, in their own truth, in a limited time, or only in one faith. The divine truth must be embraced in the different religions, indeed in all phenomena, in sexuality, in civilization, even in everyday experiences, in the most ordinary objects, and even in heresy, as another poem in the *Interpreter*, perhaps the most famous one, has it:

> My heart has become capable of every form: it is a pasture
>   for gazelles and a convent for Christian monks,
> And a temple for idols and the pilgrim's Ka'ba and the
>   tables of the Tora and the book of the Koran.
> I follow the religion of Love: whatever way Love's camels
>   take, that is my religion and my faith.[47]

It is astounding that C. G. Jung did not know Ibn Arabi when he asked whether one might also choose to believe 'that God has expressed himself in many languages and appeared in divers forms and that all these statements are *true*.' But then it is not so astounding after all, for Jung formulates an insight which is at the core of all religions, even Christianity, although Christianity makes a more definite claim to exclusivity than any other religion. I quote from his book on *Psychology and Alchemy*:

> The objection raised, more particularly by Christians, that it is impossible for contradictory statements to be true, must

permit itself to be politely asked: Does one equal three? How can three be one? Can a mother be a virgin? And so on. Has it not yet been observed that all religious statements contain logical contradictions and assertions that are impossible in principle, that this is in fact the very essence of religious assertion? As witness to this we have Tertullian's avowal: 'And the Son of God is dead, which is worthy of belief because it is absurd. And when buried He rose again, which is certain because it is impossible.' If Christianity demands faith in such contradictions it does not seem to me that it can very well condemn those who assert a few paradoxes more. Oddly enough the paradox is one of our most valuable spiritual possessions, while uniformity of meaning is a sign of weakness. Hence a religion becomes inwardly impoverished when it loses or waters down its paradoxes; but their multiplication enriches because only the paradox comes anywhere near to comprehending the fullness of life. Non-ambiguity and non-contradiction are one-sided and thus unsuited to express the incomprehensible.[48]

Here I will once again pass over the conclusions to be drawn from religious scholarship in regard to present-day debates: that the struggle against ambiguity impoverishes not only religions but likewise societies, cultures, literatures and identities. Nonetheless, I would like to remind those who publicly represent Islam, or pass judgement on it, that one of the greatest, perhaps the greatest scholar in the history of Islamic philosophy finds, in conformance with tradition and supported by many Quran verses, that God reveals Himself precisely in diversity and contradiction. Is it not written in a *ḥadīth qudsī*, an extra-quranic word of God in Islam, 'I agree with the view that My believer has of Me'? And did not the Prophet say that the paths to God are as numerous as the breaths of a lifetime? To Ibn Arabi, the rational incongruity of experiences of God and images of God is, in its totality, God, Whose reality surpasses human understanding:

> This explains why we are required in our all-embracing religion to believe in the truth of all religions. They do not cancel one another out – that would be the opinion of the ignorant.

By setting the very diversity of beliefs in relation to the unity of God, Ibn Arabi not only resolves the irreconcilability of monotheism and polytheism, recognizing even those religions which orthodox Islam considers pagan, but he goes so far as to teach that every single person's faith is a unique arrangement of an unlimited number of possible states of consciousness which, in their totality, refer to God.

> Every seeker of God is ruled by the property of one of God's names. This name is revealed to him and makes the divine self-revelation a personal, individual faith.

In Ibn Arabi's religious conception, the paradigm of this self-revelation, and of the ultimate paradox, is Jesus Christ: God, the abstract, all-embracing One, is perceptible and effable only in His reification and particularity, and hence diversity – God, man, and their union. This trinity persists even in Hegel's phenomenology and in Marxism as dialectic, which must also be driven by a world spirit, or, in secularized terms, by the cunning of reason. The 'brothers' in the chorus of Beethoven's Ninth Symphony, who incorporate the common genealogy of all humanity, and hence the monotheistic heritage of the Enlightenment, become 'comrades' in socialist rhetoric, united by their membership in the Party, that is, by an act of will. Soon the siblinghood of our day will have completely instrumentalized the language

– for a good cause, it goes without saying. Moreover, trinity is also the fundamental structure, not only of human development, but of all development on Earth: man, woman, and their love which makes them creators. Not only two cells, but also their drive to unite. Ibn Arabi writes:

> Nothing arises from one alone. Therefore the first true number is two. And nothing arises from two unless there is a third to unite them and relate them to each other.

As God incarnates Himself in Jesus, Jesus must in turn unite all opposites: be a man with feminine features, a child with all the insignia of the Lord, attractively beautiful and at the same time repellingly severe – in his perfection a paradigm for all people, who are made in God's image. He is Mary's son but, at the same time, in his godhead, her Creator; thus St Bernard worships the Mother of God in the last canto of the *Divine Comedy* as the 'daughter of your son', and in many old pictures Mary is painted as younger than her son. As early as the Revelation of John, Jesus Christ is a *complexio oppositorum*, as for example in the paradoxical image of the wrathful lamb. C. G. Jung interpreted Christ in this same comprehensive sense, which few Christians today bear in mind, as the most highly developed and differentiated symbol of the Self besides the figure of Buddha. The symbol places the individual human consciousness in a meaningful relation to the outside world without denying the world's enigmatic, arbitrary character: the believer hears the divine word, 'Behold, it was very good'; he accepts as truth, although it contradicts his experience, that the world is arranged without even the slightest flaw. At the pinnacle of faith, the believer denounces God, as Job does, and yet adheres to Him. The only higher paradox is reserved to God Himself, Who becomes a suffering human.

You would have to be blind, C. G. Jung remarks in his *Answer to Job*, one of the most profound religious studies of the twentieth century – you would have to be blind not to see the glaring light that Mount Golgotha casts on God's character. For a father to sacrifice his own son – a terrifying idea to every one of us, one which disturbs us deeply in the story of Abraham as well – contradicts the notion of God as the *summum bonum*. As man experiences the world in its terror *and* its beauty, without the one cancelling out the other, as grace in ecstasy, as punishment in distress, the dreadfulness of Christ in the Apocalypse complements His love in the Sermon on the Mount. In other words: in its paradoxical image of God, the Bible is consistent with reality. And, in any case, the holy scriptures are perceived as divine not because they conjure up supernatural phenomena, things outside reality: on the contrary, it is because they capture sensory experience in its totality. The Bible is divine – one might say in another paradox – the Bible is divine in the extreme inasmuch as it is human. For the drama of Job and the consummation of Jesus take place not just in history, whether real history or salvation history: they take place in every one of us.

Permit me, dear analysts, ladies and gentlemen, to cite at this juncture another good friend, the philosopher Carl Hegemann, who for many years was head of dramaturgy at the Volksbühne theatre in Berlin. In his book on identity and self-destruction, Hegemann defines drama in the theatre as the consequence of contradictory conditions to which human beings are necessarily subjected. The following sentences, although written in regard to consciousness, could just as well refer theologically to Job, who rebels against the God in Whom he believes:

> Consciousness experiences itself as distinct from the world only when that world has a determining influence on it, and

when it does not submit to that influence, but resists it or rebels against it. When it fights oppression without questioning the necessity of the oppression. In the moment when that happens, self-awareness arises as the pain of pressure or friction against the other which resists the self. This feeling of external resistance is fundamental to the subject and cannot be done away with – even though we work all the time, necessarily, at eliminating that resistance, in the theatre just as we do in the world. We must accept what opposes us, for, without it, we would not exist as beings conscious of ourselves.[49]

If the Gospel had been something completely new and unheard of, it would hardly have spread so rapidly. In fact, it was consistent with the psychic conditions of ancient man; it made the transcendent and hidden God, already known in Judaism, visible in the human form of Christ. In doing so, Christianity went beyond the pagan religions, in which God merely manifests Himself in animal or human forms, and likewise went beyond Judaism, which has a concept of the deification of man in such figures as the Son of Man but knows no humanization of God. Only the Incarnation makes it possible to say that Christ dwells in the person who believes in Him. This, as C. G. Jung notes, is psychologically the same relation that exists in the Indian conception between Atman and the individual consciousness: on one hand the Self as the totality of the psyche, which encompasses the unconscious, including its collective, prenatal and mythical connections; on the other the ego, which merely represents the individual consciousness and its transitory content. And it is by no means probable, Jung continues, that this connection between the universal foundation of being and the individual, which is anchored in the structure of the psyche, is broken with the advent of Christianity. Christ himself assures his disciples that he is always with them, indeed in them; and, as if that were not enough, he promises to send them a paraclete, that is, an advocate, in his place. And Jesus reminds the Jews, who accuse him of making himself into a god, of Psalm 82:6, in which God has said to them, 'Ye are gods.'

For that reason, Jesus in Islamic mysticism stands not so much for the unique occurrence of God's incarnation as a man, but the reverse: for man's – every person's – potential to unfold the divinity that is in our nature. Jesus is the model of a holy man who is so completely filled with God that he cries out in ecstasy, as the mystic al-Hallaj did, 'I am God!' But Jesus is not only the unique model of the saints: in the formula 'die and live anew',[50] the Incarnation is the model of all knowledge. Ibn Arabi extends the idea of a continuing revelation, one which does not end with the death on the Cross, by relating it to every single moment of life; he sees Creation renewed with every breath. After all, the word for 'breath' is contained in the Arabic word *rūḥ*, which stands for 'spirit', as it is in the Sanskrit word *Ātman*, and thus every person has a holy spirit which connects them with God. Every person inhales and exhales, with every breath, 'the breath of the Merciful', *an-nafas ar-raḥmāni*. Ibn Arabi writes:

> Man does not realize that with every breath he ceases to exist, and then exists again. And when I say 'then', I do not mean a temporal delay but a purely logical sequence. In the 're-creation in every breath', the moment of annihilation coincides with the moment of creation of a likeness.

For, according to both biblical and quranic teaching, God reveals Himself not only in the prophets; He is visible in all creatures and natural phenomena. In this context, Ibn Arabi reminds us that the Prophet Muhammad had the habit of standing outdoors with his head bare as soon as it rained, and that the Prophet said the rain came fresh from his Lord. 'Is there anything more full of light, more sublime and clear?' asks Ibn Arabi. 'Thus the noblest of men enchanted the rain with its nearness to his Lord; the rain was as the celestial messenger who brought him the divine inspiration.'

One might object that seeing God in every soul, in a drop of rain, or in the sexual act implies dragging him down to the level of humans and material things. In the mystic's view, however, the opposite is the case: people and things are absorbed in God the moment the believer, to use Hölderlin's famous expression from *Hyperion*, is 'one with all that lives'.[51] The unity of being, *waḥdat al-wujūd*, which underlies all existence, is a key concept of Ibn Arabi's teaching. Or, to put it in C. G. Jung's words:

> I have been accused of deifying the soul. Not I but God Himself deified it.[52]

Certainly, C. G. Jung was not trying to prove the existence of God. Much less was he interested in setting one religion above another. Rather, he was exposing the religious structure of the psyche, which exists independently of specific faiths and regardless of whether the individual person believes. The atheist too is confronted, by the very fact of birth and death, with situations that transcend his earthly existence. Even if he explains man's fate rationally in terms of 'chance' or 'nothingness', he relates to it. 'The competence of psychology as an empirical science only goes so far as to establish ... whether for instance the imprint found in the psyche can or cannot reasonably be termed a "God-image",' writes Jung in *Psychology and Alchemy*. That does not imply any assertion, 'positive or negative ... about the possible existence of God, any more than the archetype of the "hero" posits the actual existence of a hero.'[53]

Nonetheless, our relation to the world and to those around us changes when we see them in their relation to God. According to Jung, the religious attitude does not prove the existence of God, but, from a psychotherapeutic perspective, it helps people to affirm life and contributed to the recovery of many of Jung's patients. Ibn Arabi recounts in the *Meccan Revelations* how, as a young, already respected scholar, he once carried a basketful of rotting, horribly stinking fish across the market. His companions thought he was carrying the basket as a penance, or in an effort to purify his soul by performing an unpleasant and embarrassing service that was not in keeping with his social status. 'No', Ibn Arabi said, 'that was not my intention. I simply saw that God, for all His greatness, had not found it beneath Him to create these things. How then could it be beneath me to carry them?'

Christianity has institutionalized the idea that divine indwelling is continuously renewed in the miracle of Pentecost: it is the Church which the Holy Spirit indwells; two or three must be gathered together in Christ's name, and there He is in the midst of them. The institution of the Church largely removes God's indwelling from the personal experience of faith, and perhaps it could not be otherwise: in taking shape, the Church had to emphasize the uniqueness of God's revelation in Jesus Christ in order to claim a monopoly on the work of redemption; otherwise Jesus' message probably would have dissolved into a multitude of sects. The notion that the divine spirit can work in each person immediately has been preserved in Gnosticism, in the Asian and pagan religious traditions of course, in Jewish mysticism, and, with a pronounced Christian connotation, in Sufism. And, as we know, ideas from Islam have certainly contributed to the development of a mysticism within Christianity as well: Meister Eckhart drew on Arabic philosophy; Mechthild of Magdeburg would hardly have developed an eroticism of prayer if the Sufis' erotic love of God, and the motif of romantic love itself, had not spread through Europe from Andalusia with the troubadours in the eleventh century. And then, in the late hymns to Christ of Friedrich Hölderlin, who was also heavily influenced by Christian mysticism, Jesus reappears as a demigod, alongside the gods turned human of classical antiquity, but also alongside the poet Empedocles:

> I alone
> Was God, and spoke it out in haughty insolence.[54]

Thus the Incarnation, the central occurrence of Christianity, is unique, and the Cross expresses the singularity of the salvation history; but, at the same time, the strength and the legitimation of Christianity lie in the very universality of its central motif: the incarnation of God, in its progression from the virgin birth to the death on the cross, is better able than any theory to encompass a universal human experience in all its contradictions. It is the experience of every child which has been pressed out of its mother's womb. As a newborn child we do not yet divide our present world from the previous one. We have no I as long as we have no Thou. We do not yet experience ourself as a boy or a girl. We experience our parents, and especially our mother, as an indefinite, omnipotent, and yet beneficent power. We cry when we are hungry, when we feel pain, and when we are afraid because we are alone. We soon smile when we are picked up and cuddled. We are afraid when we are scolded or punished. We learn the names first. We grow up and become in our turn the mother, the father, that we once thought to be God. We grow old, we decay and become, in death if not before, as helpless, and as lonely, as a newborn child. In

Christianity, God has a very human biography. C. G. Jung reminds us that it is mainly in the West that religion stands in opposition to science. In most other cultures, it is conceived as a wisdom which interprets the empirical world and is consistent with it. In fact, he writes, from a psychological perspective, the assumption of invisible gods or demons who directly intervene in life is a much more persuasive portrayal of the unconscious than a passive explanation of it as the absence of the conscious mind. Jung writes:

> The theory has to disregard the emotional values of the experience. Dogma, on the other hand, is extremely eloquent in just this respect. One scientific theory is soon superseded by another. Dogma lasts for untold centuries. The suffering God-Man may be at least five thousand years old and the Trinity is probably even older.
>
> Dogma expresses the psyche more completely than a scientific theory, for the latter gives expression to and formulates the conscious mind alone. Furthermore, a theory can do nothing except formulate a living thing in abstract terms. Dogma, on the contrary, aptly expresses the living process of the unconscious in the form of the drama of repentance, sacrifice, and redemption.[55]

Christianity has given such expression to the human incarnation of God, which is inversely accessible to every individual consciousness as the experience of God, and even to the atheist as the experience of a non-ego element of the Self, as the oceanic feeling that even Freud accords to the human consciousness in ecstasy – the Christian cross has given an anthropological experience of suffering, love and transcendence such a valid, engaging, irresistible and persuasive expression that it persists even today against all rational plausibility, and the God-Man himself is associated even in Islam with Jesus. Yet Ibn Arabi associates his beloved Nizam, in whom a higher reality is revealed, not only with Christianity. She is also a highly attractive young woman, as the *Interpreter of Desires* attests:

> She takes with a hand soft and delicate, like pure silk,
>   anointed with *nadd* and shredded musk.
> When she looks, she gazes with the deep eye of a young
>   gazelle: to her eye belongs the blackness of antimony.
> Her eyes are adorned with languishment and killing magic,
>   her sides are girt with amazement and incomparable
>   beauty.
> A slender one, she loves not that which I love and she does
>   not fulfil her threats with sincerity.
> She let down her plaited lock as a black serpent, that she
>   might frighten with it those who were following her.
> By God, I fear not death; my only fear is that I shall die
>   and shall not see her to-morrow.[56]

To Ibn Arabi, who had more women teachers than men, the beatific vision, which is necessarily communicated to humans through concrete earthly experiences – of nature, love, dream visions and, most strongly, sexuality – reaches its highest perfection in women. For women incorporate both aspects of the divine, the passive and the creative, conception and childbirth, *patiens* and *agens*, *anima* and *animus*. Men on the other hand are born but do not give birth. That means that Ibn Arabi explicitly attributes the passive, female, receptive aspect to God as well and conceives His relation to humanity as a mutual one in which we depend on Him, but He is equally dependent on our love. 'Do not blame me if I call God a bride,' Ibn Arabi writes, conscious that his teaching must be provocative in the context of Islam, insisting, in contravention of the Arabic usage, that God combines both genders or, conversely, is genderless.

Dear analysts, ladies and gentlemen, as you know, the rift between C. G. Jung and his teacher, Sigmund Freud, involved not least the question of libido. To the Swiss pastor's son – and I do believe that the different religious and cultural backgrounds played a part in their disagreement – erotic desire is a remarkably blank spot in comparison with Freud, and although the Arab mystic Ibn Arabi speaks eloquently in support of Jung's sacralization of the psyche, he also confirms Freud, who called sexuality the 'shibboleth' of his school, that is, its badge or watchword. It is certainly no coincidence that Freud uses a Hebrew word here, not only because he was a Jew, like almost all his students, Jung excepted.

In this connection, I thank Almut Bruckstein, whom I have already mentioned, for another remarkable idea: she sees the motif of the divine beloved carried forward in the form of Freud's analytical session. Shulamite or Nizam would then be the figure of the analyst himself, who sits outside the patient's field of vision – the invisible object at which desire is directed. Sexual desire enters into the analytical process. And where Ibn Arabi in the *Interpreter of Desires* retains the image of union, not in spite of but because of the intensity of his love, Freud is right after all in a certain sense. His thinking is Jewish: the messianic theme is a postponement of fulfilment. And, to follow Almut Bruckstein's train of thought further, he places it in the middle of the psychoanalytical space: the patient's couch is the lover's bed in the Song of Solomon, the bed of Ibn Arabi who aphysically desires Nizam; it is the place where desire was sublimated in language, because the fulfilment is yet to come. 'It seems to me no contradiction at all that I love God in His creatures, for that unites the two opposite realities,' say the *Meccan Revelations*:

Where God reveals Himself, the observer [the observer!] sees himself in his partner. He sees himself in the woman, and his love and her attraction are heightened all the more as his own self takes shape in her. We have already explained to you that this is the shape of the truth through which God becomes present. Thus the lover sees nothing but true being, but with an ardent, indomitable longing and with the enjoyment of physical ecstasy. He merges with the beloved in the most sublime rapture. Not only their bodies, but their being meets in complete harmony. He vanishes in her. There is nothing of him which is not her. He is flooded with love from top to bottom; his whole being is joined with her. He finally dissolves so completely in her as would not be possible in a love for something that was not himself. He becomes one with the beloved, saying, 'I am she whom I desire, and the one who desires me is myself.' At the highest point, he cries out, 'I am God!'

Sigmund Freud adhered to a decidedly patriarchal concept of God the Father, and his resistance against religious beliefs was nourished by his general rejection of dependency and passivity, which he associated, stereotypically, with femininity. His lapse in degrading the female leaves him behind even the religions which he considered obsolete. Judaism too has a feminine image of God, from the 'Wisdom' of biblical texts to the 'Shekinah' of the Kabbalah, which is described as a woman, as bride and daughter of the male power. Christianity initially took up the female dimension of God in the early representations of Jesus as a beautiful shepherd with remarkably feminine features. In Islamic mysticism as well, Jesus is associated not only with compassion but also with beauty. Only the joining of compassion with beauty allowed being to arise out of nothing, say the *Meccan Revelations*; God's mercy alone would not have provoked the desire for a correlative.

God longed to be perceived in His beauty; He not only loves but wants to be loved: that is why He created the world. Thus the Creation, to Ibn Arabi, is an expression of God's creative femininity. This is where the figure of Mary appears in Sufi Islam, psychologically representing the Jungian anima as the mother and at the same time the bride of Christ, while Jesus himself combines masculine and feminine traits. Mary represents God's femininity, while Jesus incorporates God in His entirety with His contradictions. But it is also in Mary that Christianity retained the feminine traits long after the androgyny of the early representations of Christ – such as the Ravenna mosaics I have written about in *Wonder Beyond Belief* – had been supplanted by a purely masculine *Salvator mundi*.

According to C. G. Jung, the insight that male and female are united in the original divine being is older than history, and God's wanting to become human through a human mother was known long before Christianity in the royal theology of ancient Egypt. One of the most surprising aspects of Jung's 1952 *Answer to Job* is the vindication of the Madonna, a figure Freud ignores completely. But Jung's fellow Protestants must also have been shocked to see him call the dogma of the Assumption, which Pius XII had promulgated shortly before, in 1950, 'the most important religious event since the Reformation':[57] Jung understood the bodily reception of the Virgin into Heaven, which the dogma proclaims, as an image of Mary the bride united with the Son and as Sophia united with the godhead in the celestial bridechamber. That may seem preposterous to the unpsychological mind, Jung admits, but the papal argument makes sense to the psychologist, based as it is on a 'tradition of religious assertions reaching back for more than a thousand years': 'Equality requires to be metaphysically anchored in the figure of a "divine" woman, the bride of Christ.' Hence the dogma is indeed timely, and it relegates Jung's own background, that is, Protestantism, to 'the odium of being nothing but a *man's religion* which allows no metaphysical representation of woman.'

Again, I will pass over the consequences for social policy, which would be worth considering not only for Protestantism but likewise for the men's club of Catholicism, and how much more for Islam, which accords women equal rights in almost no respect. But I am also passing over the difficulties with C. G. Jung, and still more with Ibn Arabi, that must irritate a feminism which sees masculinity and femininity as social constructs rather than as realities that work in opposite ways in each of us, whether man or woman. I prefer in closing to quote once more from the *Interpreter of Desires*, in which 'the Greatest Shaykh' of Islam so eloquently desires a Christian as a God-woman:

> Who will show me her of the dyed fingers? Who will show me her of the honeyed tongue?
> She is one of the girls with swelling breasts who guard their honour, tender, virgin and beautiful,
> Full moons over branches: they fear no waning.
> In a garden of my body's country is a dove perched on a *bān* bough,
> Dying of desire, melting with passion, because that which befell me hath befallen her;
> Mourning for a mate, blaming Time, who shot her unerringly, as he shot me.
> Parted from a neighbour and far from a home! Alas, in my time of severance, for my time of union!
> Who will bring me her who is pleased with my torment? I am helpless because of that with which she is pleased.[58]

Dear analysts, ladies and gentlemen, before you begin your scholarly discussions, permit me one postscript. In my talk, I have repeatedly alluded to social and political implications without expanding on them. But I would like to venture once into the present, although not into politics. Instead I would like to lead you into my own field, literature. You have probably wondered by now how I have so many friends – I haven't; it's just that there are not so many authors in Germany in our time who concern themselves with spiritual matters. We can't lose sight of one another, in the gigantic space between Heaven and Earth, if only because the crowd has thinned out so in literature.

When I read contemporary books, good books, important books, books I can only be envious of because mine never turn out as brilliant, I often can't help having the impression that they are missing something essential. I mean: *I* miss something essential; but of course every reader speaks only for himself. I have the impression that literature, and especially German-language literature, whose metaphysical references once constituted part of its fame and greatness, whether Gryphius or Goethe, whether Jean Paul or Hölderlin, whether Kafka or Thomas Mann – I have the impression that most of our novels today fix their gaze firmly on the ground, on our social existence. That they are contemporary and nothing else. That's my feeling, subjective I admit – but when have feelings ever been fair? – when I read a contemporary German novel that everyone else says is brilliant, or when I don't read it because according to the reviews it's only about the here and now – and the here and now is so tiny!

After all, transcendence, in the context of art and culture, doesn't necessarily mean God – or His absence, which even the earliest poets deplored. To an artist, transcendence means first of all belonging to a tradition that is so old we can't remember its beginnings. Transcendence means going beyond the world of our immediate experience. That can also mean consciously renouncing a tradition. But we ought to know the tradition first, back to its roots in myth.

> We always start with the naïve assumption that we are masters in our own house. Hence we must first accustom ourselves to the thought that, in our most intimate psychic life as well, we live in a kind of house which at least has doors and windows to the world, but that, although the objects or contents of this world act upon us, they do not belong to us.[59]

Naturally there are historic novels – which I seldom read; on history I'd choose a monograph – and novels that are set in far-off lands – I'd choose a book of reportage – yet most of those novels are merely set in the past or in a faraway place; they are not descended from it. Many novels that are praised as worldly today are written no differently from all the others: they do not incorporate foreign philosophy, themes, language into their own structure, as Kafka integrated Jewish thought or Goethe Middle Eastern literature. And the books that are being written, discussed and praised in the German-speaking countries today rarely claim a tradition more than twenty, thirty years old; sometimes they trace their lineage as far back as the sixties, the beginnings of pop (which by now is something of a forefather to much of contemporary culture, which is ironic in itself). People still read the moderns, or at most the literature of the eighteenth, nineteenth centuries, but they hardly engage with it, and when there are references, the author cannot expect them to be recognized by the critics; more likely by those of his readers who have a classical education, whom he recognizes, in their letters or at readings, by other quirks – their clothes, their letter paper. And religion has no place at all, unless it is mentioned as a political problem.

But if a book has neither a past nor another world – a distant past I mean, one that goes farther back than an individual memory, and I mean another world in the general sense that there is more than human beings can see here on Earth – if a book neither claims a tradition nor looks up to the heavens, if the immediate circumstances are all that matters, then something is missing, the essential thing, I would say, although I am surely in the minority among readers, not least as a believer. To use the Sufis' beautiful image: what is missing is that the present glows black, from within, from darkness, because in all the diversity and particularity we do not see the influence of the common origin. This is precisely the lack that I feel, in spite of all my admiration and in spite of my envy when someone writes better than I; this is the solitude that I feel as a reader today. And that makes it all the more beautiful to be with you, dear analysts, scholars, if not followers, of Carl Gustav Jung. 'We carry our past with us, to wit, the primitive and inferior man with his desires and emotions, and it is only with an enormous effort that we can detach ourselves from this burden,' he writes in *Psychology and Religion*:

> If it comes to a neurosis, we invariably have to deal with a considerably intensified shadow. And if such a person wants to be cured it is necessary to find a way in which his conscious personality and his shadow can live together.[60]

Literature too is a way of living with the shadow that falls on us from the past or from the other world.

I thank you for your attention and wish you a rewarding conference.

Statement before the Opening Reading of the Harbour Front Literature Festival

Elbphilharmonie, Hamburg, 9 September 2020

Dear Mr Director of the Elbphilharmonie, honourable Senator, dear Festival directors, ladies and gentlemen,

Before I open this year's Harbour Front Literature Festival with my reading, I would like to make a statement. As you all know, a colleague of mine, Lisa Eckhart, will not be reading at this festival. The festival directors have revoked her invitation for fear of violent protests that a so-called black block had ostensibly threatened to carry out. Since then, it has transpired that no such threats had been made, only some 'warnings from the neighbourhood'.

Some 'warnings from the neighbourhood', and a reading is cancelled – I hardly need to explain what it would mean for the literary public and for freedom of speech in general if this paradigm from Hamburg should catch on.

In the meantime, Ms Eckhart has been given a great deal of space in the media to express herself, and her novel has sold a great many copies in spite of her revoked invitation, and most likely also because of it. Hence she has not been silenced, regardless of claims to the contrary from those who are otherwise consistently opposed to an open society.

However, one issue seems to me to have received insufficient attention in the discussion. According to accounts in various newspapers, two writers were responsible for getting Ms Eckhart's reading cancelled. They did so by refusing to appear on the same stage as her. Unfortunately, the two writers concerned have not made any public statement, and so I do not know their names. Perhaps they are sitting here among us now in the Elbphilharmonie; if not, I hope someone will report my words to them. Because I would like to address them directly.

Esteemed colleagues, according to all I have been able to read, I must assume that you take issue with a television appearance by Lisa Eckhart two years ago in the satirical late-night show *Mitternachtspitzen*. I have seen the video, and yes, I too think Ms Eckhart's attempt to discredit anti-Semitic and racist stereotypes by espousing them herself in the costume and character of Marlene Dietrich, who fled the Nazi regime, was a failure. As I perceive it, the performance is clumsy and naive, and it fails because the impression it leaves is mainly of the stereotypes themselves.

Nevertheless, Lisa Eckhart was invited to the Harbour Front Literature Festival not because of her abilities as a cabaret performer. She was invited because an independent jury considered her first novel, *Omama*, a literary work worthy of nomination as a finalist for the Klaus-Michael Kühne Prize. No one to date has found the novel politically unacceptable or hateful. Apparently, esteemed colleagues, what bothers you is not the novel, which hadn't even been published yet.

Precisely here is where you disastrously confuse the issue with the person. Every broadcaster and every event organizer has the right to invite Ms Eckhart for subsequent cabaret performances, or not. But your refusal to stand on the same stage as Ms Eckhart is not a rejection of this or that specific statement; it is not a rejection of the cabaret performer: it is a rejection of the person, whom you declare contemptible. No one would have expected you to have a beer with Ms Eckhart after her reading. The stage, however, is a public space, and the fact that an independent jury selected her novel gives her the same right to enter this public space as you. Besides your political foolishness – since of course the effect you have achieved is the opposite of the embargo you intended – anonymously arranging to have a colleague you don't like turned away also demonstrates enormous self-righteousness and disrespect.

My origins are in a country where writers are not only arrested, tortured, murdered or forced into exile on account of their books. No: in that country, which I still conceive as mine, more than a few people refuse to shake the hand of a fellow human being, to look them in the face, on account of their sex, their beliefs, their religion or their sexual orientation, much less to stand on the same stage with someone who thinks differently – believes differently, lives differently, is different – from themselves. But there, of course, people who think differently, believe differently, live differently, are different, are banned from stages in the first place.

I know freedom is hard. I wonder myself why Germans or Austrians today, whose ancestors killed 6 million Jews, think they need to break the collective ice by making jokes, anti-Semitic or not, that even mention Jews. I am aware that Bernd Lucke was one of the founders of the AfD, and yet I would still advocate allowing him to lecture at the university, with police protection if necessary. I am no supporter of the FDP, and yet I find it scandalous – and I am still limiting myself to incidents that have occurred recently here in Hamburg – I find it scandalous that Christian Lindner is prevented from appearing in public, with the acquiescence of the senator responsible. Or, to look beyond Hamburg, I find it right for the MDR television network to invite Björn Höcke to its summer interview, and I find it equally right that Mr Höcke can legally be called a fascist in Germany, according to a recent court judgement. I revere the Prophet Muhammad, and would nonetheless always defend the freedom to caricature him. I do not hold with boycotting the state of Israel, and yet I oppose the ban which the Bundestag has pronounced against every actual or even suspected supporter of the BDS movement worldwide. And so on and so forth. Wherever free speech is restricted, it is we writers who have the most to lose. I find it all the more alarming for that reason if we are now starting to ban each other.

Esteemed colleagues, in this hall, as everywhere in the literary public sphere, and of course in the country at large, we have different opinions. We may be political opponents – but we are not enemies. That is a tremendous achievement but one that is no longer sure. As a correspondent, I have reported on enough wars and expulsions to know what enmity does to people. Enmity makes it impossible to understand why the other thinks, feels, believes, loves differently from me. Enmity is thus clearly opposed to literature, which is the attempt to give expression to the incomprehensible – otherwise it would be superfluous and affirmative – to what we do not yet comprehend, in our own psyche and in the world. Literature is that which, in religion, would be love for one's enemy. But you, I, Lisa Eckhart, the people here in this hall, the guests and spectators of the festival being opened today, the citizens of this state – including the supporters of right-wing parties – we Europeans: we are no longer enemies, and we should repudiate that view of ourselves, because otherwise we risk slipping into a condition like that of a civil war.

The current pictures from the United States are not the first to illustrate how quickly opposition can turn into enmity: our own European history is full of violence between citizens who just yesterday were peaceful neighbours. Respecting the basic rules of civility is not accidental but fundamental to a democratic polity. It is fundamental to look at one another; it is fundamental to listen to one another; it is fundamental, at least in the cultures on both sides of the Atlantic, or will be again as soon as the pandemic is past, to greet each other by extending our hand before we engage in debate, and *so that* we can engage in debate. Besides, maintaining decorum makes intentional insults all the more effective when there is more at stake – just recall Beate Klarsfeld's slap in the face of Chancellor Kurt Kiesinger, or the bouquet thrown down at the feet of the newly elected Thuringian minister-president Thomas Kemmerich – when there is more at stake than a failed television sketch.

You would have had every opportunity, esteemed colleagues, in the context of the Harbour Front Literature Festival, to say publicly, and in the presence of Lisa Eckhart, what you think of the censured video. You could have confronted her with her statements, engaged with her criticism of the sham morality of the liberal-bourgeois milieu, or expressed your disapproval – even if just by your facial expressions – during the joint reading. All of that would not only have been legitimate; it might also have been productive. Instead, you have – no, not just rejected dialogue; you have declared a colleague an unperson by refusing to be anywhere near her. The least you could have done, esteemed colleagues, would have been to say who you are.

The fact that the directors of the Harbour Front Literature Festival have fulfilled your demand casts a shadow over this event, including the reading which now follows.

On Receiving the Hölderlin Prize of the City of Bad Homburg vor der Höhe

Schlosskirche, Bad Homburg vor der Höhe, 1 November 2020

Dear Mr Mayor, dear Ms von Suffrin, dear Mr Kaube, dear members of the jury, ladies and gentlemen,

What would Friedrich Hölderlin think if he could see us here? If he walked into this church now? The parish church of the town of Homburg vor der Höhe in his day, where he must have said a prayer now and again, although more likely during the week, in silence, than during the Sunday worship service. 'I am not shy because I am afraid of being disturbed by reality in my self-absorption; I am so because I am afraid of being disturbed by reality in the profound concentration with which I am wont to devote myself to other things,' he wrote to his friend Neuffer from his home at Haingasse 36, just a few paces from this church, on 12 November 1798. 'I am afraid the warm life in me will be chilled by the icy-cold happenings of everyday-life.'[61] We may assume this much: Hölderlin would shiver in our midst.

> And woe to the stranger who wanders out of love, and comes to such a people, and woe three times over to him

who comes to such a people as I did, driven by great sorrow, a beggar of my kind![62]

For Hölderlin, if he were to come down from heaven for our celebration – his celebration – Hölderlin would think our seating arrangement was a reflection of our society. He would think we, the people of today, were so concerned with our solitude that we must make sure, down to the centimetre, that we won't touch each other, even with outstretched arms. Though he might have laughed as we arrived and greeted each other by leaning away and proffering our elbows, he would notice now the tension that can still be seen in the eyes of any audience when they laugh or applaud because, in enclosed spaces, even the air can no longer be trusted. He would be alarmed at the masks that you are all wearing, and that I will put on again as soon as I leave the lectern. He would probably think I was the pastor, bereft of all consciousness of form, and he would think you, ladies and gentlemen, were the scattered flock of remaining Christians in Homburg. And he would certainly suspect a connection between the uniform spacing, the clumsy greetings, the earnest faces, the ugly masks and also the church, which is no longer full even on Sundays:

> Celebrate – yes, but what? And gladly with others I'd sing now,
> Yet alone as I am nothing that's godlike rings true.
> This, I know, is it, my failing, a curse lames my sinews
> Only because of this, making me flag from the start,
> So that numb all day long I sit like a child that is moping
> Dumb, though at times a tear coldly creeps out of my eyes,
> And the flowers of the field, the singing of birds makes me sad now,
> Being heralds of heaven, bearers of heavenly joy,

> But to me, in my heart's dank vault, now the soul-giving
>   sun dawns
> Cool, infertile, in vain, feeble as rays of the night,
> Oh, and futile and empty, walls of a prison, the heavens
> Press, a smothering load heaped on my head from above![63]

Certainly we might put Hölderlin at ease: the oddities are on account of an infectious disease, and they are easier to bear at least than the plague ordinance of his time. Next summer, or autumn at the latest, we would explain, our scientists will have defeated the pathogen and we will once more be able to meet without fear. And you, ladies and gentlemen, will be able to set me straight that 'Menon's Lament for Diotima', of which I have recited an excerpt, for all its ambiguity, cannot be interpreted in relation to Covid. But if Hölderlin were to look around our world today, we might also take his foreign gaze seriously.

It may be merely by chance that the pandemic falls in his commemorative year. Nevertheless, his poems sounded new and altogether alarming when, from one week to the next, the most familiar things became strange to us: a simple greeting, our own street, a playground, a canteen, a flirt, a lecture hall, a visit to our grandparents, a funeral, an accident and emergency department. And I do not mean his notorious question 'What are poets for in these meager times?'[64] from the elegy 'Bread and Wine', which occurred to many commentators when Amazon dropped books from its distribution in favour of hygienic articles – and which will be raised again starting tomorrow when the state, officially declaring culture a branch of entertainment, closes theatres, museums, concert halls – what are poets for in these meager times? – while shopping malls are considered essential. I do not mean the two lines from the hymn 'Patmos' – 'But where danger is, / Deliverance also grows'[65] – which might give form to the hope of a vaccine or prop up the illusion that now the world would finally join together because the virus doesn't recognize any national borders either. No, I mean the breaks and stops, the faltering and sputtering in Hölderlin's late work, when for us too life stood still. I mean the feeling of being at the mercy of an unidentified higher power, when people holed up like shadows in their homes, two, three full months long in Spain, in northern Italy, in Tehran and New York and, most eerily, in the elderly care homes, their sinews lamed by a curse, flagging from the start; numb all day long, sitting like a child moping, dumb, though at times a tear coldly crept out of their eyes. I mean that alienation as a fundamental experience of the modern era which Hölderlin captured, anticipated, transformed into landscapes, dream visions, breath, grieving tone and unequal rhythms, alienation of the language, alienation of people, alienation of work, alienation first and foremost of nature.

The flowers of the field, the singing of birds makes me sad now, Menon laments in the stanza I quoted. The sun, which is supposed to breathe the soul into a person, dawns chill and fruitless in his shuddering breast like rays of night. The sky, the open, unbounded, splendid heavens, now hangs like prison walls over his head, now become a bending load, and at the same time null and bare. And why? Hölderlin hints at the reason at the beginning of the stanza: 'Alone as I am nothing that's godlike rings true.' It is the isolation of modern individuals, who no longer feel the common origin of all creatures since they see themselves as the creators of reality: 'This, I know, is it, my failing.' Still in Homburg, half a year after his letter to Neuffer which I quoted at the outset, Hölderlin wrote to his brother Karl:

> But we have long been in agreement that all the meandering rivers of human activity flow into the ocean of nature,

just as they begin from it. To show people this path, which they mostly go down blindly, sometimes crossly and reluctantly and all too often in a base and vile fashion, to show it to them so that they may go down it with eyes wide open, joyfully and nobly, that is the job of philosophy, art and religion, which themselves proceed from this creative impulse.[66]

It may be just by coincidence that the pandemic falls in Hölderlin's commemorative year. But it is no coincidence that the Holy Spirit entered Hölderlin just as people were beginning to subdue the Earth, not as God intended, but by plundering, raping and destroying it. The previous speaker, Jürgen Kaube, has described so succinctly in his recent biography of Hegel the world in which, a few kilometres away, his contemporary Hölderlin was born in 1770: the incipient industrialization, which was accompanied by increasing division of labour and rapid urbanization; the development of the steam engine, the first ascent of Mont Blanc and the first expedition to the South Pole; simultaneous measurement of the solar system by observatories all over the world; globalization, long before the word would gain currency; the discovery of the chemical elements – hydrogen in 1766, oxygen in 1772, carbon in 1775, sulphur in 1777; and in between, in 1775, the last witch trial.

The technical, scientific and civilizational progress which humanity has made since then is undeniable, indeed spectacular. But if we abstain for once from using the criteria of our own human development and look instead at the plants, at the animal world, the seas, the natural forests, the air, the glaciers, the polar ice caps, the soil that we are contaminating with our nuclear waste for a million years to come, then the tiny quarter of a millennium since the birth of Hegel and Hölderlin is a story of loss and disaster without precedent in all evolution. 'Everything is useful', the motto Hegel once propounded for the Enlightenment, thus heralded the ruthless exploitation of resources which seems to be inherent in the growth logic of capitalism. Conversely, the mystical 'to be one with all that lives', which Hölderlin saw as the divine purpose of human beings, becomes a political programme when human beings threaten to destroy their means of life along with creation: 'To be one with all that lives, to return in blessed self-oblivion into the All of nature.'[67]

Hölderlin did not enjoy Nature on excursions, discover it on expeditions, observe it from a passing coach, analyse it in the laboratory as Goethe did. If for no other reason than that he had no money, but was always travelling, he walked more than any other poet of the German language through the natural landscape, freezing, shivering, hungering, fearing, feeling as he traversed it, surviving it many times over; along the Neckar, the Rhine, the Main, the Danube; from Homburg to Frankfurt for Susette on the appointed Thursday evening every month and back the same night; over the Alps in light clothing; the length and breadth of France in winter, and back again, half mad, in the summer; sleeping hundreds of nights by the wayside, his face tanned like that of a peasant, his legs scratched, his hands cracked; climbing over chasms, trembling through thunderstorms and blizzards, helplessly exposed to eagles, lightning and robbers.

The reader of Hölderlin's poems and letters knows the names of the rivers, mountain ranges, trees, forests, seas, animals in them, feels his racing heart, which was not at all figurative, and in *Hyperion* and *Empedocles* the reader also gazes on the landscapes of Sicily, Greece and Asia Minor, which Hölderlin dreamt so boldly that they appear to us more lifelike than the cities, transport routes and industrial zones which make up our own reality. In the early 'Fragment of Hyperion' he writes:

I don't know what it does to me when I look at it, this unfathomable Nature; but it is holy tears of bliss I weep before my veiled beloved. My whole being falls silent and listens when the soft, mysterious breath of evening wafts over me. Lost in the vast azure, I look up incessantly towards the Aether, and out to the holy Sea, and I feel as if the gates of the Invisible are opening to me, and I pass forth, with all that is around me, until a rustling in the bush awakens me from that blessed death, and recalls me, against my will, back to the place from whence I started.

My heart is at ease in this twilight. Is it our element, this twilight? Why can I not rest therein?[68]

Hölderlin did not romanticize nature: he felt deeply its menace, mindless fury, destructiveness, in which no will, no love is at work. A pacific, gracious Nature, a shaped Nature, was his ideal: the gardens, fields, shorelines, ponds; not the open, strange Atlantic beyond Bordeaux but the more civilized sea of his 'Archipelago', the 'beautiful islands' Tina and Calauria; not the wilderness, not the raw, but the harmony of human beings with plants and animals, as for example in *Hyperion*, when the view downwards from the mountain heights to the plains of Asia Minor is like a landscape painting; only as form, as image, is nature soulful and divine, as Hölderlin explains in his famous 1802 letter to Böhlendorff: the thunderstorm not as a mere phenomenon but 'seen as power and figure'; the light as 'shaping nationally and as principle and destiny, so that something is holy to us'; the forests in their characteristic aspect 'and the coincidence in one region of different characters of nature'.[69] Likewise the ancient gods which Hölderlin continually invokes must be understood, not as primitive elements and hence equivalent to feelings, but as nature cognized and associated with specific traits. They are both divine and human, like Jesus

Christ, and thus embody the equalization of the opposing forces which tear mortals apart, the 'anorgic' and the 'organic'; that is, the chaotic and the ordered, predisposition and education, chance and determination, instinct and culture, body and mind, sensuality and rationality, freedom and necessity, form and indeterminacy. 'Art is the flowering, the perfection of nature', Hölderlin wrote in 'The Basis of *Empedocles*':

> Nature becomes divine only when allied with art, which differs from it in kind but is in harmony with it, only when each is everything it can be and when each allies itself with the other, supplying what the other lacks, and lacks necessarily if it is to be everything it can be as a particular; at that point perfection is achieved and the divine stands at the midpoint of the two.[70]

For all its idiosyncrasy, what speaks out of Hölderlin's poetry is not the state of mind of an individual I. It is Being which becomes the subject, just as Diotima describes in reference to Hyperion, to whom the whole destiny of his time indelibly clings, 'because he is not rough enough to drive it out and not weak enough to weep it out.'[71] And repeatedly, a similar course from harmony to rupture to longing, completed in the novel, drafted in the tragedy, condensed into two short, contradictory stanzas in 'Half of Life'; perfected in its very fragility in the elegies and the late hymns; present only as a reminiscence in the poems from the Tower. I would like to illustrate this by three examples: one from each of his poetry, his letters and his prose.

Hölderlin's purest expression of the human being's unconscious harmony with nature, that of childhood or a time before birth, is in an undated, untitled poem which was preserved only in manuscript:

When I was a boy
A god rescued me often
from the shouts and whips of men,
It was then that I played
Safely and well with woodland flowers
And the winds of Heaven
Played with me.

And as you delight
The hearts of the plants,
When to you they extend
Their delicate arms,

So you delighted my heart,
Father Helios, and like Endymion
I was your darling,
Sacred Moon!

O all you faithful
Friendly gods!
If only you knew
How my soul loved you.

True, in those days I did not
Call you by name, and you
Never called me as men do, as if
They knew one other, with names.

Yet I knew you better
than I ever knew men,
I understood air, its stillness,
Never the language of men.

The whispering woodland's
Harmony taught me,

And I learned to love
Among the flowers.

I grew tall in the arms of the gods.[72]

Then the rupture, the trauma of separation and hence alienation, isolation, which is also predisposed by nature, however, because human beings strive for knowledge, dominance, perfection. Hölderlin explained this negative dialectic in detail in his letter from Homburg to his brother:

> Why don't they [that is, human beings] live like the deer in the forest, content with little, limited to the ground, the food at their feet, where the connection with nature is like that of the baby to its mother's breast? Then there would be no anxiety, no toil, no complaint, little illness, little conflict; there would be no sleepless nights etc. But this would be as unnatural for man as the arts he teaches the animals are to them. To push life onwards, to accelerate Nature's endless process of perfection, to complete what he has before him, and to idealize – that will always be the instinct that best characterizes and distinguishes man, and all his arts and works and errors and tribulations stem from it. Why do we have gardens and fields? Because mankind wanted a better world than the one it inherited. Why do we have trade, ships, cities, states, with all their turmoil and their good and bad? Because mankind wanted a better world than the one it inherited. Why do we have science, art, religion? Because mankind wanted a better world than the one it inherited. Even when they chafe against one another in a headstrong way, it is because the present is not satisfactory, because they want things different, and so they fling themselves sooner into nature's grave, and accelerate the march of the world.

What is greatest and what is smallest, best and worst in mankind, grows from one root.[73]

Finally, after unity and division, the longing for restored and now consciously experienced spirituality, 'more divinely at peace with all', which is possible at most in brief moments of rapture, of love and the experience of beauty, and otherwise only in annihilation, in which case, however, consciousness is probably lacking. 'We die so as to live,' murmurs Diotima, the symbol of the divine nature in *Hyperion*, in the last lines before her death:

> I will be; I do not ask what I will become. To be, to live, that is enough, that is the honor of the gods; and therefore all that lives in the divine world is equal, and in this world there are no masters and slaves.[74]

Hyperion, who stands for the Faustian merely-human, destructive and destroyed, alienated from nature, remains behind. Unreachable the gods, who walk up there in the light on soft ground; only an inkling now the blessedness of the babes asleep, when we too, like the celestials, fateless breathed. But to him, the sufferer in Hölderlin's time – as in ours, if not from the very first – it is given to find no resting place, to faint, to fall:

> Blindly from one
>   To the next moment
>   Like water flung
>   From rock to rock down
>   Long years into uncertainty.[75]

Three weeks ago, likewise on a Sunday, I lay on a bed in the evening with my two daughters in the student flat which the older one had moved into a few weeks before. It had been a strange, exciting day because the younger one had been put under quarantine, luckily with no symptoms of infection. We had just heard that her test, for which I had driven her to the airport just in time before the official order, had turned out negative. And because the family doctor had pointed out that the incubation period was past, we dared to lie side by side again.

Of course, there have always been epidemics. But as humankind ultimately did learn a thing or two from the plague, which turned out not to be the fault of the Jews or the witches, it may well come to understand Covid-19 – whose name alone sounds like something from science fiction – as a sign, although not a sign of a natural phenomenon to be done away with in the same way as rats, mice and faecal matter, but as a sign of progress turning into self-destruction. The virologists pointed out early on, and they had warned long before, that our growing vulnerability to infectious diseases has an underlying cause in population growth and the destruction of natural habitats, through massive clear-cutting, for example, which drives animals that carry germs closer to human settlements. Specifically, as we now know, the outbreak of the current pandemic may have been caused by what are called 'wet markets', where living or freshly slaughtered wild animals are bought and sold. Industrial meat production and factory mink farms also offer ideal conditions for the transformation of microbes into deadly pathogens. This means that Covid is an immediate consequence of our disgraceful abuse of nature. And hence it is also logical that the virus, whether by chance or otherwise, brought the very mobility, mass culture, supply chains, food economy and urbanity that are characteristic of our lifestyle to a standstill. 'Yes, indeed! It was an extraordinary project, to plant my Elysium with a band of robbers,'[76] says

Hyperion, and the war of which Hölderlin's novel tells refers at the same time to humanity's war with nature 'within me and outside of me':[77]

> Do you call me dispirited? Dear maiden! there is too much catastrophe. Furious crowds burst in on all sides; rapacity rages in Morea like a plague, and he who does not seize the sword is hunted down, slaughtered; and the raving men say that they thereby fight for our freedom.[78]

The present state of emergency will not last, and we may hope the Schlosskirche will be filled once again at the next awarding of the Hölderlin Prize. But even if they remain unharmed, tormented at worst by boredom, our children, and how much more those in northern Italy and Spain, in New York or Tehran, will one day tell about the great pestilence as our parents or grandparents told of the ruin and deprivations of the war. A whole generation will remember that once they could not leave the house, although the menace could be neither seen nor felt. And they will associate the memory with their already substantial trepidation that they were born into a future that can no longer be saved, but at most survived.

The children and I lay on the bed in the student flat, relieved, but the younger one still facing eight days' quarantine. The older one suggested watching a naturalist's documentary, which she said was being talked about a great deal, on Netflix on her tablet. After all, David Attenborough, as the researcher was called, had set a record on Instagram: no one else had ever found a million followers so fast – in just over four hours; no pop star, no footballer, no leader. The fact that Attenborough, my daughter added, only joined Instagram at the age of ninety-four, and until recently had not possessed an e-mail address, made us still more curious to see his film.

In the first scene we see how the old man walks through the abandoned town of Chernobyl, which, thirty years after the nuclear reactor accident, has been reconquered by nature. The growing trees reach into the tower blocks; the suddenly abandoned funfair is a paradise of flowers; and where the cars used to pass, wild horses graze. From here, from Chernobyl, which will never again be inhabited by human beings, Attenborough looks back on his life devoted to nature:

> Where, ah where shall I find
> When winter comes, the flowers,
> And where the sunshine
> And shadows of the earth?
> Walls stand
> Speechless and cold, in the wind
> The weathervanes clatter.[79]

'Half of Life' is not a nature poem, though the reader might think so after the first stanza, in which the land hangs in the lake with yellow pears and wild roses. Nor is it the winter that causes woe in the second stanza. It is an abandoned city, or rather one bereft of its soul, without the beauty of the flowers, without the natural light and the warmth of the sun, without any kind of plant at all to cast shade; in short, dried up and barren. Only the walls, built by people, are left, as speechless and cold as if after – well, not a nuclear accident – as if after the explosion of a neutron bomb. If we have been, in the 'Celebration of Peace', a discourse,[80] it has fallen silent; and where, in the same poem, we soon shall be song, only the iron clattering of a weathervane is yet audible, its staff swaying back and forth in the wind. It is the winter of humanity, which comes early now, arriving at the 'Half of Life'.

I would like to tell you about one sequence, which, admittedly, is designed for effect in the Hollywood style but which nonetheless touched me to the heart as I lay on the bed beside my two daughters: using old footage, Attenborough shows what species still ran free ten, thirty, fifty, ninety-four years ago, how far south the glaciers extended, how the polar ice has melted especially in recent years, so that just this summer, as you have probably heard, a ship reached the North Pole for the first time without the help of an icebreaker. All that was impressive enough, especially as we saw the same old gentleman, both friendly and earnest, looking into the camera in the old footage, so that a single life, a ninety-four-year life in nature and for nature, flashed before our eyes as if in the last seconds before death, as if the spectator were dying:

> Ripe are, dipped in fire, cooked
> The fruits and tried on the earth, and it is law,
> Prophetic, that all must enter in
> Like serpents, dreaming on
> The mounds of heaven. And much
> As on the shoulders a
> Load of logs must be
> Retained. But evil are
> The paths, for crookedly
> Like horses go the imprisoned
> Elements and ancient laws
> Of the earth.[81]

Nature, from which we live, has become threatening in 'Mnemosyne': these are the last days of the harvest, ripe is the fruit, dipped in the fire of the sun, roasted in the summer heat. The familiar law that all the substances and forces of the Earth, the air, the sun go into the fruits as taste and nutrition has, in its metaphysical reflection on the mounds of heaven, the reality of a nightmare or a prophecy of doom: the penetrating elements are poisonous, like serpents. Although they bear on their shoulders a burden of failure, the people must go on, must bear as Atlas did the weight of the vault of heaven. But there is no longer any orientation; the paths, the very paths which were something reliable, comforting, have become evil. Earth's elements and old laws no longer move in their own, harmonious cycle but have been harnessed by human beings like horses for a progress that is crooked.

But then Attenborough drew up a projection, one which, he said, is grounded in science, based on facts, a shiny, technically animated look ahead at how the Earth will appear in thirty, fifty, ninety-four years if the current development continues – and today, sadly, there is reason to believe that it will accelerate. Then we were really in a science fiction film, which is what reality around us has felt like for months. In ninety-four years – my youngest daughter may still be living then. But how? In 2114, large parts of the world will be deserted, and more and more people will crowd into the inhabitable remainder until finally the ecosystem collapses completely. Yes, and then someday, a day not so far off any more, yet another species will become extinct, the human one – if it doesn't find a way to adapt. Nature, however – nature will not die out with us. It will recover from humanity and will gradually reconquer our cities, transport routes and industrial zones, as it has in Chernobyl. 'Or is it not divine, what you Germans mock and call soulless?'[82] Hyperion asks, after having seen in Germany the Earth that humanity began to plunder, rape and destroy.

> 'Is not the air you drink better than your chatter? are not the sun's rays nobler than all you shrewd men? the earth's wellsprings and the morning dew refresh your grove; could you do that? O! you can kill, but cannot bring to life, not

without love, which does not come from you, which you did not invent. You worry, and scheme to escape destiny, and do not comprehend when your childish art is no help; meanwhile, the stars move harmlessly above. You degrade, you destroy patient nature where she tolerates you, yet she lives on in infinite youth, and you cannot banish her autumn and her spring, you do not spoil her ether.

O she must be divine, because you may destroy and yet she does not grow old, and in spite of you the beautiful remains beautiful.[83]

It is one of the secrets of Hölderlin that individual paragraphs, stanzas, lines, phrases, torn out of the poet's conceptual world, which is full of difficult paradoxes, seem in quite different and distant contexts and times to be so immediately obvious that they become aphorisms for a collective perception, generally agreeable and suitable for everyday use. That is how it is when the Holy Spirit has spoken. The 'meagre times' when poets are no longer needed do not refer to any political or cultural state of affairs. Intellectually, Hölderlin's era, the turn of the nineteenth century, was not at all meagre; in Germany it was, rather, the heyday of literature, philosophy, the sciences, and after the French Revolution it offered at least the hope of liberty as well. The 'meagre times' in the seventh stanza of 'Bread and Wine' refer to the world from which the gods have withdrawn, in which Nature – the plants, the animals, the resources, the far-off peoples – are no more than mere lifeless material for the human beings who have become self-aware. Lying on the bed, my two daughters beside me, on the tablet the film of a ninety-four-year-old naturalist who is breaking all the records on Instagram, I too repeat the two lines from 'Patmos': 'But where danger is, / Deliverance also grows'.[84] They are also engraved in this church upon the crypt of the Landgraves of Hesse-Homburg.

On a Concert by the WDR Symphony Orchestra in the Broadcast Series 'Music in Dialogue'

Philharmonie, Cologne, 25 March 2021

Dear symphony orchestra of Westdeutscher Rundfunk,

I'm addressing you directly because I am almost alone with you this evening. Of course there are many people listening to us on the radio, but in here in the Philharmonie in Cologne, where I would normally be lost in the crowd, today I am the only person in the audience. A moment ago, I felt as if you were playing just for me! That is a gift, and at the same time it gives me the rare opportunity to try to explain to you why you are so important in my life, dear symphony orchestra.

As some of you may know, I travelled a great deal when that was still possible, and among the places I visited were far-off countries and regions where wars are going on. It's easy to think our life in an industrialized society is alienated, materialistic and noisy; to think people in other countries may be poor, but at least their lives are more authentic and closer to nature. I won't say that such a quiet, contemplative life no longer exists anywhere. But many more people in Southern

Asia, in Africa, in the Middle East and in Latin America live in megacities that make our European capitals look almost like villages. And even many of the villages in the South have grown into insatiable behemoths where noise, exhaust fumes and swarms of people overload the senses of anyone who is not accustomed to so many simultaneous impressions. That is to say nothing of the war zones and regions in crisis, where the word 'quiet' always suggests 'graveyard'.

What did I do on my travels when I needed to escape the din for a half hour or an hour, to rest from a day's commotion? There are few parks in such cities; the cafés and tea houses spill over onto the unprotected pavement; very rarely does one come upon an enchanted courtyard. What would I do? I would walk into a temple, a mosque, a monastery or the mausoleum of a saint, and, from one step to the next, there would be peace. And yet the inside of the building would also be swarming with people, and they would be singing, reciting, teaching or playing music; they would be eating, strolling, conversing, sleeping or meditating. It was the opposite of dead; it was life at its most alive – only it was filled with beauty, with idleness, breathing and prayer, while the streets outside were ruled by the survival of the loudest. It was an unbelievable experience every time, that leap from this world into another, into a world that seemed to be enchanted, and too little attention has been given, I believe, to the eminently therapeutic function which such places of refuge have for the soul in countries where there are hardly any points of rest any more.

Where would I go in Germany, where would I go in Cologne, if I wanted to step out of my accustomed era and calendar? I could step inside one of the Romanesque churches, but even before the pandemic they were almost always deserted during the day, and what I sought, and seek, is not only peace but the opposite, a different kind of community, a closer one than is possible through words. Nor has the stately new mosque become a place, sadly, where a person can walk in without a second thought. And if I were to arrive during a prayer service ... oh dear. Where could I go, then? In Cologne, there was no place I went more often than to the Philharmonie.

What happens when we listen to music? We step outside of the order of our day-to-day lives, which are organized by utility. By that I mean not just work-related matters or material things. Even longing, grief, care have a physiological or emotional utility; even love strives for union or at least closeness. But what is the objective when we listen to music, music such as we are listening to this evening, which serves neither to celebrate an occasion nor to raise our working morale, nor even to tell stories from which we might learn something?

Relaxation, one might suppose; enjoyment. Music relaxes us; we can enjoy it. But this answer only begs the next question: What is it exactly that evokes such an enjoyment which does not seem to serve any interest? After all, our sense of taste or smell is not being stimulated, and there is no one standing behind us massaging our shoulders. Our ears are being caressed, someone might say, just as the eyes are pleasantly stimulated by looking at the sea or the desert. Beauty, harmony, silence: it gives us relaxation and enjoyment. But is this really what happens to us, is this all that happens to us, when we listen to music, or at least the kinds of music played in a symphony hall or a jazz club, at a religious ritual or a rock concert? Were beauty, harmony and silence the attributes we thought of just now as we listened to 'Signals from Heaven' by Tōru Takemitsu? After all, it was not harps that we heard, but only brass wind instruments, which are the opposite pole to silence in a symphony orchestra. And even the sound of a harp consists of a violation of harmony – one that is less obtrusive, to be sure, but constant and necessary

– that is, a break with the expectations that a chord or a melody intuitively evokes. Music, all serious music, arises out of form and the deviation from that form.

Our day-to-day life is subject to laws which we don't always obey, but whose sense consists in being generally obeyed. Music, or, in more general terms, aesthetic communication, is also subject to laws. But their sense, on the contrary, consists in being consciously, that is, purposely, adeptly, surprisingly violated. In everyday language, a phrase such as 'the dog is mewing' would be nonsensical. Translated into the language of music, however, the fact that the dog is mewing instead of barking, as we would expect, is precisely what makes the phrase interesting. In other words, there needs to be the expectation that dogs bark, and there needs to be a break with that expectation.

Forgive me, dear symphony orchestra, for translating the musical process onto, and admittedly dragging it down to, the level of words, and the most humble words at that. Because the nature of your art consists precisely in the fact that we cannot capture its message, its sense and its purpose in our everyday language. That does not mean that it has no message, sense and purpose; not in the way that dumping out a pitcher of water would make no sense, or spinning around in circles. No: when we listen to music that speaks to us, we receive a message, we understand a sense, we feel a purpose – and in fact we feel something quite compelling; it can only be just so; it cannot be otherwise than it is. But whatever we want to call it, or however we want to define it, we would not be able to say everything about it, no matter how many words we wasted. Because there is something inexhaustible in it, something infinite.

Why is that?

The question is as inexhaustible as the music itself, and everyone who loves music finds their own answer to it.

Myself, I would like to try once more on the level of words: just as we set the principle of utility aside when we listen to music, we also step outside of our accustomed verbal sense of order, which is aimed at making ourselves understood. In the order of music, the relations between sounds and meanings are no longer fixed. It is as if we were listening to a language that we do not know.

Anyone can learn this language, of course; musicians can also express themselves in it. But not even the composer with whom an expression originates can explain exactly what is being communicated. The composer can't even limit the field of possible meanings. This is a fundamental difference from the language in which I am addressing you at the moment, dear symphony orchestra. You too may understand me differently, but my ambition is to express myself as clearly as possible, and thus it would be a failure on my part if I could not make myself understood. But music, all serious music, is consciously ambiguous, removed from all definable meanings, all pragmatic use. And when we listen to it, at least in the most profound, the most moving moments, we can't state any message at all, any sense, any purpose, because we have set language aside, and, with it, thought. And then we are nothing but hearing. That is a point, dear symphony orchestra, which my art never attains. Literature, even where it chooses paradox to escape from conceptual logic, always remains bound to concepts. In the case of the mewing dog, we still think of a dog and a cat. We do not think of nothing.

This doesn't mean that we are unconscious when we listen to music; on the contrary: we are so filled with consciousness that, for a moment, there is no room left for reflection, for seeing ourselves from outside. This is what characterizes aesthetic euphoria and, still more, musical euphoria, that is, the rapture directly evoked by a sensory impression: not blindness, deafness, muteness, but maximum vision, maximum hearing, maximum presence of mind. The transcendence takes us to ourselves.

I need you, dear symphony orchestra, I need you as urgently as, in far-off countries and regions where wars are going on, people need temples, mosques, monasteries and the mausoleums of saints.

On the 75th Anniversary of the Founding of the State of Lower Saxony

Stadthalle, Hanover, 1 November 2021

Dear Mr Minister-President, dear Madam President of the Landtag, ladies and gentlemen,

On the 27th of August, the last German soldiers came back from Afghanistan. Since then, Germany has held parliamentary elections, public life is returning to normal, for the time being, in spite of growing numbers of new infections; spectators are returning to the stadiums and theatres, one German state after another is celebrating its 75th birthday, the winners of the election are negotiating to form a coalition government while the losers are tearing each other apart, and a speed limit on the German autobahn is still nowhere in sight. And Afghanistan? Two months later – did anyone expect otherwise? – it's no longer an issue. The 160,000 German soldiers who served in Afghanistan will just have to deal with the fact that their mission has been made virtually meaningless overnight by the agreement between the United States and the Taliban and the inaction of European diplomacy. More drastically left to fend for themselves are the 45 million Afghans, of whom a rapidly increasing six million are in exile by now. They have to cope with the fact that their country has suddenly regressed to its condition of twenty years ago – tyranny, religious extremism, misogyny, contempt for human rights, contempt for culture, contempt for any kind of difference – except that, this time, one crucial thing is missing: the hope of liberation.

Ladies and gentlemen, you may ask: Why Afghanistan? Haven't we heard enough about that recently? Why am I not talking about the state of Lower Saxony, as is fitting on such an anniversary? Well, I may be many things – I am an Iranian by parentage, a Westphalian by birth, a Rhinelander by choice, a grateful German, a staunch European – but Lower Saxony appears nowhere in my portfolio of skills and backgrounds.

That is why I at first politely declined the minister-president's invitation to give the commemorative speech today. His office promptly replied that there would be enough speeches about Lower Saxony on this occasion and what was wanted was, rather, some thoughts on a general political topic so that the ceremonies might rise above simple narcissism. Very well, I thought, I could talk about federalism, about what it contributed to the success of post-war West Germany and what challenges it faces as a result of globalization. But then I saw the people clinging to American aircraft as they took off from Kabul and falling hundreds of metres to the ground like stones, and I can't get these images, this whole, unbelievable, macabre occurrence, out of my mind. I can't remember a political event in recent years that upset me as much as the Taliban's return to power. That is no doubt because of my own memories of the country, so beautiful, so abused, that has been a football to world politics since the invasion of the Soviet Army more than forty years ago. It is also because of my Afghan acquaintances in Germany, whom I have hardly dared look in the eye since August, because every one of them is in despair and uncontainable worry about their relatives, especially their female relatives. But another reason for the numbed feeling is that, with the failure in Afghanistan, every intercession for democracy all over the world, for the development of civil societies, for liberation, seems to be irrelevant. Ladies and gentlemen, I have struggled throughout my intellectual life to turn our gaze outwards, for us to see ourselves, for all our love of our respective countries, as citizens of the world. But now the tenor of many commentaries, and especially those in the social media, is this: if our help does so much harm, it would be better for everyone if we didn't intervene anywhere any more. Accordingly, practically nothing was heard during the recent electoral campaigns about our foreign policy, about global responsibility, about international engagement. And I resolved to speak on precisely that political topic which has moved me the most during these days. For Afghanistan certainly does have something to do with Lower Saxony – and not just because the returning German soldiers landed in Wunstorf, barely 22 kilometres from this auditorium.

The founding of the state of Lower Saxony on the 1st of November 1946 took place thanks to an overseas military deployment and was carried out by an occupying force. In other words, what we are celebrating today is the phenomenal success of a military intervention. And what we saw two months ago, 20 kilometres away, was the end of a spectacularly failed military intervention. Are the two missions comparable? Certainly not in scale. But, in both cases, numerous and very diverse states joined together to topple an extraordinarily bloodthirsty regime. Of course the countries involved, in both cases, were also following their own selfish interests – of strategy, economy, security policy – the world has never yet been ruled by altruism. Nonetheless, both in 1939 and in 2001, the realization prevailed internationally, after long hesitation, that a fascistoid ideology must be opposed by force to keep it from spreading further – and the militant Wahhabism of the Taliban is nothing else but a religious variant of fascism, not based on some centuries-old Pashtun traditions, but an original creation of the modern era.

'Nothing is good in Afghanistan,' said a leading citizen of Lower Saxony in 2010, then the state's bishop and chair of the Lutheran church council, Margot Käßmann. The events since the fall of Kabul would seem to confirm her assessment. And yet, when she said it, the statement was false and a slap in the face to all those who were dauntlessly working in Afghanistan for peaceful development. And the sudden failure of those twenty years of effort, wilfully precipitated by outside forces, does not make it true retroactively. For what we are now witnessing is not the consequences of the Western mission – its consequences were problematic enough, and I myself have been one of the most vehement critics of the NATO strategy since my first journey through Afghanistan in 2006. What Afghanistan is now undergoing is the immediate effect of our withdrawal. What has happened – although it was carried out more dilettantishly and irresponsibly than anyone would have thought possible – is in fact exactly what more than a few groups on the left and right ends of the political spectrum had been demanding for years: end the war in Afghanistan! The war has ended, all right. But is anything in Afghanistan the better for it? No – on the contrary. The little good that the Western military intervention had made possible has now been destroyed: women's rights, access to education, a free press, the formation of a civil society, international dialogue, the development of art, literature, music. And the United Nations reports that food supplies to more than the half the Afghan population are unsure, and 3.2 million children are already in danger of acute malnutrition. 'Afghanistan is now among the world's worst humanitarian crises, if not the worst,' said David Beasley, the head of the UN's World Food Programme, last week. 'We are on a countdown to catastrophe.'

Now there is no question of a new military engagement, and so all I can do is to appeal to the world not to forget Afghanistan again. But the words would tie my tongue in knots because I know, as everyone here in this auditorium knows, that that is exactly what will happen: Afghanistan will be forgotten again; it practically is already, two months after the return of our soldiers. Forgotten like Yemen, Ethiopia, Madagascar, Burma, Syria, to list just some of the most devastating wars and famines that are not given the least attention in German politics, on German television. But the question that our soldiers' deployment in Afghanistan has raised: that will not go away; it may even be discussed – if you consider the developments in Mali – in our crisis meetings and talk shows in the weeks or months to come. I mean the question whether the West, whether Europe, whether Germany's armed forces specifically, should intervene in a conflict.

No blood for oil: everyone in this room would probably agree with that – even the business leaders, at least in public. But what if a genocide is in progress, women are being raped by the thousands, or a dictator uses poison gas against his own population? On a day like today, when we are celebrating a freedom that was fought for and won for us by foreign soldiers, we should not take the easy way out, after the debacle in Afghanistan, by retreating to the position that it's just not possible to export democracy. The lesson to be learned from both dates, the 1st of November 1946 and the 27th of August 2021, is rather that there is no easy answer. The soldiers who fly out of Wunstorf not only risk losing their own lives; they also run the risk, even though it is not their intention or that of their commanders, of further increasing the suffering of a population. But it can also bring death, and in some cases thousands, millions of deaths, when soldiers stay in their barracks.

The invasion of Iraq in 2003 was not only a breach of international law; it was at the same time a disastrous mistake, and we can be grateful – no, we must be grateful today to Gerhard Schröder, to name a second prominent citizen of Lower Saxony, for keeping Germany out of that criminal war – against the will of the opposition leader at the time, Angela Merkel. The no-fly zone and the air strikes in Libya in 2011, when millions of insurgents in the eastern part of the country were threatened by the advance of government troops – I admit I was at first unsure whether Germany had been right to abstain, the only Western nation to do so, in the UN Security Council. The German press, the opposition, with the exception of Die Linke, and even his own partners in the coalition government had nothing but criticism for the foreign minister who had brought Germany to a position of isolation. Today we know, and I know too, that Guido Westerwelle, may he rest in peace, was right in his doubts about the Libyan opposition and the motives of the West.

On the other hand, the disappointment after the lies about Libya had the result that, a short time later, no one in the West was willing to protect the rebelling population in Syria against the Assad regime's barrel bombs and poison gas. Unlike the case of Iraq or Afghanistan, what was proposed then was not an intervention by ground troops. The Syrian opposition, which was still in its secular beginnings and led among others by a Christian, Michel Kilo, called for the global community to establish a no-fly zone to stop the military from bombing its own population from the air. After the outbreak of the civil war, there was also the proposal to supply weapons to the Free Syrian Army. Both were rejected; the opposition was left to its fate. Other foreign powers subsequently got involved, especially Saudi Arabia, Turkey, Russia, Iran; foreign jihadists entered Syria, the so-called Islamic State grew stronger, the democratic revolution increasingly turned into a sectarian conflict, millions of Syrians lost their homes and hundreds of thousands their lives; the country has been made a rubble heap for decades to come. In hindsight we can say with some certainty that an early engagement by the West in the form of a broad-based diplomatic initiative, massive economic pressure and the use of limited military resources – difficult though it is to calculate consequences – would have prevented such an apocalyptic scenario. Neither would IS have temporarily conquered half the Middle East, nor would the refugee crisis of 2015 have divided Europe to the point of Great Britain's withdrawal from the EU. Yazidis and Christians would not have been driven from their homes; European capitals would not have been afflicted with a series of severe terrorist attacks.

There are many more examples in which our inaction made a war go on longer, increased the violence – most drastically probably in Rwanda, currently in Yemen. Or remember the siege of Sarajevo, the massacre of Srebrenica, which took place literally before the very eyes of NATO. And there are other countries – I just mentioned two, Iraq and Libya – where it was intervention that led to a conflagration – or where we utterly failed, as in Afghanistan. Every conflict is different, and often enough the alternatives to be weighed are both wrong because it is too late for the right decision, as it was in 2016 when IS threatened to conquer all of Iraq. At that time, the West quickly decided to provide weapons to the Kurdish Army and to support the Shiite popular militias with air reconnaissance, and that was exactly right in that dramatic situation because a genocide against Yazidis and Christians, Kurds and Shiites was imminent. It is unimaginable what would have happened if IS had penetrated Baghdad and the refugee camps in northern Iraq: the mass rapes, beheadings, crucifixions, enslavements.

As I said, these are not debates of the past. Only last May, Robert Habeck's question whether Ukraine would not have to be supported with weapons in a war against the more powerful Russia caused a commotion, and just this month Germany faces a decision – although it is hardly visible in the news – whether to withdraw the Bundeswehr from Mali. Let us recall: the military mission under French leadership began when jihadists had conquered large parts of the country, up to the legendary city of Timbuktu, subjugating the population, suppressing the local, mystical Islam, and prohibiting practically all aspects of the rich Malian culture. The European military deployment was able to repel the jihadists but failed to achieve essential goals; the country is far from stable, and the recent coup against the civilian government this summer did away with the remnants of its democracy. But weren't the goals too ambitious to begin with? And what if Europe leaves Mali to its fate? Will it be Afghanistan all over again? Will the next refugee wave be rolling towards us? Will the next terrorist bombings be planned in Mali? Frankly, I don't know. I know only that we have to ask ourselves precisely those questions that make us uncomfortable. We all have enough easy answers.

Ladies and gentlemen, my political socialization took place with the German peace and environmental movement, with the resistance against the nuclear waste repository in Gorleben, and with the sit-in blockade in front of the Defence Ministry in Hardthöhe. My first car for many years sported a sticker that shouted pictographically 'Fuck the Army'. Since then, however, I have travelled a great deal, and as a reporter I have seen war and violence up close. In Afghanistan, in particular, I know both the view from the Western tanks and the view of the Western tanks, because I travelled in the country both with NATO and as a civilian. When I speak today about Germany's responsibility in the world, at this jubilee celebration of a German state that owes its existence, its freedom, its prosperity to a foreign military intervention, I cannot say we must always oppose foreign deployments. At the same time, I have seen with my own eyes what weapons do, and as a writer I have an allergic reaction when NATO dresses up carpet bombing as 'humanitarian intervention'. War is not humanitarian, and one of the cardinal mistakes of the Western strategy in Afghanistan is that the civilian mission was subordinated from the start to a military logic. NATO, the German Army – they are not there to introduce new political systems, consolidate state power and unite war-torn societies. And, nevertheless, the alternative cannot be to look away when populations are being destroyed, dispossessed, enslaved. The alternative cannot be to refuse all involvement in the world. What is it then? I believe the alternative lies in that broad field between inaction and war that is commonly called politics.

Politics, in this case foreign policy, does not begin with military missions and does not end with talking to dictators, although it includes both of them. Politics means looking for solutions precisely where a situation seems hopeless. It means not shrugging your shoulders when basic human rights are violated – freedom, peace, enough food, housing; politics means diplomacy, it means dialogue, it means knowledge of the world, it means soul-searching, perseverance, patience. Politics can also consist of sanctions, threats and, yes, in some cases clearly circumscribed, strictly limited military action. Politics means studying not only our own interests but equally those of others, if only for the simple, selfish reason that we won't be able to preserve our own peace, our own prosperity if large parts of the world are dominated by hunger and violence. Because the concerns of others soon become our own: in the form of refugees, in the form of attacks, in the form of horrific scenes that we could tolerate only at the cost of our own souls and the civility of our polity.

Not just since this summer; no, for years now we have seen in Germany a dramatic decline in the importance given to foreign policy, both in politics and in the media. Paradoxically, this apathy towards the world seems to have been accelerated yet again by the Afghanistan debacle. The foreign minister used to be, just ten, twenty years ago, the second highest office in the government. Today, it is Heiko Maas. International politics was absent from the electoral campaigns, and now nothing is heard from the negotiations on a coalition government to indicate much interest in the world across the Mediterranean. Foreign policy is the last thing mentioned in the tentative position paper of the three future governing parties.

At the same time, our lives are more and more dependent on outside factors, down to the most mundane day-to-day activities, and we don't even need to think of the pandemic or climate change or the migration movements that, the United Nations predicts, are going to expand severely in the coming decades. All we need to do is to look at our petrol prices, look at our export volume, look at our phones, whose inner workings require rare earths and lithium. Afghanistan is thought to have some of the world's largest reserves, and that alone is a reason for China not to withdraw from the country by any means. Only the Chinese involvement is not likely to bring the Afghans any closer to freedom. If we do think it's not possible to export democracy – which sounds all the more absurd on this day, in this place – then we should at least take an interest in where our imports come from and where we will be able in future to sell our automobiles. After all, it was a Lower Saxon – to mention yet a third child of your beautiful and colourful state – who brought the word 'cosmopolitanism' into the German language: Gotthold Ephraim Lessing. It is to him, for many years the director of the library in Wolfenbüttel, that we owe the concept of the *Weltbürger*, the citizen of the world, which is my compass today.

Ladies and gentlemen, I realize that today is a celebration for you, a celebration for all the people of Lower Saxony. The success of our states and the whole Federal Republic of Germany is incredible when you imagine Germany's situation on the 1st of November 1946: humiliated, bombed flat, morally discredited in the eyes of the world. At least that may give hope to those countries which seem to be in hopeless situations today: the future rarely follows the course we expect, and it can take turns we could never anticipate – for the worse, but sometimes for the better too. In spite of everything that was and is deserving of criticism in Germany, recent German history seems to be just such a miracle. I don't just know this abstractly; I feel it deep in my core every time I return from an assignment, and I would like to urge you, and our children, and every new citizen to be conscious of this good fortune. We owe it very directly to those British soldiers who risked their lives, and those who lost their lives, to liberate what was then the states of Brunswick, Oldenburg, Schaumburg-Lippe and Hanover. No matter what you choose to compare it with, historically, geographically – it is a good country we live in.

Only, as the world citizen I try to be, my feeling is not just for Germany, and so I would like to end with – yes, with a wistful sentence, I suppose, but one which I hope will not dampen the joy of this day of celebration very much. It is a line spoken by the eponymous Fräulein in the second act of *Minna von Barnhelm*, the play Lessing wrote in that splendid library in Wolfenbüttel: 'It is so sad to be glad all alone.' That is true of individuals, but it is also true of peoples, of continents, of humanity, and if you like, ladies and gentlemen, hear in this sentence not only the sigh, but also the engagement, the vision. It is so sad to be glad all alone.

I thank you for your attention and congratulate the State of Lower Saxony on the 75th anniversary of its founding.

Epilogue:
On My Bookseller,
Ömer Özerturgut

I've done the sums: for twenty-eight years, from the time I came to the Eigelstein area in Cologne until his death, I bought my books from Mr Ömer. He liked the young woman I brought with me one day; he saw my children grow up, as I did his son; he put my very first book in his shop window, and from then on always reserved a stack in his display for my growing oeuvre; he never praised even a single line of mine in those twenty-eight years; that just wasn't his style; but he did once hang a poster of me in the window. Whenever I showed off our neighbourhood to visitors, I always came to Eigelsteinplatz and said, Look here, in our town even the German bookseller is a Turk. Then we went inside, and the visitors were always surprised at the classical music that played from morning till night, often Vivaldi, sometimes opera, or in the mornings the 'Klassikforum' programme on WDR3, which is going to be cancelled with the next broadcasting reform, if not before, because the new radio director doesn't want even symphonies to run longer than three minutes and thirty seconds. Sometimes Mr Ömer also put on French singers, and he was fonder of Cesária Évora's Cape Verdean music than he was even of Beethoven.

He isn't really called Ömer – that is, his surname is not Ömer, as I thought it was for twenty-eight years, as I even wrote in the trade journal of the German Publishers' Association in a series in which writers present their favourite bookshop; there too I called him Mr Ömer, and even poked a bit of fun at him over his German because, back before I sent him my orders by e-mail, he used to get me the wrong books, Maier instead of Meier, for example, Hegel instead of Hebel or Grün instead of Greene, to offer a few examples that are somewhat more obvious than the mistakes really were, and I also caricatured his manner, writing that he often commented on my orders, and even scolded me for being interested in the latest Pamuk, whom he considered a passing fad, oriented towards Western tastes; I wrote chaffing anecdotes of that sort in my sketch, so that I looked forward somewhat anxiously to the moment when he would read the article, but then he was pleased with it after all, I thought; he said nothing, but he held up the magazine with a smile when I came into the shop, seemed to be a little bit proud, and silently ignored the fact that he had been called Mr Ömer even in the trade journal, although Ömer was of course his given name. It was hard to figure that out, though, because for twenty-eight years I had been unsure about how to address him: sometimes he addressed me with the formal pronoun *Sie*, and then the next time he used the familiar *du*, so that I sometimes said *du* to him and sometimes *Sie*, and I got the feeling that he called me *Sie* whenever I called him *du* and vice versa.

He had that kind of innate contrariness, was always dissatisfied with the course of development that the world, Turkey and the Eigelstein quarter were taking, and he admitted of Islam, the subject of some of my books, at most the mystical tradition, Yunus Emre and so on, which was seven hundred years ago. The mayor of Istanbul, later prime minister and now president Tayyip Erdoğan was a fascist, my bookseller said, while I was still pleading progress towards democratization; he rudely chased away any customer whose face he didn't like; he ranted about everyone buying crime novels – out loud, while the crime novel buyer was still in his shop. Okay, Mr Ömer had me. At times I had the impression I alone was financing his bookshop. Once, as I was browsing through the shelves, I was afraid when I heard him ask two women what they were doing here. Oh, just looking, said the women. Then look, and then leave, said Mr Ömer, who didn't care whether the two women thought he was a macho or even an Islamist – and all they had done, probably, was look for the wrong books.

Just as I neglected his surname, by the way, he ignored my given name. *Du*, Kermani, book is here, he shouted across Eigelsteinplatz when I walked past the shop, or sat with my daughters in front of the ice cream parlour across the square. Perhaps that's why I thought Ömer was his surname. Say, Ömer, has the book come? Or, if I wanted to tease him: Say, Ömer, the new Pamuk is really not bad. Whereupon Mr Ömer would pull the novel of a Turkish social critic or early modern author from the shelf for me to read instead of that cheap stuff. Oh, how I would have loved to send the new radio director to his shop, because I'm sure she's a crime novel buyer. Then he'd have thrown her out of the shop as a philistine, and she would have been irked about multicultural problem neighbourhoods.

He really didn't speak German well, after twenty-eight years as a bookseller – a bookseller! – although I don't know how long he had been in Germany before that, or how many years he had had the shop already before I moved to Eigelstein. When I copied and pasted a bibliographical item from Amazon into an e-mail, he always sent back just three words: dozens – no, hundreds of e-mails with always the same three words: *Morgen ist da*, 'Tomorrow is here'. He was staunchly left, that was plain; he had a polite and very pleasant-natured son, who is a German teacher by now – a German teacher! – but no wife, or at least not a visible one; there were often other Turks his age there, also somehow left-looking, helping out in the storeroom or drinking tea with him; for the rest, he said next to nothing about himself.

I sensed, though, that there was a political and intellectual biography behind him, but even his second son, whose existence I hadn't even known about, told me at his graveside that he had had to find out everything for himself: leader of the '68 movement, resistance against the military dictatorship, prison sojourn, Workers' Party; he said he would send me the translations of the articles that were appearing now in Turkey about his father. There were even a television camera and a number of radio microphones at the funeral in the Muslim section of Cologne's West Cemetery, and more than two hundred mourners, many of whom had come a long way. The big photo in the mourning hall showed Mr Ömer, with a melancholy smile, almost as young as I had met him twenty-eight years before, when I had practically just finished school and he was a Turkish intellectual who had emigrated to Cologne.

A French neighbour from Eigelstein played the guitar and sang a song; a visibly very mystical imam, who admitted all religions and suggested to the few German guests that they might recite the Lord's Prayer while he recited the Islamic prayer for the dead, because it was not important now to ask God to forgive our guilt towards Him, God would do that of Himself, we could count on His mercy; our problem was our guilt towards our fellow human beings, not God, but our fellows should forgive us our sins before we go to the next world, otherwise we would go heavily burdened, and that is expressed just as well in the Christian Lord's Prayer as in the Islamic prayer which he would recite in Turkish, because the Most Merciful said in the Quran that everyone should address Him in their own language – because the Most Merciful understands no matter what prayer. I saw, admittedly only in my imagination, how the few German guests were left speechless by the candour and the gentleness of this imam, who climbed down into the grave himself to bed Mr Ömer facing Mecca, at the prescribed azimuth and altitude, and to hammer the boards into the sides of the grave over him so that the earth would not fall on his body. We the funeral guests didn't throw a discreet handful of earth into the grave, but took shovels and filled it to the brim, as the Turkish tradition apparently requires.

Before the white shroud with the body was lifted out of the coffin, the imam had said first in Turkish, then in German, that every person should go as they had lived, with what they loved, and so we would now hear a song, whereupon the younger son connected his smartphone to the loudspeaker, and everyone, the two hundred Turkish, mostly older, likewise left-looking guests listened to Cesária Évora, Cape Verdean music, in the Muslim section of Cologne's West Cemetery.

In the funeral hall, which is equipped with crosses, although it is used by the faithful of all religions, and by unbelievers – that didn't bother me, it merely struck me; and taking down the cast-iron rear panel with the crosses on it would have been wrong too – I had given one of the eulogies, although without a text, so there is no manuscript and this book of speeches closes with the recollection of a speech; Mr Ömer's older son, whom I knew, had asked me just the day before, so that at least one person would speak in German to the funeral assembly, and so that at least one of his customers could say something, and said I had been his best customer (which is certainly true). I praised Mr Ömer as the good neighbour he was, and admitted that I had learned hardly anything personal about him over the twenty-eight years, as is often the case with neighbours; I did not fail to mention that Mr Ömer could be gruff, whereupon the front row nodded collectively, but that I relied on him implicitly; I knew that he would watch out, that he kept an eye on the children when they were in the square; that he asked after my wife if he hadn't seen her in a while – How is she? Is she well? – that he always, always had presents for the children, Turkish sweets, posters, sample copies of books, once a real throne, the reading throne from a publisher's promotional event, red and sky-blue, which I had to carry right across the square and all the way home along Lübecker Strasse, although I knew my daughter had no room for it, but she had been glad nonetheless.

I also spoke of his German, and caricatured it again, told about the confusion of authors' names and the orders that I later copied and pasted into e-mails, and about the answer that always arrived a few minutes later: '*Morgen ist da*', 'Tomorrow is here'; dozens and hundreds of times, 'Tomorrow is here'. That is why I was immediately worried when one day he didn't answer right away 'Tomorrow is here', or 'Saturday is here' or 'I have to order from publisher' or whatever it might be; nothing came back; not the next day either, and so, because after all I was his neighbour too, and not just he ours, I tried in vain to ring him a few times and then went to the shop, where other neighbours had already laid flowers and candles in front of the door. I said that I would hold these three words in my heart, since Ömer Özerturgut would not send them to me any more, three beautiful words, in fact, glad, hopeful, no less than utopian words, which fit his political biography, which I am looking forward to reading: 'Tomorrow is here'. May his soul rejoice: Ömer Özerturgut, born the 12th of July 1946 in Alaşehir; died the 8th of March 2016 in Cologne.

Notes

1 '4 Sophia' by the Durutti Column. From the album *Rebellion*, Artful Records 2001.
2 '[A]usgestattet mit seinem eigenen namen und allen seinen Daten': Ingeborg Bachmann, *Frankfurter Vorlesungen: Probleme zeitgenössischer Dichtung*, in *Werke*, vol. IV, p. 221.
3 Quran 5:28, trans. Arthur J. Arberry. *The Koran*. Oxford: Oxford University Press, [1964] 2008, p. 104.
4 Cecile Massie, 'La Communauté de Deir Mar Moussa (Textes de l'exposition photographique)', 18 October 2016, www.cecilemassie.com/5788-2/.
5 Yohanna Petros Mouche, 'Morgen wird der IS auch bei euch sein', interview by Fouad el-Auwad, *Frankfurt Allgemeine Zeitung*, 9 July 2015, www.faz.net/aktuell/feuilleton/debatten/der-irakische-erzbischof-petros-mouche-ueber-den-is-13689957.html.
6 Massie, 'La Communauté de Deir Mar Moussa'.
7 Rupert Neudeck, 'Rettung auf Hoher See: Cap Anamur', in Michael Albus (ed.), *Rupert Neudeck: Man muss etwas riskieren; Menschlichkeit ohne Kompromisse*. Munich: Claudius, 2015, p. 86.
8 Rupert Neudeck, 'Dominierend ist die Freude: Zwei kurze Fragen noch', interview with Michael Albus, ibid., pp. 96–7.
9 Quran 2:286, trans. M. A. S. Abdel Haleem. *The Qur'an*. Oxford: Oxford University Press, 2011.

10 Certain passages of this and the following speech appeared in the chapters 'Third Day' and '45th Day' in *Along the Trenches*. Cambridge: Polity, 2020.
11 Primo Levi and Leonardo de Benedetti, *Auschwitz Testimonies: 1945–1986*, trans. Judith Woolf. Cambridge: Polity, 2018, p. 99.
12 Marcel Reich-Ranicki, *The Author of Himself: The Life of Marcel Reich-Ranicki*, trans. Ewald Osers. Princeton, NJ: Princeton University Press, 2020, p. 152.
13 Ibid., p. 155.
14 Heinrich Himmler, Tgb.Nr. 38/33/42 g v, 16 February 1943, quoted in Léon Poliakov and Josef Wulf, *Das Dritte Reich und die Juden*. Berlin: Arani, 1955, p. 170.
15 Reich-Ranicki, *The Author of Himself*, p. 182.
16 Martin Walser, 'Experiences while Composing a Sunday Speech', in Thomas A. Kovach and Martin Walser, *The Burden of the Past: Martin Walser on Modern German Identity; Texts, Contexts, Commentary*. Rochester, NY: Camden House, 2008, pp. 85–95, at p. 91.
17 Ibid.
18 Marcel Reich-Ranicki, 'Ich bin kein Deutscher, und ich werde es nie sein', interview with Herlinde Koelbl, *Die Zeit*, 15 September 1989, www.zeit.de/1989/38/ich-bin-kein-deutscher-und-ich-werde-es-nie-sein/komplettansicht.
19 Margarete Susman, *Vom Geheimnis der Freiheit: Gesammelte Aufsätze, 1914–1964*. Darmstadt: Agora, 1965, p. 172; quoted in Marcel Reich-Ranicki, *Über Ruhestörer: Juden in der deutschen Literatur*. Munich: Piper, 1973, pp. 48–9.
20 Reich-Ranicki, *Über Ruhestörer*, pp. 53–4.
21 Ibid., pp. 47–8.
22 Reich-Ranicki, 'Ich bin kein Deutscher'.
23 Neil Young, 'Campaigner', on *Decade*, Warner Bros., 1977.
24 In 'Das Lied der Deutschen', by August Heinrich Hoffmann von Fallersleben, now the German national anthem:

'Einigkeit und Recht und Freiheit / Sind des Glückes Unterpfand.'
25 Quran 55:13, trans. Arberry (translation modified).
26 A line from FC Cologne's official fan anthem, which is in Cologne dialect: 'The feeling that unites [us].'
27 Jorge Luis Borges, 'Epilogue', in *Professor Borges: A Course on English Literature*, ed. Martín Arias and Martín Hadis. New York: New Directions, 2014, p. 252.
28 Michel de Montaigne, *The Complete Essays*, trans. Donald Frame. Stanford, CA: Stanford University Press, 1965, p. 297.
29 Fernando Pessoa, *Fernando Pessoa & Co.: Selected Poems*, ed. and trans. Richard Zenith. New York: Grove, 1998, p. 266.
30 Fernando Pessoa, 'ANÁLISE', in *Obra Poética e em Prosa*, vol. 1. Porto: Lello, 1986, p. 162; http://arquivopessoa.net/textos/2871.
31 Friedrich Hölderlin, 'Bread and Wine', in Hölderlin, *Odes and Elegies*, trans. Nick Hoff. Middletown, CT: Wesleyan University Press, 2008, p. 141.
32 Friedrich Hölderlin, 'Dichtermut', ibid., p. 113.
33 Fernando Pessoa, *The Book of Disquiet: The Complete Edition*, trans. Margaret Jull Costa. London: Serpent's Tail, 2017, p. 267.
34 Borges, 'Epilogue', p. 170.
35 Quoted in English in Efraín Kristal, *Invisible Work: Borges and Translation*. Nashville: Vanderbilt University Press, 2002, p. 159, n. 116.
36 Fernando Pessoa, 'Death is a bend in the road', in Pessoa, *A Little Larger than the Entire Universe: Selected Poems*, ed. and trans Richard Zenith. London: Penguin, 2006, p. 319.
37 Adam Smith, *The Wealth of Nations*, Book 4, chapter 2.
38 Quoted in *Demetrius of Phalerum: Text, Translation and Discussion*, ed. William W. Fortenbaugh and Eckart Schütrumpf. New York: Routledge, 2018.

39 Karl Marx, *Capital: A Critique of Political Economy*, vol. 1, trans. Ben Fowkes. New York: Vintage, 1977, p. 638.
40 German constitution, Article 72, para. 2; here from the Bundestag's translation, www.gesetze-im-internet.de/englis ch_gg/englisch_gg.html#p0326.
41 A widely reported speech to the party's youth organization on 2 June 2018; see, for example, 'Gauland: Hitler nur "Vogelschiss" in deutscher Geschichte', *Frankfurter Allgemeine Zeitung*, 2 June 2018, www.faz.net/aktuell/polit ik/inland/gauland-hitler-nur-vogelschiss-in-deutscher-gesc hichte-15619502.html.
42 Muḥyi'ddīn Ibn al-'Arabī, *Tarjumān al-Ashwāq: A Collection of Mystical Odes*, ed. and trans. Reynold A. Nicholson. London: Royal Asiatic Society, 1911, I. All quotations from the *Tarjumān* are from this translation. The book is online at the Internet Archive: https://archive.org/details/tarjuman alashwaq029432mbp/page/n3/mode/2up.
43 Jacques Lacan, *The Seminar of Jacques Lacan*, book 20, trans. Bruce Fink. New York: W. W. Norton, 1999, p. 44.
44 *Tarjumān* XII: 4.
45 *Tarjumān* II: 4–9.
46 *Tarjumān* XXXIX: 7–8.
47 *Tarjumān* XI: 13–15.
48 C. G. Jung, *Psychology and Alchemy*, Collected Works, vol. 12, trans. R. F. C. Hull, 2nd edn. Princeton, NJ: Princeton University Press, 1968, pp. 15–16.
49 Carl Hegemann, *Identität und Selbst-Zerstörung: Grundlagen einer historischen Kritik moderner Lebensbedingungen bei Fichte und Marx*. Berlin: Alexander, 2017, p. 266.
50 Johann Wolfgang von Goethe, 'Selige Sehnsucht', in *West-Östlicher Diwan*, 1819.
51 Friedrich Hölderlin, *Hyperion or the Hermit in Greece*, trans. Ross Benjamin. New York: Archipelago, 2008, p. 12.
52 Jung, *Psychology and Alchemy*, p. 13.

53 Ibid., p. 14.
54 Friedrich Hölderlin, *The Death of Empedocles: A Mourning-Play*, trans. David Farrell Krell. Albany: SUNY Press, 2008, p. 53.
55 C. G. Jung, *Psychology and Religion: West and East*, trans. Gerhard Adler and R. F. C. Hull, *Collected Works*, vol. 11. Princeton, NJ: Princeton University Press, 1969, p. 46.
56 *Tarjumān* XXII: 6–11.
57 Jung, *Psychology and Religion*, pp. 464–5.
58 *Tarjumān* XLIX.
59 C. G. Jung, 'Anima and Animus', in *Two Essays on Analytical Psychology*, trans. R. F. C. Hull, *Collected Works*, vol. 7, 2nd edn. Princeton, NJ: Princeton University Press, 1966, pp. 205–6.
60 Jung, *Psychology and Religion*, pp. 76–7.
61 Friedrich Hölderlin, *Essays and Letters*, ed. and trans. Jeremy Adler and Charlie Louth. London: Penguin, 2009, p. 109.
62 Friedrich Hölderlin, *Hyperion or the Hermit in Greece*, trans. Ross Benjamin. New York: Archipelago, 2008, p. 211.
63 Friedrich Hölderlin, 'Menon's Lament for Diotima', in Hölderlin, *Poems and Fragments*, trans. Michael Hamburger. London: Anvil Press Poetry, 1994, 241.
64 Friedrich Hölderlin, 'Bread and Wine', in Hölderlin, *Odes and Elegies*, trans. Nick Hoff. Middletown, CT: Wesleyan University Press, 2008, p. 141.
65 Friedrich Hölderlin, 'Patmos', in Hölderlin and Eduard Mörike, *Selected Poems*, trans. Christopher Middleton. Chicago: University of Chicago Press, 1972, p. 75.
66 Hölderlin, *Essays and Letters*, p. 136.
67 Hölderlin, *Hyperion*, p. 12.
68 The 'Thalia Fragment', in German in *Neue Thalia*, ed. Friedrich Schiller, 1794.
69 Hölderlin, *Essays and Letters*, p. 214.

70 Friedrich Hölderin, 'The Basis of Empedocles', in Hölderlin, *The Death of Empedocles*, p. 144 (translation modified).
71 Hölderlin, *Hyperion*, p. 174.
72 Friedrich Hölderlin, 'When I Was a Boy . . .', in Hölderlin and Mörike, *Selected Poems*, p. 3.
73 Hölderlin, *Essays and Letters*, p. 135.
74 Hölderlin, *Hyperion*, p. 199.
75 Friedrich Hölderlin, 'Hyperion's Song of Fate', in Hölderlin and Mörike, *Selected Poems*, p. 5.
76 Hölderlin, *Hyperion*, p. 157.
77 Ibid., p. 119.
78 Ibid., p. 158.
79 Friedrich Hölderlin, 'The Half of Life', in Hölderlin and Mörike, *Selected Poems*, p. 73.
80 'Since we have been a discourse and have heard from one another': Friedrich Hölderlin, 'Celebration of Peace', in Hölderlin, *Poems and Fragments*, p. 461.
81 Friedrich Hölderlin, 'Mnemosyne: Third Version', ibid., p. 519.
82 Hölderlin, *Hyperion*, p. 208.
83 Ibid., p. 209.
84 Friedrich Hölderlin, 'Patmos', in Hölderlin and Mörike, *Selected Poems*, p. 75.